Showing the
HEAVY HORSE

Showing the
HEAVY HORSE

An Exhibitor's Guide

EDWARD W. HART

J.A. ALLEN
LONDON

© Edward Hart 2004
First published in Great Britain 2004

ISBN 0 85131 827 4

J. A. Allen
Clerkenwell House
Clerkenwell Green
London EC1R 0HT

J. A. Allen is an imprint of Robert Hale Limited

A catalogue record for this book is available from the British Library

Photographs on pages 16, 26 (lower), 29, 31, 33, 39, 41, 42, 43, 44, 45, 46, 48–9, 52–3, 137, 138, 140 (upper), 141, 164–6, 168–9, 170–5, 189, 193, 194, 195, 199, 200 (lower), 202, 204 (upper), 213, 220, 231, 239, 247, 256, 260, 261, 265, 267, 269, 270, 272, 275, 276 (upper), 278, 280 (lower), 286, 287, 288, 292 and 326 (lower) by Roy Fox; on page 205 (lower) by Fleet Fotos; on pages 40, 65 (lower), 204 (lower), 232–8, 268, 280 (upper), 285, 290 and 319 by Audrey Hart; on pages 295, 296 and 301 by Sue Everson; on pages 34, 294 and 302 by Robin Everson; on pages 143(lower), 154, 155 (lower), 206, 276 (lower) and 300 by Janice Gordon; on pages 19, 26 (upper) and 248 by Trevor Meeks; on pages 325, 329 and back jacket by Adrian Legge; on pages 184 and 297 by Brian Robinson; on page 104 by Roger Clark; on page 298 (upper) by Skyla Consultants Ltd; on page 326 (upper) by Farmer and Stock-Breeder; on page 55 by Gavin Cole; on page 58 (lower) by Gwen Johner; on page 229 by Monty; on page 289 (upper) by The National Shire Horse Centre; on page 304 by Betty Peacock; on pages 64 (right) and 65 (upper) by The Dales Pony Society; on page 330 (upper) by Wally Talbot; on page 64 (left) by Sue and Jennifer Millard; on pages 314 (lower) and 334 by Claudia Steele; on page 63 courtesy of the Fell Pony Society Archive; on pages 60 and 61 courtesy of The Irish Draught Horse Society of Great Britain; on page 298 (lower) courtesy of Tina Reaney; other photographs by, or the property of, the author

Colour print on front jacket and all prints of pictures by Malcolm Coward supplied by Sally Mitchell Fine Arts; print on page 119 by Joe Gooderidge; painting by Nina Colmore on page 277 and the photograph on page 6 courtesy of John Young CBE

Line illustration on page 199 by Roger Clark and line illustrations on page 198 by Maggie Raynor, based on sketches provided by Kevin Flynn

Design by Judy Linard
Edited by Martin Diggle
Colour separation by Tenon & Polert Colour Scanning Limited, Hong Kong
Printed in China by New Era Printing Company Ltd.

Foreword by John A. Young CBE

Having taken a keen interest in heavy horses for over half a century, I am well aware of the depth of affection and interest they still command in Britain and many other parts of the world.

When I was privileged to be President of the Shire Horse Society it was evident to me that the perpetuation of the breed at the highest level depends not only on the esteem we feel for these great horses, but equally important is the depth of knowledge available in handling them effectively.

There were times in post-war Britain when it seemed that the breeds of heavy horse were seriously endangered. There is bound to be a risk in our fast-changing society that knowledge of such traditional skills as showing heavy horses effectively could be lost or eroded. For this reason I especially commend Edward Hart's new book.

Edward has drawn on a lifetime's experience and observation to produce a work which will be enjoyed and valued by current and future generations of heavy horse enthusiasts. I am sure that experts will find much of interest here, and it will be especially worthwhile for those seeking to enter the fascinating world of heavy horse showing in all its forms.

It is patient, effective preparation beforehand which wins equine showing classes of all kinds. Edward Hart provides valuable insight into the selection, training and maintenance which must take place with heavy horses to ensure success.

No matter what technology provides as distractions in the 21st

John Young CBE, Chairman of Young's Brewery, with his champion black Shires.

century, I am confident there will continue to be many people finding enjoyment and refreshment in showing heavy horses – or simply watching them. Edward Hart has made a significant and, I am sure, long-lasting contribution to ensuring that this is so.

John Young

Acknowledgements

This book is a compilation of the views of a number of leading horsemen and women, without whose unstinted help it would never have appeared. They gave not only their time, but also a distillation of their knowledge and experience gained over a great number of years. Some of this expertise was handed down to them by previous generations, now often unidentified but deserving of our thanks.

I would like to thank: Audrey Hart, Bernard Adams, Billy Cammidge, Bob Langrish, Bob Stobbart, Carl Boyde, Denis Oliver OBE, FRCVS, Diana Zeuner of *Heavy Horse World*, Graham Ward, Harry Tomlin and his daughter Ann Jones, Jim Yates, John Peacock, John Ward, the late Keith Chivers, Ian Misselbrook, Libby Archer of the Horserace Betting Levy Board, the late Mervyn Ramage, Norman Jones, Patrick Flood, Paul and Walter Bedford, Roger Clark, Rosemary Cooper, Sinclair McGill Seeds, Ted Cumbor, Warwick Aldersley, Tom and Ronald Brewster, Harry Ranson, Kevin Flynn, David Coffen, Mike and Colin Horler, Dick and Mary Fuller, Bruce Smith, Owen Garner and Terry Keegan.

Special thanks to Walter Bedford for staging the plaiting demonstration, to Audrey Hart for photographing the sequence, and to Kate Lugsden of Baileys Horse Feeds for the latest research details on feeding the heavy horse, and on its disorders.

Also to Roy Fox for so many excellent photographs taken with skill and enthusiasm at a wide range of events, to Sue Everson of Hayfield Coloured Shires and to all others who supplied photographs, and particularly to Sally Mitchell Fine Arts and Malcolm Coward for paintings which capture the atmosphere of the heavy horse scene so well. And finally thanks to my editor Martin Diggle for his unstinted and detailed help, and to Judy Linard for bringing it all together.

Contents

Adjustments; The Finish

INTRODUCTION

The Lure of Showing

A new show season is always around the corner. Once, when Shire breeder Denys Benson and I were chatting around the turn of the year, he observed wryly that his Spring Show schedule should arrive any day, and that there seems no let-up between one season and the next.

Suspended from a bacon hook in the back kitchen was an elderly bridle dripping neatsfoot oil into a container below. I came to accept its ornamental presence as part of life, like a climbing plant. A non-horsy household would shun such embellishments, and regard us with a measure of truth as mad.

So why do we do it? Why can't we live in 'normal' households where chairs are used as seats and not as handy places to drape a set of breechings? Why keep an animal with an appetite nearly as big as an elephant's? Why regard vet's bills under £100 as friendly, and why plead with a farrier to hold up a big foot onto which the whole weight of a mature Suffolk or Clydesdale is somehow concentrated?

Why do we admire such basically exaggerated forms of animal life as heavy horses? A strong cob would do much the same work as most. A pair of piebald ponies in a scurry must be tremendous fun, and far cheaper.

An earlier writer on the horse show scene referred to 'a curious little knot of exhibitors, tucked away in a corner of the horse world'. They were the Hackney exhibitors of some decades ago. Today's heavy horse people are less tunnel-visioned – but not much. We may find turnout drivers admiring private driving at the Highland or East of England Show, or watching the coaches leave. But 'pony people' – especially some of the mums – are not usually in our top ten, and as for showjumping . . . At one Wembley show a group of us stood in the

In Britain, the Royal Family takes a keen interest in equestrian events. Here, HRH Prince Philip, who competed in carriage driving at the highest level, chats to Colin Jordan of Grovesmere Shires.

alleys while the world's best puissance performers gained deserved applause in the main ring. We, however, were discussing The Bomber, the famous Shire stallion of the 1950s, deaf to the excitement a few yards away.

Let's be honest. It's the heavy horse people that we like. The breeds may contain a quota of rogues, but they are likeable ones of the sort that we can cope with and understand.

For the heavy turnout exhibitors, spring means another round of late nights and early mornings. Whose fault are the late nights, by the way? I have yet to hear a groom who didn't blame someone else's groom for them. For we correspondents, it is the start of another round of result sheets to be sought, checked and copied. No one ever comments on a correctly produced prize list. Make one mistake, however, and the whole heavy horse world picks it up.

Each season, there is the consideration of which horses have retired or died and, still more sadly, which competitors will no longer exchange banter while the judge is at the far end of the line. There will be new faces to learn to recognize. As Dr Johnson advised: 'Keep your friendships in repair'. Failure to do so means fewer and fewer acquaintances year by year.

The National Shire Show at Peterborough, known to all Shire participants as the Spring Show, will, in March, be bathed in mild sunshine or end in a blizzard. We don't know. We only know that it will be followed by the Clydesdales' big event when their Stallion Show raises the curtain up north.

Then, in May, come the gleaming Suffolks in their seven shades of chesnut (as that breed's coat colour is spelt), and the black and grey Percherons for a jolly and festive occasion. There will be the usual minor essentials left behind, easily remedied through the heavy horse brotherhood. Some will win, some will lose, some will grumble and others smile.

Win or lose in the coming heavy horse season, the scene has much more to commend it than most of the inane ways of spending time so lauded by non-horsy people. Let's all enjoy our good fortune. Only recently, we were all robbed of a season through the foot-and-mouth catastrophe; let's try to make up for this in the current and future seasons.

At any major show, the heavy horse lines are a place apart. They buzz with the throng of fascinated spectators, with horses looking over stable doors, the summer air echoing to the thump of great feet against the gentle rustle of hay being systematically torn from the net.

Above all is the air of companionship. The heavy horse world constitutes a fairly tight-knit community, its competitors invariably ready to

The East of England Show has magnificent Turnout classes.

help each other with anything from a length of forgotten ribbon to replacing a broken pole.

Exhibitors on the circuit meet repeatedly during the show season, which extends from the National Shire Show in mid-March to the Horse of the Year Show in October. Their summer routine means they see little of home, so all endeavour to make the itinerant life as pleasant as possible. To this end there is 'open house' down the lines, with tea or something stronger readily available.

At one-day shows, transporters arrive early and are directed into line in their own section. This soon takes on the atmosphere of the heavy horse stable, even though the base is a lorry, the floor of which is reached only after a stumbling clatter up the ramp. Horses are usually tied up outside when being prepared.

The open field is quickly transformed into an intriguing and busy scene. Skeps containing brushes, combs, wood flour for drying and a selection of buckets are set nearby, and the brushing and braiding begin. Yet there is somehow time for an inspection of neighbours' horses, with comments on how they are summering, while any previously unshown horses very soon attract a knot of spectators.

Foals suckling their dams are a favourite target for amateur photographers. Such is their affinity with their dams that young foals are not always tied up, and for city spectators this may be one of the few opportunities for close contact with a growing animal; the horse world provides an invaluable public relations service here. The effect upon the foals is also beneficial; they will never forget those early lessons trotting up the resounding ramp alongside their clattering dams, being stroked by strangers, or hearing the crowd clap as they dance on green showground turf. One day they themselves will be seniors, perhaps with foals of their own, and first experiences help them to qualify for that endearing term 'diamond', the highest accolade that owner or groom can bestow on the heavy horse.

Then it's on to the actual showing, starting at 8.30 or 9 a.m. with the In-hand classes. At county or national shows, these classes are usually staged on the same day for all the heavy breeds. Since a reveille at 4 a.m. is not unusual to give time for the final washing, grooming and braiding, the preceding evening is usually quiet. The previous night's (relative) abstinence and bleary-eyed industry are

This Malcolm Coward painting recaptures the peaceful summer show scene. Suffolks in the foreground, with Shires nearer the grandstand.

All the colour and life of a heavy horse Grand Parade, captured by Trevor Meeks.

Samuel Smith's hitch of ten grey Shires was popular at pageants and galas, but not shown competitively.

then rewarded as exhibitors display their immaculate charges for spectators and judge.

The In-hand classes are usually followed by the Turnout classes, perhaps augmented by novelty and speciality classes – Harness, Best Decorated, Young Handler, Riding (Heavy) Horse, topped off with a Stallion class or Grand Parade. The Turnout classes may encompass every combination from a single horse and vehicle to teams of three, four, six or even more. The 'six' came to prominence as the pinnacle of North American horsemanship. To see those massive six-horse teams swooping through the narrow arch of the Toronto Winter Fair at a fast trot makes crossing the Atlantic worthwhile for that alone. In common with other aspects of the heavy horse revival, the 'six' is spreading from North America to become a major part of the British summer scene.

All the bigger turnouts are expensive to exhibit in terms of transport and manpower, yet they are such crowd-pullers that many shows offer grants to help exhibitors compete in what would otherwise be an exercise beyond most private pockets. If showing holds its own lure for the real enthusiast, these spectacular turnouts prove that the public is still lured willingly to the world of the heavy horse.

PART ONE

Choice and Care of Heavy Breeds

CHAPTER 1

The Heavy Horse Breeds

Many distinctive breeds and a whole range of colours await the heavy horse exhibitor. In Britain, the Shire, Clydesdale and Suffolk could be considered the traditional native 'core' breeds, with the Percheron growing in popularity from the 1920s onward. More recently, the Continental Ardennes has also found favour, and this low-slung horse now has more and more show classes in Britain, as it does in its native France. In North America, the Belgian is a highly popular show horse, and it is now appearing in the United Kingdom also.

In addition to these main breeds, we might also consider the Irish Draught, an admirable breed used traditionally for farm work and ploughing matches. Although now the basis of a breeding programme producing top-quality event and performance horses, and perhaps thought of more readily in that light, it is, in fact, the dominant heavy breed of both the Republic of Ireland and Ulster (despite the fact that there are some excellent Clydesdales in the latter region).

Finally, although they are not, by definition, 'heavy horses', it is worth considering the Fell and Dales ponies, since both are used in ploughing matches and particularly in classes featuring haymaking machinery – a purpose for which these sturdy breeds were traditionally employed.

Choice of Breed

The heavy breeds are basically lowland breeds; fertile soils are their natural home, and on sparse, wind-swept uplands the native breeds of pony are more likely to thrive. This point aside, which breed is the most suitable for the newcomer? To a certain extent, this is unanswerable, since all have their adherents and strong points. However, for those looking for horses with the avowed intention of showing them, geography is one major consideration. There are two related reasons for this. The first is that, historically, the different breeds developed in (or were introduced to) areas to which they were best suited as working horses. For example, the clean-legged heavy breeds, Suffolk and Percheron, both have strong East Anglian links. The former originated on the heavy clays of its home county, where copious feather on the legs would be a distinct disadvantage. The latter, a native of France, arrived in Britain in numbers during the 1920s and immediately found a niche on the Fens, where fast-walking, neat-footed animals were required for the comparatively light but accurate row-crop work between small plants drilled in straight lines.

Although this relationship of breed to area has moderated somewhat down the years, it still has a significant impact upon overall distribution. In general terms, the distribution of the main heavy breeds throughout Britain might be summarized as follows. The Suffolk is still based in East Anglia, although there is a sizeable Suffolk community in the south-west, particularly in Dorset. The greatest concentration of Percheron breeders and exhibitors is still to be found in the East Anglian Fens, although Percheron stables have made their mark from Sunderland in the north-east to Hampshire in the south. The Shire is found throughout England and Wales, but only rarely in Scotland, where the Clydesdale is first choice. Cumbria is another Clydesdale stronghold, and the breed was, historically, in direct competition with the Shire in northern England above a wavering line from Kendal in Cumbria to Whitby on the North Sea coast. Northern Ireland is another region with a high regard for the breed (and some of the best examples). It has some excellent studs, and turnout exhibitors cross the Irish Sea to compete in Scotland. There's keenness for you! Nowadays, there are also Clydesdale enthusiasts in southern England.

This discussion of distribution brings us to the second reason why geography is a major consideration in choice of breed. It is the pragmatic point that there is much to be said for choosing a breed already found in one's own area. The way of the pioneer is hard, and to establish a Percheron stud in North Wales, for example, would be to saddle oneself with costs that would not apply in East Anglia. Travelling to suitable shows would be far more complicated and costly, as would the expense of taking a mare to a top stallion. If you plan to keep heavy horses for fun, that aspect is easier when like-minded people live within range.

Of course, if there were no pioneering spirit, no breeds would ever spread beyond their existing ranges and, as we shall see, there can be certain attractions to involvement with a numerically small breed. However, the difficulties inherent with going out on a limb should not be underrated.

Breed Characteristics

If you intend to acquire a heavy horse, of whatever breed, with the intention of showing it, it is imperative that you are conversant with the standards laid down by the relevant breed society. Even though not all classes are judged exclusively on the horse's type and conformation, these are inevitably major factors, and there is little chance of success with an animal that is a poor specimen and does not conform to type. (If you already own a horse, and have recently decided that showing might be fun, comparison with the breed standard may help you decide upon the most appropriate classes.)

The characteristics and standards of the main heavy horse breeds are as follows.

Shire

To the general public, all heavy horses tend to be 'Shires'. This is, of course, completely wrong and causes much resentment among Clydesdale, Percheron and Suffolk breeders, who are driven to put notices on their stands reading: 'This is NOT a Shire'. Matters can become more serious, and relationships further strained, when Shires are blamed for accidents caused by horses of other breeds!

Such issues aside, the hairy-legged Shire is numerically the most

Three of the best Shire stallions of the 1990s: Walter Bedford's Deighton Commodore (centre) takes the King George V Cup for best stallion, 1994, followed by John Williamson's Snelson Magnus (left) and David Worthington's Walton President.

Philip Moss's champion Shire, Walton Supreme, one of the most successful and influential stallions in modern times.

common heavy breed in Britain, and is popular not only in England and Wales but also in North America, Australasia and, more recently, in Europe. It is found in bay, brown, black and grey, and suitable specimens abound, albeit sometimes at a price.

A mature Shire is a magnificent animal. It is excellent for showing in-hand, or in halter classes as Canadians, Americans and Australians term them. It is the most popular turnout horse, with well-developed action and flowing movement. For Working Harness or Decorated Harness classes the Shire is admirable, its long, fine feather making an added attraction, its length of mane lending itself to plaiting. In recent times, especially in Europe, it has become sought after for riding, and many big shows now have Ridden Shire classes.

The Shire is a 'town and country' horse, equally at home in front of the plough or in crowded city streets. To show one at either your local village event or at the East of England Showground's National Shire Horse Show near Peterborough is a thrill unlikely to be forgotten.

The Shire Horse Society is an active and forward-looking organization, welcoming newcomers. It will assist in finding a suitable Shire, and issues a list of members with stock for sale. The Shire world is a highly competitive one, however, and rivalry at the top, in all classes, is very keen indeed. Both skill and money are needed in any attempt to join the top Shire ranks.

Ever since its formation in 1877, the Shire Horse Society has endeavoured to keep up with modern requirements, and its standard of points for Shire horses has been amended when necessary. For instance, years ago, a great characteristic of the Shire was the wealth of hair, or feather, on the legs. Today the demand is for a cleaner-legged horse, with straight, fine, silky hair.

The standard of points as laid down by the Shire Horse Society Council is:

STALLIONS

Colour: Black, brown, bay or grey. No good stallion should be splashed with large white patches over the body. He must not be roan or chestnut.

Height: Standard 17 hands and upwards. Average about 17.2 hands.

Head:	Long and lean, neither too large nor too small, with long neck in proportion to the body. Large jawbone should be avoided.
Eye:	Large, well set and docile in expression. Wall eyes not acceptable.
Nose:	Slightly Roman, nostrils thin and wide; lips together.
Ears:	Long, lean, sharp and sensitive.
Throat:	Clean-cut and lean.
Shoulder:	Deep and oblique, wide enough to support the collar.
Neck:	Long, slightly arched, well set on to give the horse a commanding appearance.
Girth:	The girth varies from 6 ft to 8 ft [189–244 cm] in stallions of from 16.2 to 18 hands.
Back:	Short, strong and muscular. Should not be dipped or roached.
Loins:	Standing well up, denoting good constitution (must not be flat).
Fore-end:	Wide across the chest, with legs well under the body and well enveloped in muscle, or action is impeded.
Hindquarters:	Long and sweeping, wide and full of muscle. Quarters well let down towards the thighs.
Ribs:	Round, deep and well sprung, not flat.
Forelegs:	Should be as straight as possible down to pastern.
Hind legs:	Hocks should be not too far back and in line with the hindquarters, with ample width broadside and narrow in front. 'Puffy' and 'sickle' hocks should be avoided. The leg sinews should be clean-cut and hard, like fine cords to touch, and clear of short cannon bones.
Bone:	Of flat bone 11 in [28 cm] is ample, although occasionally $12^{1}/_{2}$ in [32 cm] is recorded – flat bone is heavier and stronger than spongy bone. Hocks must be broad, deep and flat, and set at the correct angle for leverage.
Feet:	Deep, solid and wide, with thick, open walls. Coronets should be hard and sinewy, with substance.
Hair:	Not too much, fine, straight and silky.

Ray Williams' Moorfield Edward, every inch a Shire stallion. Ray is one of many heavy horse enthusiasts who have to take care that their hobby does not take precedence over their business!

Proven Shire stallion, Bodernog Master, shown by Bryan Banham.

The Official Standard continues:

A good Shire stallion should stand from 16.2 hands upwards, and weigh from 18 cwt to 22 cwt [914–1118 kg] when matured, without being overdone in condition. He should possess a masculine head, and a good crest with sloping, not upright, shoulders running well into the back, which should be short and well coupled with the loins. The tail should be well set up, and not what is known as 'goose-rumped'. Both head and tail should be carried erect.

The ribs should be well sprung, not flat sided, with good middle, which generally denotes good constitution. A stallion should have good feet and joints; the feet should be wide and big around the top of the coronets with sufficient length in the pasterns.

When in motion, he should go with force using both knees and hocks, which latter should be kept close together. He should go straight and true before and behind.

A good Shire stallion should have strong character.

MARES
Modification or variation of the stallion standard of points for mares reads:

Colour:	Black, brown, bay, grey, roan.
Height:	16 hands upwards.
Head:	Long and lean, neither too large nor too small; long neck in proportion to the body, but of feminine appearance.
Eyes:	Large, well set and docile in expression. Wall eyes are acceptable, except for animals in Grade A or B register.
Neck:	Long and slightly arched, not of masculine appearance.
Girth:	5 ft to 7 ft [152–213 cm](matured) according to size and age of animal.
Back:	Strong and in some instances longer than a male.
Legs:	Short, with short cannons.
Bone:	9 to 11 in [23–28 cm] of flat bone, with clean-cut sinews.

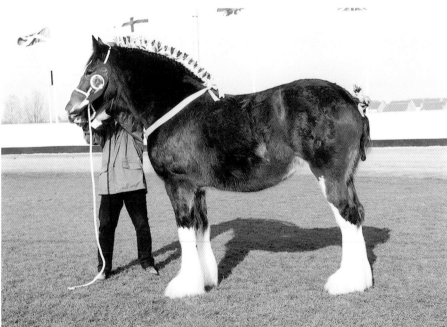

Fine examples of modern Shires. Paul and Walter Bedford's Harwoods Commander, (top) bred by A. H. Brown in Ely, Cambridgeshire, was both Junior and Supreme champion stallion at the 2003 National Shire Show. At the same show, the Bedfords' Deighton Deborah (bottom) was champion female – and went on to be Nonsuch Shire Horse of the Year in August 2003.

A mare (says the Standard) 'should be on the quality side, long and deep with free action, of a feminine and matronly appearance, standing from 16 hands and upwards on short legs: she should have plenty of room to carry her foal'.

GELDINGS

A similar modification or variation of stallion standard points for geldings reads:

Colour:	As for mares.
Height:	16.2 hands and upwards.
Girth:	From 6 ft to 7 ft 6in [183–228 cm].
Bone:	10 to 11 in [25.5–28 cm] under knee, slightly more under hock and broadside on, of flat, hard quality.

A gelding should be upstanding, thick, well balanced, very active and a gay mover; he should be full of courage, and should look as though he can do a full day's work – an impression he should be able to confirm in practice. Geldings weigh from 17 to 22 cwt [864–1118 kg].

One point arises from the current standard for hair: 'Not too much, fine, straight and silky'. Around the end of the nineteenth and into the early twentieth century, Shire breeders had a fetish for 'feather'. This involved masses of long hair covering the hoof and stretching upwards – almost to the knee in some cases. This hair was equated with bone and strength, and clever grooms could make a great display of it, hiding other faults. If the horses had been walked through a pond before judging, they would have looked very different! It is important to be aware of this background since, despite the current standard, some judges were brought up to believe in the value of hair from their fathers and grand-fathers. To some extent we can sympathize with them on seeing a few modern foals that have little more bone than a heavyweight hunter.

Regarding colour, the dearth of true blacks in the Shire is a cause of some concern. Arlin Wareing, who imported the Shire stallion Jim's Chieftain into the USA in 1970 and helped start the revival, found too many Shires of the late 1990s were muddy brown rather than black. You must use your eyes, and note the true blacks, then compare them with others claimed to

The grey Shire colt, Isles Fields Grey King, winning at the Peterborough Spring Show as a two-year-old. Grey stallions of quality are essential to the breed since, to breed a grey, at least one parent must be that colour.

Mr J. F. McCormick's eye-catching yearling colt, Goosegreen Apache, at the Midland Shire Foal Show.

Sue Everson of Hayfield Coloured Shires on her striking part-bred Shire mare, Hayfield Razzle Dazzler, a winner both in-hand and under saddle.

be black but which are not really so. Fortunately the 2002 National Shire Show saw the return of some excellent black stallions.

Bay is, by definition, brown with black mane and tail. In the Shire, this colour occurs in a wide range of pleasing shades, from light to dark bay. A brown horse has a mane and tail that match its body colour. The brown body colour should be deep and solid, not tending to roan or splatched with white. However, the beginner should not be put off if these less desirable colours occur at a reasonable price. The main thing is to be in the ring or on the box seat, taking part in the spectacle rather than watching it. Horse, harness and vehicle may all be improved upon as time goes on.

Clydesdale

This is the other British hairy-legged heavy breed. It evolved in the mid-eighteenth and early nineteenth centuries from imported Flemish stallions used on sound native stock. Its course has run parallel to the Shire's, at times closely, at others more distantly. Ferocious arguments arise about each breed's influence on the other. Yet John M. Martin, writing in *Horses of the British Empire* in 1907, best summed up the position:

> It cannot be claimed that the Clydesdale is an indigenous, native, or pure breed, in the sense in which the White Cattle of Chillingham, or the black, red or dun West Highlander, are so styled. The modern Clydesdale is unquestionably of mixed origin and has continued to be mixed, until the compilation of the Stud Book (1878).

The great foundation sires of the Clydesdale breed, Darnley and Prince of Wales 674, both had English blood in them. In the draught horse's heyday in the latter nineteenth and early twentieth centuries, dealers took large numbers of both Clydesdale and Shires across the England-Scotland border both ways.

In terms of numbers registered, the Clydesdale reached its peak in the early 1920s. Clydesdale stud books for the three years from 1919 to 1921 have a combined width of almost seven inches, and contain the registration of 700 stallions and 5,000 mares. Many more thousands were unregistered, even though many were sired by the pedigree stallions that travelled the country each spring in one of the best breeding organizations the world has ever seen.

In the inter-war decades, the Shire and Clydesdale breeds were more distinctive, the Shire being heavier-legged with masses of feather, the Clydesdale more active. These distinctions led to heated discussions between their adherents.

In the late 1940s and early 1950s heavy horse numbers reduced rapidly. During this period of the Great Slaughter, whole stables were emptied overnight as mechanization took over. The heavy horse seemed indeed doomed to extinction and, at this time, Clydesdale blood was undoubtedly a factor in 'cleaning up' the ample Shire feather which found no place in an era of more expensive labour and of keeping horses for fun. Trying to clean and dry a bushy-legged Shire after a day on wet clay was certainly no fun, especially as hair dryers were not then used on farm animals!

The nineteenth-century Clydesdale champion, Darnley, was a founder of the Clydesdale breed. Note the massive weight, and the three dark legs seldom seen today.

The nineteenth-century Clydesdale stallion, Flashwood, carries the physical attributes of his illustrious sire, Darnley. The way the groom holds him could not be bettered.

Clydesdales tend to show more white than other breeds, as in this bay, and roan is an accepted Clydesdale colour. Leg feather is a very important Clydesdale feature.

During this difficult period, some pedigree faking seems to have taken place. At the time there was no blood typing and some animals appeared in both Shire and Clydesdale stud books under different names. This caused a furore at the time and, with so few animals being registered, an outstanding sire of either breed might be used, along with an inaccurate pedigree. In the 1960s and 1970s it took a real horseman to be able to differentiate between Shire and Clydesdale, and even then they could be proved wrong! In his book *The Shire Horse*, Keith Chivers wrote: 'Some breeders who wished to speed the cleaner-legs campaign in their own way found it hard to resist the temptation to fake certificates of breeding to gain entry for the produce into the Stud-book'.

Whatever one may think now of such practices, almost everyone in that small remaining band of heavy horse enthusiasts knew at the time what was going on. And it is well to remember that they and they alone kept the two breeds alive when all seemed lost.

Subsequently, the two breeds drew apart once again, particularly after blood typing was introduced to prove or disprove parentage. This was done first by the Shire Horse Society and later by the Clydesdale

Society. Many excellent Clydesdales were exported, and those remaining included rather too many light colours and mealy roans. After considerable discussion the register was opened in 1992 to allow in 'other' blood. This invariably meant Shire, since the clean-legged Percherons and Suffolks were not considered for the register.

If Shire breeders formerly had a fetish for hair, the same may be said of modern Clydesdale exhibitors. Fine, silky hair being combed out to perfection seems to be the main show ring activity; it is not uncommon to see one helper at each foot, teasing out the fine feather.

As previously mentioned, Clydesdales are spreading from their traditional northern strongholds down into southern England. In recent times, several newcomers to showing have obtained nice coloured working geldings, which may well have been cheaper than Shire alternatives. This is all to the good, and the two breeds will often compete against each other in Heavy Horse or Agricultural classes at smaller shows.

The most common Clydesdale colours are black, brown, bay and roan. Grey is uncommon. The modern breed includes some striking blue roans and roan-and-whites, which the interested lay public can readily identify – surely an advantage when so much of the heavy breeds' future depends on audiences who are prepared to pay to see them. A conspicuous roan is a real crowd-puller; hard colours are the breeder's rather than the public's delight.

Roans are said to trace back to Dunure Footprint, a famous stallion foaled in 1908, who won every possible trophy. He had a light splotch on one side, but after he became famous he was never photographed from that side! Footprint served a mare every two hours day and night during the covering season. Two cows were kept solely to provide him with milk. Richard Mitchell, a friend of Footprint's groom, told me that the great horse collapsed spread-eagled on the floor after every service.

A bald or white face occurs occasionally in Clydesdales. The poet Will H. Ogilvie knew their broad blazes:

> *But for me the giant graces,*
> *And the white and honest faces,*
> *The power upon the traces*
> *Of the Clydes!*

The Breed Standard for Clydesdales makes the following require-ments:

The head must be strong, intelligent and carried high. The forehead open, broad between the eyes, wide muzzle, large nostrils, bright, clear eyes, big ears and a well arched long neck springing out of an oblique shoulder with high withers.

The body should be deep, the back short and the ribs well sprung. The kidneys should be below the level of the withers and the tail placed high but well set in.

Mature stallions should be 17.1 to 18 hands and mares 16.3 to 17.2 hands.

Forelegs must be planted well under the shoulders. There should be no openness at the knees, or tendency to knock-knees. Knees should be big and broad at the front. The ankles [the Clydesdale Horse Society use this term for fetlocks] should be fine, of medium length and set at an angle of 45 degrees. The foot should be large and strong, the hoof wide and springy.

Hind legs must be set close together with the hocks turned inwards. The thighs must come well down to the hocks, clean and well packed with muscle and sinew. The cannon bones again must be long. The hocks should be broad, clean and sharply developed. The ankles should be fine, of medium length and at a lesser angle than the fore ankles. The feet should be large and sound with a tendency to strength on the outside.

The [cannon] bones should be broad and flat with an abundance of long, silky hair from behind the knees and from the hocks to the ground. The front of the bones should be clean, but the hair should again spring from the hoof head to the ground.

The front action should be straight with the fetlock and knee joints being well utilized. The hind action should be close, clear and defined. When moving, the horse should lift its feet cleanly off the ground so that someone standing behind it can see the inside of every shoe.

The overall impression created by a well-built typical Clydesdale is that of strength, power and activity.

In its general comments the Clydesdale Horse Society stresses:

The outstanding characteristics of this renowned horse are a combination of weight, size and activity. What is looked for first and last by a Clydesdale man is the exceptional wearing qualities of feet and limbs. The former must be round and open with hoof heads wide and springy, for any suspicion of contraction might lead to sidebones or ringbones.

Further requirements of this breed vary somewhat from the orthodox and should be noted. The horse must have action, but not to an exaggerated degree, the inside of every shoe being made visible to anyone walking behind. The forelegs must be well under the shoulders, not carried bulldog fashion. The legs, in fact, must hang straight from shoulders to fetlock joints, with no openness at the knee, yet with no inclination to knock. The hind legs must be similar, with the points of the hocks turned inwards rather than outwards, and the pasterns must be long.

Hugh Ramsay of Kirkudbrightshire exhibits a team of Clydesdales. Hugh is a prominent dealer in turnout horses and many of his Millisle Clydesdales are for sale, so he is frequently introducing new horses into his teams.

Clydesdales in the busy collecting ring at the Highland Show.

More detail is given concerning the face, which 'must be flat, neither dished nor Roman'. Expanding on colour, the Society lists 'bay, brown or black, with much white on the face and legs, often running into the body. It should be noted that chestnuts are rarely seen.' The last remark has become outdated, for Dr Christine Wallace Mann's lively team of chestnut Clydesdales became part of the summer show scene.

Anyone contemplating purchasing a Clydesdale must pay special attention to hock action and hair. Regarding the former, it is fashionable nowadays for the hocks to be so 'nipped' together that they almost brush one another at the walk or trot. I have watched Clydesdale devotees at the Highland as a horse 'leaves' them during its show, and they appear to concentrate on the hocks and nothing else. It should be noted, however, that veterinary surgeons condemn this fashion, saying that it offends against the laws of dynamics, and that stress is placed in the wrong areas when a heavy horse walks with its hocks in and its toes out. Uneven wear on the shoes also comes into the equation, and the shoeing of Clydesdales is discussed in Chapter 5. On the second matter, however lovely the silky feather, combed and brushed so assiduously in the show ring, it should never be allowed to take precedence over points of conformation.

Percheron

The British Percheron Horse Society is a small but friendly body. It has a high proportion of farmer-breeders and, while competition at shows is keen, it is less cut-throat than is the case with some other breeds. The main breed show has had a variety of dates, but at present takes place in either April or May.

The *History of the British Percheron Horse* in the Society's show programme tells us:

The breed originated in the Le Perche area of north-west France. Here in 732 AD Arabian horses abandoned by the Moors after their defeat in the Battle of Tours were crossed with massive Flemish stock, and

Mark Morton, whose father Geoff's Hasholme Carr Farm relies largely on horsepower, with their champion Percheron stallion, Lime George. Lime George was one of the last foals bred by Roger Peacock, importer and breeder of many excellent Percherons.

E. Garner & Sons' black Percheron mare, Hales Uni.

Gordon Bailey with his champion Percheron mare, Willingham Phoebe, a multiple winner at major shows and the dam of other champions.

M. J. Bradley's black gelding, Lynside Baron, as a three-year-old. This is about as much feather as is usual in the breed.

from this cross came the Percheron type which has endured for twelve centuries. During the Crusades, further infusions of Arab blood were made. Arab sires procured in the Holy Land were bred to the Percheron and in the early 1800s the French Government's Stud at La Pin introduced further Arab blood into the Percheron breed by covering selected mares with two outstanding Arab sires, and now all contemporary Percherons share this common heritage descending from the foundation stock which originated in Le Perche.

The Percheron Horse Society of France was formed in 1883, and the British version in 1918. The latter's main aim was to encourage the breeding of a clean-legged draught horse with short legs, short back, ample bone, powerful, active and quick in work, with a good temper and easy to handle. 'The docility of the breed was very important as experienced horsemen were declining on farms', stated the Society.

Today, this is a very valid point for new owners. They may also consider the Percheron's considerable advantage in having an available

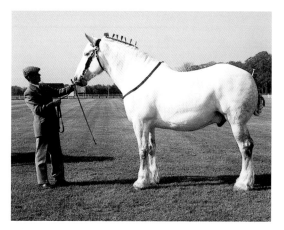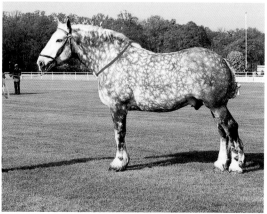

There are many variations of grey and, while grey coats tend to lighten over time, this process varies from horse to horse. Jim Barker's Prince, a dark grey when he arrived in England from the USA, is pictured here aged nine, and nearly white. The other horse, Vaux Breweries' Scorpion, remains deeply dappled at age ten.

supply of new blood from across both the Channel and the Atlantic. Various importations have been blended successfully into British bloodlines, and following their progress is a source of interest at any major show. There is also close and friendly cooperation among Percheron breed societies worldwide, with a periodic World Congress.

For those accustomed to the 'feather' on Shire and Clydesdale, clean-legged breeds such as the Percheron and Suffolk may appear insubstantial. Bone measurements prove that this is not the case. In pure black or a range of greys from dapple to iron and steel, the Percheron is an attractive animal.

Its Breed Standard reads:

General: The British Percheron Horse is essentially a heavy draught horse possessing great muscular development combined with style and activity. It should possess ample bone of good quality, and give a general impression of balance and power.

Colour: Grey or black, with a minimum of white. No other colour in stallions is eligible for entry in the Stud Book.

Skin and coat: Should be of fine quality.

Size: Stallions should be not less than 16.3 hands in height and mares not less than 16.1 hands, but width and depth should not be sacrificed to height at maturity.

Head:	Wide across the eyes, which should be full and docile; ears medium in size and erect; deep cheek curved on lower side, not long from eye to nose; intelligent expression.
Body:	Strong neck, not short; full arched crest in case of stallions; wide chest, deep, well-laid shoulders; back strong and short; ribs wide and deep, deep at flank; hindquarters of exceptional width and long from hips to tail, avoiding any suggestion of a goose rump.
Limbs:	Strong arms and full second thighs, big knees and broad hocks; heavy flat bone, short cannons, pasterns of medium length, feet of reasonable size, of good quality hard blue horn. Limbs as clean and free from hair as possible.
Action:	Typical of the breed; straight, bold, with a long, free stride rather than short, snappy action. Hocks well flexed and kept close.
Weight:	On average, stallions 18 to 20 cwt [914–1016 kg]: mares 16 to 18 cwt [813–914 kg].

The old description of the Percheron as 'a heavy horse that can trot' is exemplified by Owen Garner's Hales Quintilian.

In 1999 Warwick Aldersley startled the turnout world with his importation of black Canadian Percherons. They were of a lighter coaching type than the usual English version with flowing, sprightly action and plenty of speed. Some traditionalists feared that these horses would be incapable of a long day's work, but they certainly did not lack stamina when circling the ring under a hot sun. 'Exciting to drive' was the verdict of Tom Brewster, seen here driving a pair and a unicorn hitch.

Of all our heavy breeds, the Percheron is probably the most suitable to cross with a Thoroughbred, Cleveland Bay or other active breed to produce performance horses, eventers, showjumpers or spanking driving animals. The cross is usually free from feather, and of acceptable colour. Whereas the chesnut (see next section) often found in Suffolk crosses is not everyone's favourite colour, the Percheron's grey or black gives rise to very saleable animals, and if an exhibitor must subsidize showing costs by breeding a cross-bred foal for sale, there is much to be said for the Percheron dam.

No Percheron breed show in Britain is complete without a working demonstration by the Sampson family's fire engine, horsed by a Percheron pair at a really flying pace (see photograph on page 143) Where power combined with speed is essential, the Percheron is difficult to beat, and the original military reason favouring ' a heavy breed that can trot' is vindicated when watching the style and strength of today's greys and blacks.

Suffolk

Like that of the Percheron, the Suffolk Horse Society is a comparatively small, but well-organized and friendly body. In 1993 the tally was some 80 registered mares but, at the time of writing, that figure had more than trebled, with 19 stallions also registered. Although a far cry from the days when the breed supplied the motive power over much of East Anglia, it is evident that, with assistance from the Rare Breeds Survival Trust (based at the National Agricultural Centre in Stoneleigh), the breed is beginning to expand once more. One attraction of involvement with a breed in the throes of expansion is that there are sufficient fresh faces in evidence to ensure that the newcomer does not feel out of place.

Expansion is also occurring in the United States, where there are now approximately 900–1000 registered Suffolks, an increasing number of which are also registered with the American Suffolk Horse Association. The increasingly international aspect of the breed was highlighted in December 2001, when Dorset breeder Randy Hiscock imported the registered Suffolk colt Garrettland's Golden Eagle from an Amish breeder, Sam Yoder. This ended a thirteen-year search by Randy, who found Golden Eagle's pedigree 'impeccable.'

The British breed show is part of Woodbridge Horse Show Society's major event on the Suffolk Showground, Ipswich, in early May. The whole show attracts some 700 entries, and the Suffolk section is vital to the breed's well being. One rule enforced by the Suffolk Horse Society is that no yearlings may be shown. Members of very wide equestrian experience decided long ago that forcing a yearling into show condition may do lasting harm.

This is not the only lead they give. At one time Suffolk feet were notoriously bad. The breed was much more an agricultural rather than a town horse, which latter environment would immediately induce lameness in faulty hooves. The Suffolk Horse Society became aware of the problem, admitted it, and tackled it in practical fashion. Foot classes for stallions and mares were instigated – although for some obscure reason none was provided for geldings until 1993. Farriers and vets were chosen as judges, and the improvement over the years is such that the Suffolk can now claim parity with any other breed, and is probably the leader in this respect.

Feet are judged separately from the main ring classes. The judge wanders around the collecting ring or anywhere a Suffolk is unboxed, and inspects feet and shoeing. Thus there is no hold-up in the main ring when other judging is taking place.

Although the Suffolk has only 'one coat colour' – chesnut – this comes in a number of shades, a variety of which are illustrated here.

The mare Sandford Gem, with owner Philip Ryder-Davies, a former Secretary of the Suffolk Horse Society.

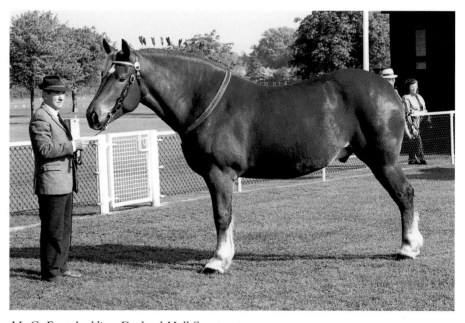

Mr G. Evans' gelding, Donhead Hall Senator.

J. S. & S. A. Geller's filly, Lindsay Magic.

Philip Morley's champion mare, Milden Tess.

The breed has only one basic colour, of which 'chesnut' is the accepted spelling. However, it comes in seven shades, and none can better the description laid down by Hermann Biddell in Volume I of the Suffolk Horse Society Stud Book (1880):

> Of the chesnut there are seven shades – the dark, sometimes approaching a brown-black, mahogany, or liver colour; the dull dark chesnut; the light mealy chesnut; the red; the golden; the lemon; and the bright chesnut. The most popular, the most common and the most standing colour is the last named. The bright chesnut is a lively shade, with a little graduation of lighter colour on the flanks and at the extremities – but not much. It is, in most cases, attended with a star on the forehead, or thin 'reach', 'blaze', or 'shim' down the face.

The flaxen mane and tail prevalent some hundred years ago and occasionally found at the present day, is usually seen on the bright chesnut. This shade is also not infrequently shot with white or silver hairs, a hereditary factor distinctive of certain strains.

The red chesnut is a very popular colour; and a red chesnut is almost sure to be a whole-coloured horse. There is no variation of shade in it, not even at the flanks, quarters, or extremities.

The golden is a beautiful colour, not many removes from the bright chesnut, but is not infrequently faced up with a white heel behind. The lemon is a very light golden shade; sometimes known as the 'yellow' chesnut. The dark chesnut is favourite with some breeders, but is mostly a changing colour, varying with the season of the year, from almost a black to a dark cherry red.

The light mealy chesnut is condemned by all. Commencing with a dull chesnut body, the flanks and underline are a mottled ash colour, gradually shading off to a dirty white at the extremities, which are usually covered with soft hair of the same hue. (As a consequence of its unpopularity, this shade has now virtually disappeared.)

Biddell points out that 'Sorrel was the name by which the chesnut was known many years ago' and, in North America, this term is still applied. But, as Biddell stresses, 'Black, white, grey or dun is never mentioned in connection with a Suffolk horse.'

The Scale of Points for Suffolk Horses was adopted on 11 November 1919, and has stood the test of time. It is as follows:

Colour:	Chesnut; a star, little white on face, or few silver hairs is no detriment.	5
Head:	Big, with broad forehead.	
Neck:	Deep in collar, tapering gracefully towards the setting of the head.	
Shoulders:	Long and muscular, well thrown back at the withers.	25
Carcass:	Deep, round ribbed from shoulder to flank, with graceful outline in back, loin and hindquarters; wide in front and behind (the tail well set up with good second thighs).	
Feet, joints and legs:	The legs should be straight with fair sloping pasterns, big knees and long clean hocks on short cannon bones, free from coarse hair. Feet to have plenty of size with circular form protecting the frog.	50
Elbows:	If turned in, regarded as a serious defect.	
Walk:	Smart and true.	
Trot:	Well balanced all round with good action.	20
	TOTAL	100

Probably no judge ever follows this points system implicitly in assessing an animal, but its descriptions of the various physical characteristics are noteworthy. These had also been summed up earlier by Manfred Biddell in the aforementioned Volume I of the Stud Book:

Height varying from $15^{3}/_{4}$ h to $16^{1}/_{2}$ h on short flat legs with short strong pasterns, free from much long hair: hard clean legs with bone of compact quality being desired, rather than soft large legs. Shoulders very long, lying rather forward to suit draught purposes. Hindquarters long, heavy, well and close coupled with loin and back, having the legs well under the horse. Girth should be large, and flanks well dropped. If the forehand is a little low, it is not objected to provided the neck is strong and the head well formed, and carried with spirit.

The following sequence shows some aspects of conformation as they relate to the Suffolk. Although there are some variations of conformation between breeds, most of these points are pertinent to all heavy horses.

A well-shod Suffolk foot.

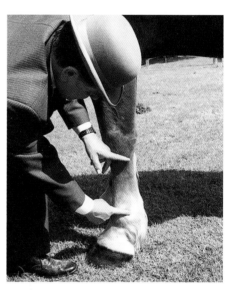

Measurement of the cannon bone, which should be short.

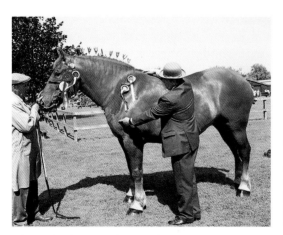

The angle of slope of the shoulder.

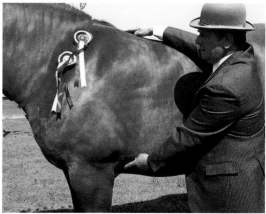

Depth through the chest, or girth. In a Suffolk, this should measure almost the same as from the demonstrator's left hand to the ground.

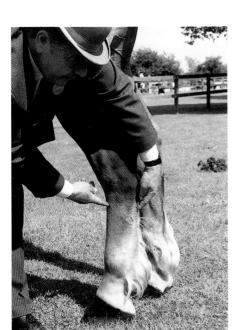

The amount of 'bone' is measured round the circumference of the cannon bone at this point.

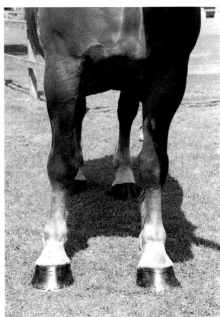

Excellent feet, straight legs and a broad chest.

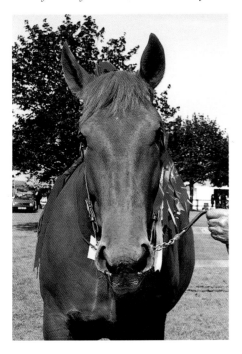

Broad muzzle and forehead, amenable disposition, kind eye.

If you study old prints of Suffolk horses, or visit the admirable Suffolk Horse Museum at Woodbridge, you will be immediately struck by the close similarity in type compared with today's horses. This continuity applies to the Suffolk breed more than any other. There is one major difference, however; Manfred Biddell's standard of a 16 hands average is no longer acceptable for the show ring, and especially for turnout horses. 'Big is beautiful', and Suffolk exhibitors competing in inter-breed classes stress that they cannot beat a team of Shires or Clydesdales standing 18 hands with 16.3 hands Suffolk geldings.

Although a strong case can be made for the more chunky type of animal for draught (especially land) work, there is no doubt that size attracts the judge's eye. A team of really big Suffolks makes a truly impressive picture, their shiny chestnut coats glistening against the black of harness, gold of brass and green and gold of vehicle.

The Suffolk's height, however, comes from its depth of body rather than length of leg. Its admirers claim that with Suffolks you are measuring the horse, not the air beneath it! A wide chest is sought, to give ample heart room and this, coupled with depth of body through the chest, gives the capacity for food enough to see the working animal through one long shift rather than two shorter ones. Big, flat knees and good, sound feet are essential to give that freedom of movement so sought by the discerning judge. Shoulders should be nicely sloping, and hocks flat. The Suffolk should be short in the cannons, giving that impression of Punch, the short, thickset man. By nature the Suffolk should be quiet. This is one of the breed's strengths, and must always be to the fore in any breeding programme.

Prices of Suffolks are probably lower than in the Shire world for the top class, but good fillies are much sought after. One reason is that, as with the Percheron, the breed's clean legs are a distinct advantage when producing heavyweight hunters. When John Bramley managed the Hollesley Bay stud near Woodbridge, Suffolk, he told me that a pure-bred Suffolk filly would be at least as valuable as a Thoroughbred-cross one, but that a half-bred gelding was worth much more than a pure-bred one. As a starting point for breeding police horses, showjumpers or eventers, the Suffolk has much to commend it, a noteworthy point when trying to balance the books.

Ardennes

Although the Ardennes is more a working horse than a show horse, it does have its own classes in the United Kingdom. Originating in the border country between France and Belgium, it is an old breed that has long been popular in northern Europe, and now has its own breed society in Britain. The society's members are helpful and enthusiastic. They recognize that their chosen breed differs from a tall, upstanding Shire, stressing rather its virtues as a low-slung and economical pulling animal.

The Breed Standard is as follows:

A family group of Ardennes – mare, foal and stallion – at Geoff Morton's Hasholme Carr Farm, East Riding of Yorkshire.

General: The Ardennes is essentially a compact heavy draught breed, possessing great muscular development combined with style and activity. Good posture and conformation, with plenty of quality bone. Should give an impression of balance, strength and power.

Height: Height must not be at the expense of bone and/or fine quality musculature.
Stallions 15 to 16.3 hands. Mares 14.2 to 16.2 hands.

Colour: All colours permitted, except part-coloured (skewbald/piebald). No white markings permitted except on the head in stallions. A little below the fetlock is allowed in mares (but not to be encouraged). Nowhere else except on the head.

Head: Intelligent expression, flat (snub) nose or rectilinear profile. Pronounced eye sockets; eyes large and docile. Ears pointing forwards. Forehead flat or concave. Large, well opened nostrils. Must avoid long heavy heads, drooping lips, misshapen ears, and domed foreheads.

The sweet face of the Ardennes filly, Forge Wood Alpine Poppy, champion at Chertsey as a three-year-old.

Neck: Medium length, well set on, with full arched crest in stallions.

Body: Stocky, expressing mass, density and power. Chest ample and deep, close to the ground. Back and loins, powerful and well supported. Haunches large and wide. Hindquarters long and well muscled. Low-set tails are common but not to be encouraged.

Limbs: Long, sloping shoulders. Arm, forearm and legs very muscular, short and hard. Joints set wide and well defined. Clean-cut tendons. Neat, round feet with hard blue/brown horn. Not excessively hairy. Avoid fat and puffy joints, spindly limbs, lumpy or spongy bone, hollow knees, knock knees or outward-turning toes.

Action: Correct and above all active and energetic.

Carriage: Powerful, proud and purposeful.

Champion Ardennes filly, Forge Wood Alpine Poppy, being shown at walk.

American Belgian

A few of these attractive horses have arrived in Britain from the United States, where they are a dominant showing breed. Their sorrel (chestnut) coat colour makes a spectacular contrast with their flaxen mane and tail, and the numbers coming into Britain may well increase.

The breed is virtually clean-legged, with just a little feather allowed. Big geldings topping 19 hands are in demand for American hitches (teams). The breed evolved from the Ardennes type imported into North America from Belgium, but selective breeding for colour and size has made it unrecognisable from its origins.

There appears, at the time of writing, to be no set Breed Standard for the American Belgian, nor is there yet a British breed society. However, the website of the Belgian Draft Horse Corporation of America, http://www.belgiancorp.com, gives the following description of the breed:

Belgian Ardennes.

'Many of the breed's first imports were roundly criticized for being too thick, too low headed, straight shouldered, and round boned. There was even an expression for it . . . 'the Dutchman's Type'. But even with his faults, those early Belgians made friends because they were easy keepers and willing workers with an amiable disposition.

'The American farmer decided that the breed's assets far outweighed its faults and the American breeders set out to retain what was right and remedy what was wrong. The success of the effort has been one of the great success stories in animal breeding. Today's Belgian is a big, powerful fellow that retains the drafty middle, a deep, strong

A typical Belgian: big, docile and with attractive colouring.

foot, a lot of bone, the heavy muscling and amiable disposition possessed by early Belgians. His qualities as an easy keeper, a good shipper, and a willing worker are intact.

'What then have the American breeders done to change him? They have developed a horse with far more style, particularly in the head and neck, with more slope to both shoulder and pastern, and the good clean, flat bone that goes hand in hand with such qualities. The modern Belgian is still a great worker . . . and has become a great wagon horse.

'Along with these changes in conformation has come a colour change. The original imports came in many coat colours, with a predominance of bay. About half of the first imports were bay and bay-brown, followed by roan, chestnut/sorrel, black, and even a few greys. There was no particular Belgian colour at the outset.

'By the 1920s and 30s, when the breed really hit its stride in the USA, the colours had pretty well come down to 'sorrels and roans'. Nowadays, although there are a few roans and even the odd bay now and then, for all practical purposes the American Belgian has become a chestnut/sorrel breed. This has long been the colour preferred by Americans . . . the Cadillac of colours being a chestnut/sorrel team with snow-white manes and tails, with a white strip [blaze or stripe] on the face and four white socks.'

Irish Draught

Females of this lovely breed are expensive, as they are so much in demand for cross-breeding to produce showjumpers and eventers as well as maintaining the pure stock. Geldings may be comparatively cheap. Irish Draughts make splendid animals for hauling agricultural vehicles and implements, and they are often well suited to ploughing matches. Their temperaments are usually sound, and they have neat feet that fit nicely into the furrow. If you want a ride and drive horse, they may fit the bill, although it's a long way to fall off the taller ones!

The Irish Draught (GB) Breed Standard is as follows:

Type and character:	The Irish Draught Horse is an active, short-legged powerful horse with substance and quality. It is proud of bearing, deep of girth and strong of back and

Irish Draughts are seen competing in the National Ploughing Championships each year, helped by their neat feet.

quarters. Standing over a lot of ground, it has an exceptionally strong and sound constitution. It has an intelligent and gentle nature and is noted for its docility and sense.

Height: Stallions to mature at15.3 hands to 16.3 hands approximately; mares at 15.1 hands to 16.1 hands approximately.

Bone: Good, strong, clean bone.

Head: Good, bold eyes, set well apart, long, well set ears, wide of forehead. Head should be generous and pleasant, not coarse or hatchet-headed, though a slight Roman nose is permissible. The jawbones should have enough room to take the gullet and allow ease of breathing.

Shoulders,   Shoulders should be clean-cut and not loaded, wither
neck, front: well-defined, not coarse, the neck set in high and carried proudly. The chest should not be too broad and beefy. The forearms should be long and muscular, not caught in at the elbows.

The knee should be large and generous, set near

the ground; the cannon bone straight and short, with plenty of flat, clean bone, never back at the knee (calf kneed), i.e. not sloping forward from the knee to fetlock.

The bone must not be round and coarse. The legs should be clean and hard, with a little hair permissible at the back of the fetlock, as a necessary protection; the pasterns strong and in proportion, not short and upright, nor too long and weak.

The hoof should be generous and sound, not boxy or contracted and there should be plenty of room at the heel.

Back, hindquarters, body and hind legs: The back to be powerful, the girth very deep, the loins must not be weak but the mares must have enough room to carry a foal. The croup to buttocks to be long and sloping, not short and rounded or flat-topped; hips not wide and plain; thighs strong and powerful and at least as wide from the back view as the hips; the second thighs long and well-developed.

The hocks near the ground and generous, points not too close together or wide apart but straight; they should not be out behind the horse but should be in line from the back of the quarters to the heel to the ground; they should not be over-bent or in any way

Patrick and Joe Fahy, from County Galway, with their Irish Draught mares, Rose's Last and Black's Last.

Mr and Mrs Kays' registered Irish Draught mare, Three Wishes.

	weak. The cannon bone, as for the foreleg, short and strong.
Action:	Smooth and free but without exaggeration and not heavy or ponderous. Walk and trot to be straight and true, with good flexion of the hocks and freedom of the shoulders.
Colour:	Any strong whole colour, including greys.

Fell and Dales Ponies

Although, as mentioned at the start of this chapter, these breeds are not 'heavy horses' as such, both are used in ploughing matches and particularly in classes featuring haymaking machinery – thus reflecting traditional use. Indeed, since they developed in areas where small family farms predominated and there was little room for specialist breeds, these versatile animals also drew the market trap and carried the farmer round his sheep – and following hounds.

The two breeds are very similar in origin but they developed, respectively, on the west and the east sides of the Pennines. Nowadays, the Dales tends to be taller, and an admixture of Clydesdale blood to some strains in the past may have been an influence here.

The following is the Breed Standard for the Fell: that of the Dales is very similar, their additional height (to 14.2 hands) being the main difference.

Height:	Not exceeding 14 hands.
Colour:	Black, brown, bay and grey, preferably with no white markings, though a star or a little white on the foot is allowed.
Head:	Small, well chiselled in outline, well set on, forehead broad, tapering to nose.
Nostrils:	Large and expanding.
Eyes:	Prominent, bright, mild and intelligent.
Ears:	Neatly set, well formed and small.
Throat and jaws:	Fine, showing no sign of throatiness or coarseness.
Neck:	Of proportionate length, giving good length of rein, strong and not too heavy, moderate crest in stallions.

Shoulders:	Most important, well laid back and sloping, not too fine at withers, nor loaded at the points – a good, long shoulder blade, muscles well developed.
Carcass:	Good, strong back of good outline, muscular loins, deep carcass, thick through heart, round ribbed from shoulders to flank, short and well coupled, hindquarters square and strong with tail well set on.
Feet, legs and joints:	Feet of good size, round and well formed, open at heels with the characteristic blue horn, fair sloping pasterns not too long; forelegs should be straight, well placed, not tied in at elbows, big, well formed knees, short cannon bone, plenty of good flat bone below the knee (8 in [20.3 cm] at least), great muscularity of arm.
Hind legs:	Good thighs and second thighs, very muscular, hocks well let down and clean cut, plenty of bone below joint; should not be sickle or cow hocked.
Mane, tail and feather:	Plenty of fine hair at heels (coarse hair objectionable); all the fine hair except that at point of heel may be cast in summer. Mane and tail are left to grow long.
Action:	Walk smart and true. Trot well balanced all round with good knee and hock action, going well from the shoulder and flexing the hocks, not going too wide or

The Fell pony mare Birkett Bank Polly, foaled in 1934, seen here put-to a pony-sized Cumbrian agricultural block cart.

The black Fell pony, Tebay Tommy, driven by Sue Millard to a Leftley Gig, taking second place at the 2003 Fell Pony Society stallion show.

A grey Dales mare, Hilton Maytime, owned, bred and shown by the late George Hodgson, a former President of the Dales Pony Society.

	too near behind. Should show great pace and endurance, bringing the hind legs well under the body when going.
General	Should be constitutionally as hard as iron and show good pony characteristics, with the unmistakable appearance of hardiness peculiar to mountain ponies and, at the same time, have a lively, alert appearance and great bone.

The scale of points by which the breed is judged is as follows:

Height and colour:	5 points
Head, nostrils, eyes, ears, throat, jaws, neck:	10 points
Shoulders:	15 points
Carcass:	20 points
Feet, legs and joints, hind legs:	25 points
Action:	25 points
General characteristics:	100 points

Mr W. Buck driving his Dales mare, Dartdale Nancy.

A Dales pony pair in a double-shafted waggon.

In summary, a good Fell should be a substantial animal, well built and powerful, but active and free moving, with plenty of pony quality and native character.

Choice of Individual

It will now be obvious that there is a range of types and colours in our heavy breeds to meet anyone's fancy. The choice of individual is helped by assessing the reasons for buying. For example, is it to compete in-hand, or drive a turnout, or to enter Decorated Horse classes? Does a desire for involvement in breeding enter the equation? If you have determined to buy a pair or a four, the ideal is to have them matching in colour and size, but that is by no means easy to achieve. Matching size is slightly less important than colour, as the bigger pair can make the wheelers, with the slightly smaller animals in front. If you had three bays and couldn't find a fourth, a grey as off leader is a possibility. I have not seen such a yoke in recent years, but it used to be practical in coaching days, as the grey could be better seen in the dark.

Moving beyond these background criteria, here are a few pointers for newcomers in search of a suitable heavy horse. First, beware of the

Long-established breeders make a safe source; the Richardson family at Bewholme Hall near Driffield, East Riding, have bred many generations of Shires.

'gentle giants' syndrome. That phrase may be basically true, but if you run into one of the exceptions you are in real trouble. A big horse with a nasty, flighty, unreliable temperament is a dangerous animal. Make sure that you buy one that you feel really comfortable with, one that will prove an enjoyable companion.

Above all, unless you really are one yourself, take an expert with you. Approach someone who understands not only the horses, but also their vendors. Some of the latter take special pride in supplying a beginner with a suitable animal. Sadly, however, a few might take advantage of ignorance, and palm off an unsuitable, unreliable and expensive animal onto the unsuspecting tyro. In a similar vein, if you don't know anyone who is an expert in the breed that you fancy, the breed society is an obvious starting point for inquiring about breeders and vendors. However, make sure that you ask for several names – in that way, you should get a genuine choice of contacts, rather than risk being put in touch with just one particular breeder or vendor.

Finally, in addition to choosing a horse that you will be happy with as a character, try to choose one that will really suit your purposes for some time. Horses tend to become 'part of the family', and a basically unsuitable one may hang around for years because no one has the heart to sell it. Also, provided you have the money, it is much easier to buy a horse than to sell one.

Selling a horse these days is an art and an achievement, so bear in mind that the horse you are thinking of buying may one day be the horse you are trying to sell!

CHAPTER 2

Feeding

'It's a very dangerous job advising anyone how to feed big horses. The rascals are all different!' Such uncompromising advice from an experienced feeder may seem to defeat the object of these pages, but appropriate horse rations cannot be weighed out in the precise manner of cattle, pig and poultry diets. (This does not apply just to heavy horses – ask any racehorse trainer!) The fundamental point to bear in mind is that each horse has a different metabolism, and it is most important that the nature of the work being done is taken into consideration.

Yet feeding horses boils down to common sense, and there is no reason for the novice to be deterred or alarmed. In the simplest analysis, if the animal has not licked its manger clean, give it less next time. If it is still clomping about, obviously hungry after a feed, give it some more. To follow this advice cuts down the risk of digestive upsets, including the very dangerous colic, although, for a number of physiological reasons, the most carefully fed horses can still succumb to this distressing condition. In the longer term, and with experience, the owner will be able to assess whether feeding is appropriate by looking at the animal's overall condition: a tendency towards gross or poor condition – too fat or too thin – suggest the need for change. The horse's attitude and temperament also provide clues: excitability or bad behaviour may suggest that too much, or the wrong type, of hard (concentrated) feed is being given for the work done, while sluggishness and lack of spirit may indicate underfeeding (or ill health).

David Lambert, a practical owner and exhibitor (see photo on pge

200), who also owns the horse feed firm Oss-i-Chaff, sums up the situation by saying 'Though scientific knowledge of feeding is always helpful, the best knowledge will always come from experience'.

However, if there is one piece of scientific knowledge that is essential to those who feed horses, this is the basic knowledge of the horse's digestive system. The key point is that horses differ from cattle and sheep in having only one stomach, and no ability to chew the cud. One practical consequence of this is that horses can digest about 30 per cent of the fibre content of hay, whereas cattle and sheep can digest 60 or 70 per cent. Furthermore, the stomach of a mature heavy horse holds only 3 gallons or so (13.5 litres) by volume, whereas the hind gut system, where most of the digestive process takes place, holds between ten and twelve times as much. This arrangement means that the horse is intended, by nature, to spend most of its time grazing and, if allowed, will do so for some sixteen hours a day, and may lie down for a few hours. There are two important lessons to be drawn from this. First, the horse is designed to draw most of its nutrition from the regular consumption of grass and grass-like feedstuffs. Grazing, whether at pasture or picking hay in the stable, is a natural, familiar and thus reassuring activity. Second, when concentrated feed is added to the diet to provide extra energy for the working horse, the small stomach necessitates that this be given on a 'little and often' basis, if digestion is to be efficient and digestive disorders are to be avoided.

This 'little and often' regime is especially important at shows, where feeding must fit in with preparation and showing time, and where the change of environment may affect the feeding patterns of more nervous or excitable individuals. However, a similar regime, including early and late feeds, also has its advantages at home, one being that it necessitates regular inspection of the horses over a prolonged period each day. The frequency of feeding the show horse in work is usually between four and six times a day. Those advocating the latter routine point out that it ensures that each horse is seen six times a day, and its dung picked up each time. The four-feeds-daily enthusiasts give a late feed just before bedtime or around 10 p.m. The horse is then racked up with sweet hay to last well into the night.

Grass

As we have seen, the horse is essentially a grazing animal and young, fresh grass is by far the best and cheapest feed. Some pointers about good pasture management are given later on (see Pasture Management in Chapter 3). 'Doctor Green' can resolve problems caused through poor wintering – although the horseman should see that these do not arise. However, it is a fact of nature that good, nutritious pasture is not available all year round, and some of the heavy horse world's most important shows take place before the new spring growth of grass has had much time to take effect. Therefore, despite its virtues, the horseman cannot rely solely on fresh grass, but must look also to its preserved forms, supplemented as necessary by hard feeds.

Hay

Hay for horses must be good. Mouldy, musty or dusty hay is very dangerous for horses, being likely to cause long-term respiratory problems, and over-ripe hay has little nutritional value. Rather than feeding such hay, it would be far better to feed clean straw (see Straw, below) and augment with concentrates. Grass for hay should be cut after flowering but before seeding, and should not contain a lot of weeds and thistles, which are signs of poor grassland management. The bale should spring apart when the bands are cut. If it clags together, it is probably mould-infected.

There are two main types of hay, meadow and seed hay. The latter comes from a sown sward, and is preferable if a range of varieties is involved. Meadow or 'old land' hay should have a wonderful herby smell, but is a scarce commodity in many areas.

Racehorse trainers, with long experience of the need for the very best, prefer to feed year-old hay, and much may be learnt from these full-time professionals. That ideal may well be impractical for some, but trainers would certainly not feed new season hay in its first year if doing so could possibly be avoided. New hay can be indigestible and a potential cause of colic.

When buying hay by the bale, weigh a few sample bales. They are very deceptive, and you may find you are paying a very high price per ton. It is often satisfactory to buy hay in the field, and then you know how it has been made, and it may never be cheaper. On the other hand, it will lose a lot of weight between haytime and February, and allowance must be made for that.

Hay must be stored dry and, although an open-sided Dutch barn is useful, care must be taken to protect the bales from wet as the stack lowers and lets in the weather. The bottom course should be stacked on pallets, stakes or poles to allow air to circulate underneath and avoid damage from damp and mould. Even so, any hay that does become damaged should not be used for horses.

This brings us to another point about buying hay in bulk, which is to buy enough to cover any spoilage and other contingencies. A good deal may be fed whilst travelling to and staying at shows when, if at home, the horses might otherwise have been turned out. In addition, it is prudent to keep a few bales per animal in reserve during the summer, in case of drought, a really wet time when horses are better housed, or sickness. If a sick horse won't eat top quality hay, it probably won't eat anything.

The turn of the year is a good time to take stock of feeding requirements, especially the provision of hay. Never forget that winter is not half over on New Year's Day, and remember that old farming saw advising having half one's fodder still on hand at Candlemas (2nd February). At the turn of the year hay requirements should be reassessed and the hay market studied; prices can rise astronomically in a late spring, especially in hill-sheep districts where hay is the main practical standby.

So far as feeding hay is concerned, it is probably best to give it on the floor. A horse's natural means of feeding is 'downwards', with its long head and neck allowing it to reach food on the ground. Although hayracks were once standard in all stables, often filled through a hole in the floor of the loft above, it has to be said that they suited the men rather than the horses. Hay nets are handy and help to save waste, but they allow dust and hay seeds to fall into the horse's eyes. Improbable accidents can also occur when a foal rears and catches its foot in the net, with disastrous consequences. If you must use a net, for example on journeys, rope is preferable to nylon, and nets should be secured to tie rings via a weak link.

Silage

Silage is essentially grass of various sorts that has been 'cut green' and placed in sealed containers, where it undergoes a fermentation process. Although it is now made by choice on a large scale, silage first came to the fore as a means of salvaging hay crops that would otherwise have been ruined by wet weather. Big bale silage, wrapped in plastic sheeting, is now a common feature of the countryside. Silage is used extensively as a cattle feed, but cattle silage is not suitable for horses, since by-products of the fermentation process may prove harmful, and the protein content may also be too high.

There are forms of silage available that are produced for horses, made with a higher than normal proportion of dry matter (high dry matter silage). This is the only type that should be considered as a horse feed but, even so, it may be richer in protein than other bulk feeds, and should be introduced gradually, with due caution.

Haylage

This is essentially a 'halfway house' between hay and silage, the crop being taken at a later stage than for silage, but a little earlier than for hay. It is then vacuum packed in waterproof bags. Haylage from reputable sources is safe for horses provided that the manufacturer's instructions are followed. In general terms, once a bag is opened, the contents should be used within a few days and any that shows signs of mould should be discarded. Any bag found to have been torn or punctured during storage should also be disposed of. One advantage of haylage is that, correctly stored, it is dust-free, making it particularly suitable for horses susceptible to respiratory problems.

Haylage is generally made from ryegrass and tends to have higher feed values than hay, so this should be considered when calculating overall quantities of feed. However, some newer products are formulated to be more or less direct substitutes for dust-free hay, and these can be sought out if they suit one's purpose.

Straw

In the heavy horse's heyday, long oat straw and chopped hay formed an integral part of the working horse's ration, as may be seen from a study of textbooks written prior to the Second World War. Both materials were readily available, especially in farm stables. Oat straw was particularly useful in northern climes, where it was cut on the green side, then left in the stook for a fortnight to mature. The crop then had a beautiful rustle and smell. Nowadays the oat acreage in Britain is considerably reduced and, since the straw is usually combined at a more mature stage, it is of less feed value than before.

Although owners would not consider it part of their horse's diet, it is a fact that some horses will eat their bedding straw, so this must be clean and dry. Oat straw, as mentioned above, is not used primarily as bedding, but barley straw is soft and suitable. Wheat straw is harder than either, and of lower feed value. Years ago I read that the nutritive value of wheat straw is less than the amount of energy used by the horse in consuming it, but this will not necessarily prevent certain horses from doing so! (Since modern wheat varieties are very different from those of times past, it may be that the nutritional values of the modern straw are also different, but I am not aware of any up-to-date analyses.)

A basic test of the quality of straw is the same as applies to hay; the bale should spring open when the bands are cut, and not stick together in flaps.

Chaff

Chaff, or 'chop', consists either of hay by itself, or mixed with a proportion of oat or barley straw (see above), and processed through a chaff cutter to cut it into short lengths. When mixed in with a hard feed, it adds roughage, encourages thorough mastication (thus preventing the horse from bolting its food) and aids digestion.

Most successful showmen have traditionally based their rations on hay and chop, prepared at home. To the chaff mix is added bran and soaked sugar beet pulp, with the emphasis on 'soaked'. A twenty-four hour steeping is essential to allow the pulp to swell in the bucket – if fed dry the swelling takes place in the stomach, with disastrous results. The advantages of such preparation – especially if the hay and straw are home-produced – are cheapness and complete control over ingredients.

However, while most equestrian establishments traditionally made their own chaff, this practice is less prevalent nowadays, with much chaff being sourced from commercial suppliers such as David Lambert's firm, mentioned earlier. These companies offer a range of chaffed feeds, some containing garlic or cod liver oil, others with vitamin/mineral supplements. Certain brands, produced from top-quality hay, are formulated specifically for certain types and breeds (including heavy breeds), and are specially processed and packed to ensure they are dust-free. Although the costs of commercial production are reflected in the price, such products can save owners the worries of finding and accessing suitable hay at times when it is of variable quality.

Hard Food

Cereals, nuts and mixes come under the heading of concentrates or 'hard' food, the purpose of which is to provide additional nutrition and energy to the horse in work.

Cereals, in particular oats and barley, are the traditional hard feed. Both grains, whilst highly nutritious, are low in fibre. Maize is another high-energy cereal, also low in fibre. In Britain, it is more likely to appear as a constituent element in a mixed feed than on its own. Wheat is not recommended as a horse feed. In its whole form it is dangerous, since it swells in the stomach. While it may be boiled and then fed safely in small quantities, there is nowadays no point in such a practice.

So far as oats and barley are concerned, they are best prepared in a way that renders them more readily digestible. Traditionally, they have been bruised, rolled or crushed for this purpose but, once this is done, and especially if it is done too severely, they begin to lose their nutritional value. Modern techniques, such as micronizing and gelatinizing, improve digestibility with less nutritional loss.

Although they are not cereals, beans, another traditional heavy horse feed, have much in common with the cereal feeds, providing high levels of energy and protein, and requiring preparation in the form of splitting, crushing or micronizing. Nowadays, beans are more commonly seen as constituents of coarse mixes rather than as individual feedstuffs.

Individual cereals can be fed with great success by those experienced in horse husbandry, but they do require a certain degree of knowledge. In the first place, in their natural form, they may vary considerably in nutritional value. (Incidentally, while cereal varieties have changed greatly in the past half-century, I suspect that many of the nutritional tables published have not been changed, and may well be misleading.) Second, their 'heating' nature can have a considerable effect on the behaviour of certain horses, especially those of an excitable or suspect temperament. Third, overfeeding (especially of barley and maize) can cause allergic skin reactions in some horses and finally, despite their nutritional advantages, cereals do not, of themselves, provide horses with an optimum mix of trace minerals (especially calcium), so some form of supplement is usually required. For these reasons, less experienced owners, and those who lack the time to prepare and mix traditional feeds, may opt for commercially blended hard feeds.

Those going down this route for the first time may struggle to find products obviously targeted at the heavy horse. Generally speaking, most of the commercial manufacturers have diversified from cattle, sheep, pig and poultry feeds into horse feeds and, in aiming at the mass market, have focused mainly on the light breeds, and on the nutritional demands of their various regimes and circumstances. This means that, compared to the number of feeds formulated for other breeds and types, there are few proprietary hard feeds on offer aimed *specifically* at the heavy breeds. There are, however, a number of commercially blended feeds that will suit heavy horses and recommendation from an experienced owner, or inquiry to the nutritionists employed by most of the reputable feed manufacturers, may provide the best guidance for the newcomer. That said, one should be mindful that, just because a particular feed has proved eminently suitable for one horse of a certain type, there is no guarantee that it will prove ideal for another (apparently similar) animal. This is part and parcel of the individual nature of feeding, mentioned earlier.

One point to bear in mind when feeding commercial blends is that, whereas individual cereals usually require some form of vitamin/mineral supplementation, proprietary brands are blended to be completely balanced and further additions are not only unnecessary, but may even upset the balance.

Minerals and Vitamins

While it is true that vitamins and certain minerals are essential to the well-being of the horse, most are required only in small quantities, and most will be available much of the time from regular food sources, provided that these are of good quality and appropriate blend, and provided that there are no underlying problems of mineral deficiency in the soil of the horse's grazing land.

Because there are nowadays a huge number of vitamin and mineral supplements on offer, many owners feel a virtual obligation to feed them without due assessment of real need. This is not advisable, since it has the potential to produce imbalances or, in extreme cases, toxic effects.

In general terms, blended hard feeds from reputable sources can be considered, as previously stated, to contain appropriate quantities of vitamins and minerals, and need no supplementation. Those who feed cereals in the traditional manner should be mindful that, despite their benefits, all contain a poor ratio of calcium to phosphorus. Bran also contains high levels of phosphorus. Although essential of itself, phosphorus inhibits the uptake and utilization of calcium, which has important functions including enhancing lactation and bone growth. In order to improve the levels of calcium, sugar beet (which has a good ratio of calcium to phosphorus) can usefully be added to cereal feeds, or the mineral supplement limestone flour can be given.

Horses in hard work, that consequently sweat a lot, will benefit from the addition of salt to their feed, and most horses will benefit from having a mineral/salt lick in their stable – many seemingly enjoying the simple process of licking. In the winter months, many owners add an eggcupful of cod liver oil daily to the feed – this provides an alternative source of Vitamin D, which is naturally made under the horse's skin during times of sunshine.

Other than these basic practices, it is sensible to provide specific supplements only once an actual need has been established. This need may be informed by veterinary advice, or by soil analysis or the analysis by sample of forage (hay) bought in bulk.

Watering

Water constitutes approximately two-thirds of a horse's bodyweight and, as with humans, an appropriate intake is essential to well-being. A large heavy horse may drink as much as 12 gallons (54 litres) daily, especially in hot weather.

Generally, clean, fresh water should be available to the horse at all times. This provision means ensuring that containers in stables are robust, kept clean, and cannot be easily be kicked over; that automatic systems are kept in good order; that field troughs are checked regularly, with ice being broken in winter and debris of any sort removed and that water is changed regularly rather than just 'topped up', to ensure that it does not become stale or affected by algae.

A constant supply of water will ensure that the situation does not arise in which a thirsty horse is given a feed and then, immediately afterwards, is offered a drink. A horse taking a long drink in such circumstances may wash the food out of its stomach before the digestive process has started, denying itself nutrition and risking the onset of colic. This is a different circumstance from the harmless one of a horse, with water freely available, taking the odd sip whilst eating. One other situation in which a horse should not be offered sudden access to a large quantity of water is if the horse has become very hot and tired. In such a case, small quantities of slightly tepid water should be offered initially, since the sudden intake of a large quantity of cold water can produce colic and shock.

The provision of water whilst at shows may require prudent planning, and it is sensible to take a large container of fresh water with you, and an adequate supply of buckets.

CHAPTER 3

Field and Pasture Management

The basic principles of field and pasture management are no different for the heavy horse owner than for owners of other breeds, but in some respects the demands are accentuated. For example, heavy horses will eat more grass and poach the ground more than lighter breeds, and their weight and strength will find out any deficiencies in fencing and other field structures. It is self-evident that horses injured by wire or nails, or whilst straying, or sickened by ingesting poisonous plants, will not enhance their chances in the show ring. It is therefore recommended that newcomers to keeping heavy horses study the comprehensive works available on equestrian field and pasture management. This category of 'newcomers' includes those who have experience of livestock other than horses since, in certain aspects, equine requirements may differ substantially from those of sheep and cattle. In the meantime, the following pointers may be helpful.

Ideal and Less Than Ideal Conditions

While, in many cases, ideal grazing conditions may be unobtainable, a knowledge of the ideal will help the horse owner work towards the best conditions achievable.

The ideal pasture, whether for rearing young horses or maintaining adults, contains a mixture of grasses. It should be spacious (two acres is a standard minimum for a single heavy horse) and preferably extensive enough to allow for grazing rotation, well drained, well sheltered and safely fenced. There should be ample lime in the soil, since this provides calcium, essential for bone growth. (Certain limestone districts are renowned for the livestock they produce, whether cattle, sheep or horses – for example, horses from Ireland's limestone districts are noted for their good quality of bone.) This is an especially important consideration for the heavy horse breeder, since big, heavy horses with poor bone are not a recipe for success.

Such ideal conditions seldom occur. You may have access to only one small paddock, without the chance of a change in summer or winter. Proper management, including periods of resting, then becomes even more important, as there is less room for error. A paddock over-grazed by horses for too long becomes horse-sick. The ground becomes badly poached, there is an increased risk of heavy worm infestation, and useless types of vegetation take over among the many bare patches. With little of nutritional value available, the horse's rations need to be supplemented throughout most of the year, and the paddock becomes nothing more than a turnout area.

If circumstances are really dire, remember that it is perfectly possible to keep a heavy horse and yet have no grazing at all. Historically, many heavy horses, especially in urban environments, were kept in this manner. W. J. Gordon's marvellous book *The Horse World of London* describes how omnibus, cab, delivery and draught horses were stabled, perhaps on more than one level, and all their feed was brought to them. It is also the case that farmers have, on occasion, plumped for a stabled regime in times of low cereal prices, when it paid them to feed a high cereal diet rather than use up grassland. When Billy Cammidge had his fascinating Open Farm at Flower Hill, in the East Riding of Yorkshire, he found it better to feed hay and corn rather than take up potential arable land for grazing horses. Of course, if a horse is permanently stabled, it must be regularly exercised. With the town horses kept for work, that was not a problem. However, if you cannot be sure of being able to exercise your stabled horse daily, the project should not be attempted. Also, it is much more fun for the horse to have access to even a small paddock, and nowadays most heavy horses are kept essentially for fun.

Fencing and Facilities

Horses are difficult to fence against. When cattle are full, they lie down and cud. When horses have finished grazing, they tend to look around for mischief, which often entails a breakout. The first consideration in this respect is that horses must be able to see a fence, otherwise they might career into it with calamitous results. The second consideration is that it must be high enough to dissuade them from jumping it – and if you think that heavy horses can't jump, think again! They will also paw, rub or push fencing by leaning with their chests, thereby exerting incredible pressure, so a strong, sound, safe fence is the first essential. Pawing in particular precludes the use of any wire fencing with low strands, in which the horse might catch a foot or shoe. Rubbing, which occurs particularly when horses are changing their coats, means that sharp protuberances on any field structure should be avoided. For this reason, all fencing rails should be nailed to the inside of the supporting posts, a practice which also provides extra strength to counter the effects of pushing or leaning. One ploy to entice horses away from rubbing on perimeter fencing is to supply an actual rubbing post. In bygone days, rough tree trunks of eighteen inches or so diameter were sometimes planted deep into the soil for this purpose, and I know of one such rubbing post that must have been in place for fifty years.

Regarding the materials of which fences or field boundaries are constructed, natural hedges without reinforcement are rarely stout enough to provide an effective barrier. They do, however, play a useful role in providing shelter and shade. Drystone walls may also afford shelter, especially since the wind tends to filter through the walls, so that they do not create the same turbulence as a solid wall. However, these walls are rarely high enough to fulfil this function adequately for heavy horses, nor are they high enough to ensure containment. Furthermore, it is by no means unknown for horses to lower them, whether by accident or design, by rubbing or pushing off the top stones with their chins.

The best fencing is correctly constructed post-and-rail, using three rails, with each rail twice as long as the gap between the posts and placed alternately so that there is a joint above a solid rail the length of the fence. As mentioned earlier, the rails should be nailed to the insides of the posts, from the field side. The life of the fencing will be greatly extended if, prior to sinking, the posts are treated with preservative and if the tops of the posts are cut at a slant to encourage rainwater to run off, and discourage chin-rubbing.

A modern alternative to wooden post-and-rail is a plastic version, now available in several forms. The advantages of plastic are that it is highly visible (usually white in colour) and solid looking, and it is also flexible yet strong. Thus horses can see it even if they are careering about, yet even if one does crash into it, it does not splinter dangerously like some timbers. It also needs very little maintenance, and does not rust or rot, crack or peel.

A cheaper alternative to full post-and-rail is a top rail with two strands of plain wire beneath. A plain wire fence with no top rail is no good, as the horses may not see it from a distance, and they will also rub it with their necks and slacken it. Even when combined with a top rail, it is a good idea to ensure that tension is maintained in the wires at all time. Also, the lower strand should be at least 18 inches (45 cm) above the ground, to guard against a horse getting a foot over it. This can be particularly dangerous if a shod horse gets the wire caught between foot and shoe, especially if the horse panics and the wire holds. For the same reasons of safety, pig netting, often used to fence against sheep, is unsafe around horses. However, the very worst fencing for horses is undoubtedly barbed wire, which has caused horrific injuries, especially when badly set and loose. Even when correctly set and kept taut, it does not fulfil the criterion of visibility, and its very nature invites injury.

In contrast to most other forms of wire, electric fencing can be a boon to horse owners, if used sensibly. It is commonly used to partition off parts of a field for grazing by rotation, for a schooling area, or for taking a hay crop. The modern type is available in the form of brightly coloured tape, which is highly visible and gives the horse every chance of seeing it before touching. If, for any reason, it is necessary to join such types with a length of plain wire, this should be adequately tensioned and preferably decorated with strips of old fertilizer sack, or something similar, to aid visibility. If a single electrified wire is run the length of the fence to prevent animals rubbing on it, this should be well tensioned and secured, and checked on a regular basis.

When electric fencing is introduced, is does no harm to engender circumstances whereby the animals receive an initial shock, in order that they learn to respect it and do not unwittingly try to charge through it. You can lay some damp grass on the live fence, and lead the horse up to it to sample, but do stand well clear. However, there is another side to this coin. Having more brains than cattle, horses may remember an electric fence in a certain place after it has been moved, and they have been known to refuse to leave a paddock long after the electric fence has gone, so be sure that they know that the exit gate is safe.

Further to this, no fencing is complete without a neat gate, functioning properly, that is both secure and safe. Gateways can be dangerous places, through which horses may tend to barge to their own and their handler's detriment so, even for hand gates, 4 ft (1.2 m) should be the minimum width. Gates that swing properly and latch smoothly are a perpetual boon, both in terms of time saving and safety. These attributes are products of correct construction, especially ensuring that the hanging post, on which the hinges are hung, is perpendicular and, particularly with regard to wooden, gates proper maintenance and freedom from abuse. It is a great advantage if the gate is not set in the lowest, least well drained part of the field, since gateways churn up readily enough in wet weather without the burden of additional run-off.

In these days of increasing crime, gates – especially those close to roadways – may need to be secured with stout padlocks and chains, and with perhaps an iron bar driven in just above each crook to prevent the gate from being readily lifted clear.

Shelter, Water and Provision of Winter Feed

Even if turned away in New Zealand rugs (see Chapter 4), there are times when horses will benefit from shelter. This may be especially the case if they are turned out periodically during the time when they are being prepared for the showing season, and grooming has thus begun. If a purpose-built shelter is provided, a concrete base will prevent the floor from becoming poached. Entrances should be wide enough to ensure that no inmate can be trapped and bullied by other horses, and the open (entrance) side should usually face southwest, on the basis that the coldest winds usually emanate from the north or east. Any existing structures pressed into service as shelters should preferably comply with these criteria, and it is certainly the case that a tall, bushy hedge provides better shelter than an inadequate shed.

Whilst discussing shelter, it should be added that actual stables for heavy horses should be both large and robust. The standard size often quoted for a loose box, 14 x 12 feet (4.34 x 3.72 m) is the minimum for a heavy horse, but recent structures measuring 20 x 20 feet (6.4 x 6.4 m) are wonderful, giving a great sense of space and freedom. Doorways should be at least 4 feet (1.2 m) wide and 7 feet six inches (2.32m) high. The propensity of certain horses to lean on things, mentioned in the context of field boundaries, may extend to stable structures, and this should be taken into account when assessing existing stabling, or planning new constructions.

Clean, fresh water is essential for all horses, whether housed or at pasture. In the field, this is usually provided by a ball-valve trough. This should be situated on a well-drained part of the field, preferably on a concrete base, and preferably away from trees and hedges to prevent falling leaves from fouling the water. It should be free from any sharp edges or projections, with any taps or fittings boxed in and the supply pipe well lagged. In severe weather, it should be checked for ice, and for continued functioning, at least daily.

If water is supplied in buckets, these should be large, robust and preferably stood in old tyres to aid stability. Very regular checking and refilling is essential at all times.

In most cases, natural sources will be unsatisfactory for watering horses, particularly as this means that the horses will soil their feather when going down to drink. Certainly, stagnant ponds and streams with sand or clay beds are unsuitable, and should be securely fenced off.

If it is necessary to feed horses at grass (for example, to provide supplementary hay during harsh winter conditions), it is best to do so in a relatively well-drained area. Where groups of horses are involved, provide more piles of hay than there are horses, and place them some way apart, to avoid any problems of fighting or bullying.

Security
In addition to using the appropriate materials for fencing, fences and boundaries should be checked on a regular basis, and any defects made

good immediately. This applies particularly to slackened wire, loose or protruding nails and broken rails. Areas where horses congregate in close proximity to field boundaries, such as beneath hedgerow trees, often require extra attention. Remember that straying horses are a danger to themselves and other road users. Furthermore, so far as English law is concerned, the owner or keeper of an animal found straying on the highway commits an offence under the Highways Act 1980 and, if an animal strays onto and damages another's property, there may be repercussions under the Animals Act 1971. Therefore, in addition to making every effort to ensure secure fencing, it makes sense for horse owners to be covered against third party liability.

Poisonous Plants

Apart from ragwort (dealt with under Weed Control), the plants most likely to concern the horse owner are those associated with the hedges and gardens of human habitation. These include laurel, privet, laburnum, box, rhododendron and yew. Although the first two mentioned would not normally prove fatal to a healthy horse, the others must be considered extremely dangerous. Therefore, be especially careful if your pasture adjoins gardens or hedged walkways, and make very sure that neighbours do not deposit clippings into your pasture under the mistaken impression that they are 'giving the horses a treat'. (Even if the clippings do not contain any poisonous plants, the short-cut grass can cause compaction in the horse's digestive system.) Remember, also, that heavy horses have enormously long and strong necks and a capacity for leaning on apparently safe barriers, and can reach forbidden fruits many feet away. This must be taken into account when fencing close to human habitation.

Yew, of course, is not simply confined to gardens, and it goes without saying that horses cannot be kept in fields containing, or adjacent to, yew trees. It is, however, the case that many horses are kept in fields containing oak, and caution is needed here. Some horses develop a liking for acorns and, particularly in certain seasons, these can cause poisoning if eaten in quantity. In most cases, this is relatively mild, but still undesirable. It is, therefore, good policy to collect fallen acorns. An alternative, if it fits your regime and you have suitable temporary fencing available, is to use pigs to eat the acorns, since they are not affected by them.

Poisonous plants more associated with meadows and hedgerows than with gardens include deadly nightshade, foxglove, hard rush, hemlock, horsetails and meadow saffron. Found in wet soils, hard rush is very tough and would usually be eaten only if the rest of the pasture was bare. Much the same applies to horsetails, although large amounts eaten in hay would be very dangerous. Deadly nightshade is usually not deadly to horses, but its consumption is highly undesirable, while foxgloves, although rarely eaten, can prove fatal in small quantities. Hemlock would need to be eaten in some quantity to cause death, but lesser quantities can cause levels of narcosis and paralysis, while meadow saffron has a markedly toxic effect, which usually becomes evident too late to save the horse.

It should be evident from this brief summary that all horse owners should familiarize themselves with the full range of plants that are poisonous to horses, and take measures to ensure that these are eradicated from the vicinity of their charges.

Pasture Management

Seed Mixtures for Planted Pasture

A hard-wearing sward is necessary for horses, which are bad grazers at the best of times, selecting certain areas and refusing others used as a latrine area, while youngstock in particular are apt to go careering around, cutting up the ground in wet times. If you are in a position to seed your own pasture, pre-planning and planting an appropriate mix of grasses can help minimize the effects of supporting a heavy horse population.

Modern grass mixtures hold many advantages over some of the older types, but the basic principle remains that a range of species is an insurance against any one succumbing to adverse circumstances such as drought, and is more palatable to the stock. Perennial ryegrass and turf-type perennial ryegrass form the basis of production for a modern sward. These are augmented by strong creeping red fescue, smooth-stalked meadow grass and crested dogstail. For still harder wear, for example if the field is to be used in part as a schooling area, the smooth-stalked meadow grass is omitted and slender creeping red fescue added. This latter mixture is designed to produce a very dense, springy sward, capable of withstanding very heavy wear. However, if used regularly for schooling, it cannot be expected to provide so much in the way of grazing.

The addition of mixed deep-rooted herbs such as burnet, chicory, wild garlic and yarrow will enhance the horses' intake of minerals and assist with the calcium and phosphorous levels. However, if you intend to use weedkiller (herbicide) on the field, then the herbs should not be mixed in with other grasses. In fact, since herbs generally flourish in infertile conditions, the same applies if you intend to use fertilizer, so the best place for herbs is usually in a strip along a particular fence line.

General Husbandry

With sufficient pasture the grazing may be rotated. Sub-dividing existing areas facilitates pasture management, helps worm control and allows the necessary resting period. While the paddock is being rested, it may be topped with a mower or, better still, grazed down by cattle. Strong store cattle about eighteen months old are ideal. By all means get some agistment (grazing fee) money for them if you can, but even if not they will level off the pasture, wrapping their rough tongues round herbage left by the more fastidious horses.

Heavily grazed areas tend to become lime-deficient, so they should be soil-tested, and the necessary lime applied. The soil may also become impoverished, resulting in thin swards and bare patches, which encourage weeds. In this case, fertilizers may be needed, but the horse keeper must avoid that over-lush growth of pasture that encourages laminitis (see Chapter 6). If nitrogen is used on the horse pasture, it should only be applied when really needed. While shepherd and cowman seek maximum production, the horse keeper requires a level growth throughout the grazing season. Remember, also, that it is pointless boosting a pasture in late spring when there is already an abundance of growth. However, small, frequent doses of nitrogen to encourage early spring, late summer and autumn growth may be invaluable. Ideally, horses should be kept off the pasture until rain has washed in the fertilizer, but in dry weather, some time can be allowed for the dews to do their work

Ideally, horse droppings should be picked up daily. Where this is not possible, harrowing with grass, chain or parmiter harrows spreads the droppings. An old method if no suitable harrow is available is to tie hawthorn branches to a horizontal five-barred gate, turn it over so that the gate adds weight, and pull it by ropes attached to the traces. Remember that harrowing is an ideal means of training and exercising young horses. When horse power is available, use it. To do otherwise is as silly as the practice once used in sheep dog trials, of having a team of men to bring off the sheep at the end of each run, instead of using a dog.

If an area of grazing is to be shut up for haymaking, it should first be harrowed and then rolled. The object of rolling is to press any stones into the soil so that they are not caught by the grass reaper blades. Molehills, which soon blunt a sharp knife, are similarly dealt with. Again, the roller is a good means of training a young horse alongside an old stager.

Weed Control

When horses are grazed alongside cattle and sheep, pasture management and weed control are that much easier. However, nowadays more and more horses are kept as the sole grazers.

Horse pastures present special problems for weed management, and weedy swards on frequently overstocked horse paddocks are a common sight on the fringes of many towns and cities. The highly selective grazing behaviour of horses and their preference for separate grazing and latrine areas in the same paddock encourage infestations of weeds, none of which are beneficial and some of which are injurious.

Where infestation becomes a problem, it may be necessary to employ herbicides. This should be done out of necessity rather than as a general measure and, where possible, knapsack spraying of weed 'blackspots' is to be preferred to blanket spraying. If spraying becomes necessary, it is important to bear the following points in mind:

1. Herbicides are toxic – some dangerously so. Manufacturers' instructions should be followed implicitly in all respects, including the use of protective clothing.

2. Horses should not be allowed to graze the sprayed pasture until heavy rainfall has washed all the weedkiller off the herbage. Again, this general rule should be supplemented with specific advice given by the manufacturer.
3. If it is necessary to spray a large area, it may be best to engage an expert contractor.
4. Spraying should never be done on a windy day.
5. Generally, the best time to spray pasture is when the grass is still young. This gives the grass the best opportunity to grow strongly and smother the wilted weeds.

It should be noted that, under two existing Acts, landowners in England are legally obliged to eradicate specific weeds from their land. If you rent, rather than own, your grazing, you may need to ascertain whether this obligation is yours or your landlord's, but the weeds in question are ragwort, dock and creeping and spear thistles.

Of these, ragwort is the most pernicious, causing dysfunction of the liver in horses, which can prove fatal. Although local authorities have a legal obligation to control its growth in public areas, they seldom seem to bother and roadside verges are often a prime source of ragwort seed. Since this seed can blow into your pasture every year, you are never free of the risk. It is also the case that many landowners fail singularly to fulfil their obligations, and it is devastating to see horses grazing bare pasture on the edge of towns, picking among a forest of the 'yellow peril'. Although horses do not generally eat ragwort as it grows, this is little comfort, since they apparently find it more palatable in its wilted state, when it is at its most poisonous. It is particularly lethal when eaten in hay.

The simplest and best way to eradicate ragwort is to uproot it by hand, which can be done readily enough, especially after rain. Since the stems are quite woody, it helps to wear a stout pair of gloves. All of the uprooted material should then be removed from the pasture and burnt. Because of the biennial nature of the weed, and its wind-borne seeds, this process will have to be repeated annually.

Sheep seem to be able to graze ragwort with no ill effects. They may be a supplementary means of control, if it suits you to have them on your pasture while the ragwort is growing. As mentioned earlier, fencing requirements for sheep differ from those of horses, so modifications – perhaps temporary netting, removed along with the sheep – may be necessary. If you have no sheep of your own, a local farmer may be persuaded to put a small flock onto the pasture free of charge.

We are all familiar with the bright green, oval-leafed weed that is dock. This is a particularly robust and hardy plant, which develops a deep taproot that expands by a phalanx growth system. As a mature dock may produce up to 60,000 seeds a year, and as these may lie buried in the soil for several years before germinating, the problems are obvious.

Dock is, in fact, fairly easily controlled by approved sprays, but for reasons previously mentioned, the horse owner may dislike spraying. If spraying is not to be the means of control, then regular cutting will eventually weaken the plant, but if you inherit a mature and thriving stand, digging up each individual plant may be possible. One Worcestershire horse owner who took over a dock-infested paddock dug up the bigger specimens with a special inverted-V shaped spade, and pulled up the smaller ones by hand right down to earth level. This, combined with liming, over-sowing with a grass/white clover mixture, and daily removal of droppings, resulted in a much-improved pasture within three years.

Like dock, thistles are readily controllable by spraying – late spring, prior to flowering being the best time. Whatever one's reservations about the method, spraying is almost certainly the most effective means of dealing with creeping thistles, which spread through subterranean systems, their seeds being mainly infertile. Where sprays are unwelcome, constant cutting and mowing will eventually weaken them, and this method is fairly effective in dealing with the large Scotch thistles, which spread by seed alone. However, so far as cutting is concerned, the old rhyme that tells us:

> *Cut them in June and they'll come again soon;*
> *Cut them in July and they'll soon die;*
> *Cut them in August and die they must.*

can be considered wildly optimistic. This principle was followed in pre-spraying days, yet thistles flourished year after year!

Other weeds, not subject to legislation, but potential nuisances, are nettles and bracken. Nettles are harmless to horses if eaten, and some animals seem to relish them. However, they can spread rapidly and take over whole areas of paddock or pasture. Frequent mowing will keep them in check, while applications of common salt will help on small, dense areas. Alternatively, they can be controlled by spraying. Either method should be carried out during their growing season between April and September, before they go to seed.

Bracken is largely a weed of upland and marginal land rather than the fertile lowlands, so it is less likely to be found where heavy horses are kept. However, although horses do not normally eat it in quantity, it is potentially poisonous, having the capacity to cause internal haemorrhage and containing a substance that inhibits the uptake of vitamin B1. Its presence on grazing land is therefore undesirable. Constant bruising will check its growth, but the best method is to plough up the mass of rhizomes that lie beneath the bracken bed. Dried bracken is used in some areas as a form of bedding, and it does not appear poisonous at that stage.

Taking a Hay Crop

'Good hay, sweet hay hath no fellow', wrote Shakespeare, and his words remain true today. Hay quality and price differ from year to year, and lucky are those horse owners with enough land to make their own. However, practical considerations of quantity and the demands of the show season must be taken into account. Missing an important event for the sake of a few bales of hay is counterproductive, so do remember that once grass is cut for hay – even if a small area – it takes over and other activities seem to take second place.

The most satisfying way of making horse hay is to use your own animals to haul a mower, even if it is powered by an auxiliary engine. Finger mowers with cutter bars are out of fashion, and may be relatively cheap to obtain, yet quite suitable for small areas. You need to learn to sharpen knives and to replace blades or sections, but both are basically simple operations.

The object of haymaking is to reduce the moisture content of the grass to a point when it may be safely stored. Rapid rates of drying are fundamental to this, but so is even drying. Any moist patches inevitably result in the growth of mould, which can affect the horse's respiratory system. Horses are far more susceptible to such problems than cattle and, when making hay for horses, it is important to remember the physiological differences between them and other livestock. Whereas cattle and sheep can digest some 60–70 per cent of the fibre content of hay, horses can digest only about 30 per cent. Thus, while grasses and clovers harvested as the flower heads are fading may be of optimum weight/feed value for cattle, that stage is too late for ideal horse hay. Hay for horses should be cut at the leafy stage, even though that means it will take longer to cure.

The more the sward is shaken out in dry weather, the quicker the drying. There are two schools of thought here. One is to follow the mower immediately or almost immediately with the tedder or turner, and continue the process as often as possible until the requisite dryness is achieved. The snag here is that the more the crop is shaken out and dried, the more damage it takes if the weather breaks. The second, now rather old-fashioned, method is to let the swathe bake on one side, and leave it untouched until the top is thoroughly dry. It is then flipped over and the underside cured. This takes longer, but is safer as the unbroken swathe will shed a lot of rain with little adverse effect.

When dry enough, the hay may be baled. If it is not dry enough the small pick-up baler will not tackle it. For just one or two horses you do not need expensive machinery; some of the best hay is made by cocking as soon as the crop is partly dry, which is well before it can be either baled or stacked. In wet districts like western Scotland and the Lake District, the grass may be put into small hand cocks as some safeguard against the weather, and then into ever bigger ones. Use of tripods, which allow air to circulate through the pike (a higher version of the haycock), is another small-scale technique that can result in excellent hay, if the amount of hand labour is discounted.

Haylage, described more fully in the previous chapter, is a term for herbage halfway between hay and silage, and is becoming more and more popular with horse owners. In recent years, it has enjoyed increasing popularity as a cash crop since, when made correctly, it is less risky than hay, and is readily handled mechanically. However, the requirement for a machine to bale the haylage, and another to bag it, means that small-scale operators will rely on a contractor to make haylage. While the contractor will try to fit in all clients as best he can, he will doubtless be very busy so, in respect of taking the crop at the optimum time, it is important to stress that high quality fodder for horses is the aim.

Samples of old haymaking implements.

CHAPTER 4

Grooming and Rugs

Grooming

Some suppose that grooming is merely a matter of prettying the animal. It would be more appropriately termed 'cleaning the skin', essential to the general health and condition of the domesticated horse. In fact, if grooming does not play its important role in maintaining condition and promoting health, then the horse's superficial appearance will leave much to be desired.

Overall, the reasons for grooming heavy horses, and the general principles and practices, are much the same as for other types being worked and shown. However, certain factors associated with heavy horses, such as the tradition of wintering out, their size, and the working and showing regime, require owners to have a thorough understanding of grooming if they are to produce horses in the peak of condition.

The first point to consider is the differing regime of the horse at grass as compared to the stabled horse in work. Heavy horses normally and advantageously run out from the end of the showing season sometime in autumn until into the New Year. Horses running out at grass are not routinely groomed. To do so reduces the coat's weather-resisting qualities, for the naturally produced grease unwanted by the showman helps keep out rain and bad weather.

However, as the days lengthen, the time comes to bring them in for the early shows. Both Shire and Clydesdale breed shows are held in late winter or very early spring, so the grooming for these breeds starts as soon as they come inside. At this point, we address an apparent conundrum: if grooming is connected to health and condition, as well as appearance, why can horses wintering out do without it? And if horses wintering out can do without it, why (other than for the sake of appearance) does the stabled horse require constant grooming? The answer to this lies not in the bare difference between living out and living under cover, but in the work being done and the food being taken.

In simple terms, the amount of grooming needed depends on the amount of food and exercise: the more arduous the work, the greater the care expended on getting the skin into perfect condition. Grooming the stabled horse may be limited when the horse is only lightly exercised, but it must be increased as the show season gets under way, to aid the pores of the skin to work at full efficiency. This applies particularly to horses that will appear in Turnout classes.

In order to understand this correlation between grooming and work more fully, we should look briefly at the structure of the horse's skin, and its relationship to the horse's overall metabolism. The skin has two distinct layers, the inner being called the dermis and the outer the epidermis. The dermis contains blood and lymphatic vessels, nerve fibres, heat sensors, hair follicles and sebaceous and sweat glands. The epidermis consists of a layered arrangement of cells, through which the hairs rooted in the dermis penetrate to form the coat and through which the sweat glands pass to reach surface pores. The sebaceous glands are closely associated with the hairs, and secrete an oily substance called sebum into the hair follicles. This lubricates the hairs and the surrounding skin and can penetrate to the skin surface. Since the hair is so closely associated with the skin, it is no surprise that the appearance of the coat reflects the health of the skin and of the whole animal. A harsh, dry coat is a sign of unhealthy skin, and very often of poor health in general.

Since the outer surface of the skin is subject to 'wear and tear', the top layer of epidermal cells is constantly being shed. To compensate for this, new cells are formed and the lower layers of cells move up to replace those that have been lost. As the cells move further away from the nutritional sources of the underlying dermis, they degenerate and die, forming scurf. This has the capacity to 'block up the drains' of the sweat and sebaceous glands and must therefore be removed from the skin surface in order that the glands and pores can operate effectively.

When turned out at grass, the horse is in a more or less natural state and will, generally speaking, take only as much exercise as grazing demands, and will feed on a laxative diet. These two factors mean that, compared to the working, stabled horse, the horse at grass will produce low levels of sweat and (although its production increases naturally in cold, wet weather) relatively low levels of sebum. Furthermore, the turned out horse can remove a significant amount of skin debris by rolling, rubbing against various surfaces and, to some extent, self- or mutual grooming.

Working horses, by contrast, are kept under artificial conditions. They receive a quantity of feed considerably in excess of what they would require in a natural state, in order to provide the extra energy to produce the work required. Also, the type of feed given places more demands upon their digestive system and overall metabolism than does grass, and it introduces to the body increased levels of proteins and carbohydrates. These changes in regime trigger the production of greater quantities of sebum and increase the activity of the sweat glands which, in addition to cooling the working horse through perspiration, also have a role in excreting some of the waste products of metabolism. It will be evident that, unless the pores of the skin are kept free of debris and the increased secretions of the glands are removed by artificial means (i.e. grooming), the pores will clog, the condition of the skin will deteriorate and the horse's general health must suffer in consequence.

Further to this, the importance of grooming as a preventative of skin disease should not be underrated. Although mange and most other skin diseases are not induced solely by dirt, it is equally true that they occur most frequently, spread more rapidly and are more difficult to eradicate where dirty conditions prevail.

It can be seen, therefore, that grooming helps to keep the body fit as well as clean. Grooming, and massage of any sort (see Strapping, page 98), is very beneficial to a horse's general condition. This aspect has always received attention from professional horse trainers. The racing trainer does not pay his staff to spend hours and hours grooming just for the fun of it. Heavy horse owners must think in the same way, whether they are full-time professionals or amateur one-horse owners. Perhaps one reason why amateurs are generally less successful than professionals in the show ring is that some tend to 'give a better grooming tomorrow'.

Routine Grooming

'If you're not in a sweat when you've finished grooming, you haven't done a proper job!' That is the old-time horseman's adage that remains as true today as ever. No modern gadgets have as yet really reduced the time and effort spent in grooming. In fact, to the usual set of grooming tools – body brush, dandy brush, curry comb, sponges, leather and hoof pick – the heavy horse groom can simply add a stout box. This is because the spine and haunches on a heavy horse are so far from the ground that the groom needs some such object to stand on, since these areas cannot be adequately brushed from floor level.

The following are some pointers for the routine grooming of a horse being made ready for the show ring.

Grooming entails use of the headcollar, and even fastening and adjusting this calls for care, since the forelock and mane are being prepared for showing. These must be adjusted under the headcollar, the forelock free and the mane swept to its appropriate side, and not simply roughed up anyhow.

Start at the head. Clean the eyes and eyelids with a sponge, or wipe them with a clean cloth, and sponge the insides of the ears as necessary. Next, give particular attention to the face. Facial grooming tends to be neglected, but a bold, clean face takes the judge's eye as soon as it enters the ring. Spend five to ten minutes brushing downwards on that part of the face below the eyes then, holding the forelock to one side, brush upwards to the near ear, taking in just the front of the off side ear. A very soft body brush is useful; a particular favourite retained for the face may last several years, whereas a brush used repeatedly for sweeps along the body may need replacing after two months. In the earlier stages of preparing a horse for the show season, a rubber curry comb may help remove some of the scurf.

Now take the near side from the ear downwards. Brush in long sweeps of the left hand, following the lie of the hair, and cleaning the brush from time to time on the curry comb, held in the other hand. Proceed down to the chest, and between the front legs. Like the face, this is often a neglected area. Any judge worth his salt is well aware of the fact, and may inspect accordingly, so don't be caught out. After the chest, proceed to the near flank, the belly and the near hindquarter. The back – especially around the loin area – often accumulates dirt and scurf, and the grooming box mentioned earlier will assist in ensuring that this is given proper attention.

The legs down to knees and hocks may be groomed, but it is not usual to brush any lower than that. The feet and lower legs may be washed It is also traditional to treat the lower limbs of the feathered breeds with oil. Various types of oil are used. Pig oil as used by the exhibition pig fraternity is a traditional horseman's favourite, but a well-tried recipe is white oil mixed with flowers of sulphur into a fairly pale yellow paste of creamy consistency. At one time waste tractor oil was used, but modern engine oil detergents make them completely unsuitable. The oil is applied once a week throughout the year. Lift the long hairs at the back of the foot and gently work in the mixture so that it reaches the skin. This helps keep the feather correct and clean, but it does tend to run down onto the hoof, which should be guarded against.

After completing the near side, the grooming process is repeated on the off side

The mane and tail must also be brushed, and the former swept onto its correct side. It is often better not to use a mane comb on the mane and tail until the time comes to plait; its action is too severe and it pulls out a lot of hair – exactly what the exhibitor seeks to avoid.

The final act of grooming is to sponge around the dock, with a sponge kept separately for that purpose. Picking out feet is not necessarily part of the grooming process, usually being done before and after exercise and last thing at night. It is, however, an essential procedure, since it can give early warning that a shoe is loose, and helps prevent lameness from being caused by foreign bodies or accumulated dirt in the foot.

The time required for routine grooming is fully half an hour in a morning, and perhaps an hour and a half later on, giving a total of two hours a day at least, and more during the height of the show season. A young horse unaccustomed to the grooming process will need to be handled with a mixture of firmness and patience. It will have certain sensitive and ticklish spots, which may vary between individuals, but the belly, sheath area, and under inside aspects of fore and hind legs may need approaching with extra care. However, while impatient and rough grooming can spoil a young horse's relationship with humans, grooming with consideration can have the opposite effect, bringing horse and groom closer together than any other operation. Therefore, talk to your horse whilst grooming, let it become accustomed to its name, and give an extra brush or rub to those parts where it obviously appreciates attention. When properly carried out, this regular close contact between horse and groom forms a bond that cannot be bettered.

For all horses, a definite routine is best for grooming. The detail may vary from person to person, but the process as outlined is based on years of experience, and horses as well as grooms will become accustomed to it. It also helps to ensure that no part of the horse's body is missed out.

Camaraderie in the heavy horse world is such that volunteer helpers keen to learn the art of grooming will be welcomed at the big stables. Practice may also be gained at shows, but if so it is better to approach the stable staff after their class, when there is less pressure on time. A few sessions will yield a surprising amount of information. It will be fun, and with the brewery teams especially there is always the chance of a sample of the firm's products by way of reward for energetic work!

Strapping

Strapping is a separate operation, additional to grooming, although the criteria of practising and establishing a routine are equally applicable. It is a vigorous workout for horse and groom – effectively a fairly powerful massage – and there's nothing like it to tone the muscles. It also stimulates the blood supply to the horse's skin, gets rid of unwanted lumps of subcutaneous fat and puts a final shine to the coat. It is far more beneficial than a lot of washing (see next section).

Strapping is carried out along the neck, the shoulders and tops of the forelimbs and on the hindquarters and thighs. A leather strapping pad, available from any good saddler, is used for the purpose. It is applied with the lie of the coat, in a rhythmical flapping motion, gently at first, but building up to a more positive action. Time taken is from about twenty minutes minimum, possibly up to one hour.

Washing

At one time heavy horses were never washed. Even mud on the feather of a Shire or Clydesdale was left to dry and then brushed out, although horses might be led through a pond to clean them. Even now, washing of manes and tails is seldom routine in most heavy horse stables (although it may be done in preparation for a show – see Chapter 11), but washing horses' bodies all over seems to have spread from the cattle lines at shows. Hosepipes have been used there for years, and now hair dryers make it easier to dry stock afterwards. While washing is much quicker than thorough grooming, it does not give the benefits to skin and circulation afforded by the latter. Also, comprehensive hosing has a different, more drastic effect than does rain. Other than in exceptional circumstances, rain does not penetrate right through the horse's coat to the skin, nor does it affect the coat under the belly. Thorough washing with a hose does both, rendering the horse unusually cold and leaving him vulnerable to the effects of cold for a considerable time. For these reasons, there is a considerable risk attached to all-over washing, especially during the weather conditions often associated with early spring shows.

If washing becomes part of your routine, be very wary, and take the greatest care, otherwise you may bring on chills and colicky stomach upsets. As a minimum precaution, once horses have been washed, they must be suitably rugged up and walked immediately afterwards.

Obviously, localized washing to remove stable stains is a different matter, and the sooner these are removed, the better. It is notable that bedding on Irish moss peat, rather than shavings or straw, tends to reduce the level of staining.

Rugs

In common with wild horses and most native ponies, most non-working heavy horses thrive perfectly well outside without rugs, but this depends on the individual rather than the breed. Some will grow much heavier winter coats than others. However, as we have noted, any horse in work should be groomed, which depletes the coat's natural oils. To redress the balance, some form of protection must be provided, hence the need for winter rugs.

The all-weather New Zealand rug will provide protection for horses turned out in winter, or during other times of particularly inclement weather. It is waterproofed, with a warm underlayer, and with fastenings designed to combine security of fit with safety. These benefits notwithstanding, it is still good practice to check on a regular basis that these rugs have remained properly in situ since some horses, perhaps aided and abetted by bushes, trees or companions, have a Houdini-like ability to effect total or partial escape from their rugs, possibly tearing them in the process.

When measuring for rugs, the measurement should be from the centre of the horse's chest to the furthest point of the hindquarters. The actual width of the chest has a bearing on overall fit, so a broad-chested heavy horse may require a bigger (longer) rug than casual assessment might suggest. This is especially significant in the case of New Zealand rugs which might be worn for days on end, since an over-tight front fastening may chafe the horse's chest quite badly. Furthermore, too short a rug may leave the hindquarters inadequately protected, with the consequent risk of chilling.

If a horse requires rugging in the stable, then stable rugs of various weights are available. One point to bear in mind is that, while horses enjoy being adequately warm, they neither need nor like to be unnecessarily hot. Many people nowadays feel a need for sky-high central heating and Arctic-rated duvets, but such practices do not translate well into the stable.

A day rug is, essentially, a light form of stable rug, often used for special occasions. So far as heavy horses are concerned, day rugs are most likely to be used when travelling to shows, to keep the coat reasonably clean before final grooming and to provide such warmth as may be necessary. At the show, clean and smartly coloured day rugs, embroidered with the owner's initials or sponsor's name, can play their part where advertising is involved.

Rugs in various forms can have uses other than to provide warmth. The summer sheet, or fly-sheet, is a very light cotton rug designed to give protection from flies. Some horses are very susceptible to the attentions of these pests, and may not only get bitten extensively, but may even bite or rub themselves out of irritation, none of which adds to appearance in the show ring. Apart from providing a measure of protection, a summer sheet also helps to keep the coat smooth and clean after grooming.

Anti-sweat rugs and cooler rugs are used to cool down a sweating horse safely, without risking a chill. In the heavy horse world, they may be used if a horse has sweated up during the fittening process, or after protracted work pulling a turnout vehicle or ploughing. The anti-sweat rug is similar to a string vest, and is usually made of cotton mesh. Placed under another light rug – preferably a woollen rug or old-fashioned jute rug – it creates air pockets next the skin which, warmed by the horse's body heat, help to dry the coat. This arrangement can also be useful in minimizing the effects of nervous sweat, as in horses that 'break out' when travelling. A modern version of the anti-sweat sheet and its supplementary rug is the cooler rug, a single rug made of 'wicking' material, that allows sweat to evaporate steadily through the rug, whilst maintaining the horse's body heat.

CHAPTER 5

Shoeing

Shoeing the heavy horse for the show ring seems to give rise to more controversy than almost anything else in that already contentious world! The owner thinks he knows how the horse should be shod, and the farrier is sure he knows best, and is unwilling to compromise. Differences of opinion can extend to the perceived requirements of the show ring, for example leading farriers may disapprove of the long feet beloved by some Shire exhibitors and judges. Clydesdales in particular have one specific regional technique, called 'calping', in which the shoe is built up on one side (the outside) and is extremely thin on the other side. This practice has been going for a very long time. One aim is to accentuate the 'nipped' or 'cow-hocked' appearance and calping is also said to reduce the risk of one hind foot brushing the fine, silky feather of the other foot – Clydesdale people tend to be fanatical about feather. If practitioners don't know what they are doing, calping can be harmful and, at the time of writing, there is some controversy about the practice. However, it may be that some of the criticism is not well informed. When Roger Clark worked for George Colson, breeder of the immensely influential Suffolk stallion, Rowhedge Count II, the stable included several Clydesdales. 'All had such tight hocks that you couldn't get a cigarette paper between them', said Roger, 'yet they received no special shoeing'.

For some owners, getting the horse shod is the most difficult part of keeping a heavy. Good light horse farriers are scarce enough, but in some areas these craftsmen shy away from shoeing heavies. (Although heavy horse shoeing competitions are well supported, it is noteworthy that few of the competitors shoe heavies as routine!) It has to be said that shoeing heavy horses on one's own can be a daunting task, and the hard work is made a lot harder by horses that have never been taught to stand and have their feet handled. If a farrier's initial experience of shoeing a heavy horse is to be thrown about or leant on, it is no wonder that some people are put off. For this reason, it is essential that heavy horses should be thoroughly accustomed to having their feet lifted from foalhood. Lift, and scrape with a blunt tool, even though there is nothing to remove. Tap the hoof gently. For those buying a mature animal, a check to see how readily it lifts and holds up its feet may be time well spent. In all cases, regular attention to foot lifting will pay real dividends on shoeing day.

Some horses, particularly Shires with 'itchy' legs, are made worse by the practice of getting hold of the hair to lift the hind feet. With such a horse, it is far better for the farrier to pull up the foot with the claw of the hammer, and then grab the toe.

Shoeing For the Show Ring

Successful shoeing for the show ring is essentially a matter of good management, for if the horse is to have sound feet it must be prepared well in advance. For the showing owner, this preparation must become part of the seasonal cycle. Traditionally, after the last show of the season, the horses are turned away for a winter's rest. Before turning away, they should have their shoes taken off and their feet trimmed. It is a bad mistake simply to turn the horses away with their shoes on. All horses benefit from a period without shoes; it enables them to put pressure on the frogs and they are better for the absence of the shoes' weight on their feet. Also, shoes are too expensive to leave on and lose! If just one is lost, that may still mean a new set all round.

During the rest period, feet should still be trimmed as necessary. Some owners keep the hooves short, others dress the foot at each trimming to match the shoe that will eventually be applied to it. As soon as the horse is brought up ready for the next season's initial show preparation a set of light shoes should be put on. If the horse has run unshod for some time, it may be a month before its feet start to show even the smallest signs of growth, so shoeing early is important if strong feet are expected in the coming season.

A sound frog and a perfect fit.

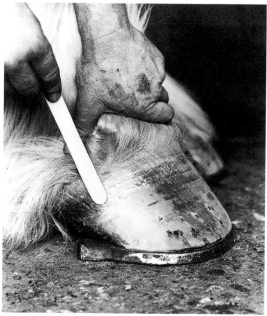

The hoof is rasped smooth and the nails neatly and firmly clinched.

Hooves fit to win a Foot class. A skilled farrier is the horseman's best friend.

Foot conformation, which affects the specifics of shoeing, varies from breed to breed. For example, Suffolks and Percherons have different foot conformation from Shires and Clydesdales and need a different style of shoe – as light as possible. For all breeds, however, the basic aim of good, strong feet remains the same. A strong foot needs to be deep in the heel, short in the toe, with bold quarters and the bars left strong.

The feet must of course be trimmed and balanced before the shoes are fitted. If the nail holes are stamped coarsely enough, then the shoe can be fitted slightly wider than the foot. It is surprising how the feet will pull out when the shoe is nailed on and drawn up. Regarding the relative size and shape of shoe and foot, the Shire Horse Society has recently introduced a new regulation that states: 'The whole ground bearing surface of the foot must be covered by the shoe', and has instigated a system of show inspections by an appointed farrier to check exhibitors' compliance.

The horse's action will be exaggerated if it is first shod light, and then shod with heavier bevelled shoes. These shoes, the main purpose of which is either to exaggerate good feet, or help enhance poor ones, are seen extensively in the show ring and most horses shown in-hand wear this type. In the bevelled shoe, the outer rim of the shoe continues at the same angle as the wall of the hoof, giving an appearance of length and depth. Some people are critical of shoeing a horse with bevelled shoes for the show ring, saying it serves no purpose. To others it is the icing on the cake and, if carried out by a good craftsman, it is almost an art form in showing. In addition to the bevel continuing the angle of the hoof wall, such shoeing should be exaggerated at the heels in length and width and have the upper surfaces of the shoes well boxed to the feet. A well-boxed shoe is one that is no wider than the foot itself. It is important to shoe a good length at the heels, especially the outer heel which can be slightly 'donkeyed' (turned out) if required, to give the appearance of more width at the heels. With the forefeet, the toe clips should be positioned to make the horse appear square and straight. Careful work by the farrier can help disguise faults such as pigeon toes and faulty movement such as dishing (throwing the feet outward in a paddling motion) and, in the longer term, expert farriery can actually have a remedial effect on such faults.

This being so, it is perhaps ironic that the farrier is often blamed by the owner or groom when a horse throws out its feet whilst giving its 'show'. This usually happens because the person showing the horse has never properly learnt his craft and, in asking the horse to move at the wrong pace, actually induces dishing, or exacerbates any natural tendency to do so. In many cases, even a horse that has a natural tendency to dish will appear to go straight if properly paced and shown. It is all a matter of homework and practice. It is interesting to note that a farrier who also shows may like to see his own horses run out by someone else; this way he can judge at what pace the horse goes best.

In some cases, a horse may move straight when in natural condition, but develop faults in stance and gait when brought into show condition. This can come about if, in attempting to show their charge to best advantage, exhibitors proceed to 'over-egg the cake'. To have an animal in top condition while keeping its legs and feet right is a major skill in the art of showing the heavy horse.

Shoeing Working Horses

Working horses will need to be shod somewhat differently from show horses. A light shoe that will last at least six weeks is best for land work. A plough horse walking in a 9 or 10 inch (approx. 24 cm) wide furrow should have the inside branch of the hind shoes narrowed to about a third of the width, and well safed off, otherwise it is apt to brush one foot against the other. Safing off means rounding the edge of the hoof to correspond with the shoe. We have to safeguard the horse from standing on its own shoe, and also from doing the same to its neighbours in the yoke.

A town horse – for example, a dray horse – requires a different style of shoeing from a horse that works the land. Shoes should withstand a month's work without wearing out, yet not be too heavy. While the shoes should be well boxed to prevent treading them off, the town horse is not working under the same constraints as the farm horse and can take a longer shoe.

CHAPTER 6

Veterinary Matters

There are excellent books available that provide detailed information on equine lameness and disease, and it is not within the province of this book to seek to emulate them. What follows are general notes on health issues that may be especially pertinent to those who own and show heavy horses, and it is hoped that the points made will assist owners in maintaining the welfare of their charges. Some diseases which are especially pertinent to breeding stock are covered in Chapter 7 Breeding and Rearing Heavy Horses.

Tetanus and Equine Influenza

These are two very different diseases, but can be considered together for our purposes. Tetanus is a dangerous disease caused by soil-dwelling bacteria. This disease is easy to prevent, but difficult and expensive to treat: all horse owners should vaccinate their stock against tetanus. Equine influenza is, as the name implies, more or less the equine equivalent of the viral illness that plagues the human population.

The reason for mentioning these two diseases in tandem is that the most common vaccination programme protects against both, through a combined flu and tetanus vaccine. In recent times, in an attempt to reduce the incidence of equine flu, it has become the practice of many equestrian organizations to require proof of up-to-date vaccination as a condition of entry to shows and events. The Royal, the Horse of the Year Show, the Royal International Horse Show and, indeed, most of the main breed shows now insist on the necessary veterinary certificate accompanying entries. Any shows or displays that take place on racecourses are almost certain to adopt the same policy. Therefore, in addition to putting horses at risk, an inadequate vaccination programme and record keeping may confound ambitions to compete at certain shows. With rules and regulations changing constantly, it is wise to keep up to date on this issue, even where local shows are concerned.

Since instigating the vaccination programme requires primary and booster vaccinations, and as there are certain constraints of timescale, owners of unvaccinated animals are advised to consult their vets well in advance of any proposed show dates. A thorough perusal of conditions of entry is also advisable.

It should be noted that some horses show a slight reaction to the flu vaccination and, in a few cases, this may be more marked, with the horse appearing distinctly off-colour. Any post-vaccination concerns should be reported to the vet, and all but the lightest work avoided, pending veterinary advice.

Parasitic Worms

Parasitic worms, of which there are many varieties, can do enormous damage to horses, and even kill them. It goes without saying that a wormy horse will never do itself well and, other considerations aside, will stand no chance in the show ring. All owners should make themselves broadly familiar with the main species of worms and their life cycles, and it is well worthwhile consulting your vet to devise a worming programme that suits your animals and your overall regime. This may involve the use of several proprietary wormers, none of which is cheap, but the cost must be viewed in proportion to the damage that worms can do. Further to this, those with past experience of, for example, worming riding horses should remember that wormer dosage relates to bodyweight, and the dose that protected a 15 hand hack will not be adequate for a 17 hand Shire stallion.

So far as overall regime relates to worming, it is well to remember that much infestation takes place in the field, and good pasture management can reduce the overall worm population. Not over-populating or over-grazing the pasture are basic measures, as is the regular collection and removal of droppings. This latter measure is made easier by the tendency of horses to use certain areas as a toilet, thus leaving most of the droppings together – although this benefit is somewhat countered by their consequent tendency to graze other areas down to the sod, which may cause problems of its own, such as sand colic.

Harrowing, carried out at the right time, can also reduce the worm population. It should be done during a settled period of dry weather, so that any droppings that have been otherwise missed can be spread over a wide area, the dry conditions then killing worm eggs and larvae. However, carried out at the wrong time, in moist conditions, harrowing has precisely the opposite effect, and it should never be considered as a *substitute* for collecting droppings.

One useful method of worm reduction is combined grazing. Worms are mainly host-specific, so worms that affect cattle and sheep do not affect horses, and vice versa. Thus, if combined grazing is possible, cattle and sheep will pick up some of the larvae that might otherwise have infected the horses, and these larvae will be destroyed within their digestive systems. Note, however, that fencing must suit the stock being grazed – see Fencing and Facilities in Chapter 3. Note, also, that while most parasitic worms are host-specific, this does not apply to lungworms, which can affect horses although their primary host is the donkey.

While simply resting pasture may help in the reduction of the worm population, it is a fact that some infective larvae can survive even over the winter so, again, this cannot be considered a substitute for more specific forms of control.

Colic

Colic is a term used to describe any abdominal pain, so it is really a symptom of a variety of different problems rather than a specific disease. Although most commonly associated with digestive disorders, it can also be indicative of other factors which impact upon the alimentary canal. These include worm damage, certain forms of poisoning, and thrombosis in blood vessels supplying the gut.

Although some cases of colic occur for unforeseeable reasons, it is a fact that the horse's digestive system and processes make it prone to this disorder, and it is consequentially true that, while good management will reduce the risk, inappropriate management will greatly increase it.

The basic point to understand is that the horse's digestive system is based around a series of tubes and organs, along which food being digested is moved by a process of muscular contraction and relaxation (peristalsis). Along its length, this tube system undergoes many changes in internal diameter and also many changes of direction, which predispose it to partial or total blockage, and to the possibility that, in certain circumstances, it can twist over itself (twisted gut). Furthermore, depending on the precise nature of the blockage, the horse's condition may be worsened by the onset of shock and a reduction in blood pressure – both of which give rise to further complications. Therefore, if anything happens to cause an obstruction, or to interfere with the digestive processes, the consequences have the potential to be very grave.

As stated, not all cases of colic can be avoided, but there are some simple management practices that can greatly reduce the risk. One basic point is to have regular checks made of the horse's teeth. Problems in this area may make it difficult for a horse to chew and break down the feed adequately before it passes down to the stomach – a common sign is 'quidding', in which partially chewed food falls from the horse's mouth at feeding time. If any dental problems are suspected, the vet or a bona fide equine dentist should be consulted. Many owners, in fact, have their horses' teeth checked on a regular basis (perhaps coinciding with annual inoculations), so that filing and rasping the teeth can be carried out as necessary.

Other good management practices are based upon the concept that anything likely to interfere with the overall digestive process should be avoided. A simple example is to water *before* feeding since a thirsty horse, having fed, might otherwise take great draughts of water and wash food out of its stomach before the digestive process had properly begun. Similarly, for the same reasons that we would not have a large meal immediately before or after hard work, neither should our horses. (Following hard work, horses can be allowed to pick at a small quantity of hay, and fed once they are clearly cooled down and calm.)

Another factor that can upset the digestive process is making any sudden changes to the horse's diet. The horse's digestive system relies in part on a population of micro-organisms in the intestines to break down specific foodstuffs. Sudden changes to the constituents of feed don't give the population of micro-organisms time to adjust, and so the food will not be digested efficiently and may cause partial or complete blockages. One example of this, pertinent to heavy horses, is that forages with high levels of indigestible fibre (such as straw) may cause problems if large amounts are eaten at any one time, or if the horse has not been used to having this material in its diet. However, if introduced to such fibrous material gradually, most heavy horses are able to digest it sufficiently well to avoid problems.

A different form of indigestion can occur if a horse eats a large quantity of readily fermentable food such as cereals. Cereals contain starch, which should ideally be digested and absorbed in the small intestine. However, if the intake of starch is too great, some will pass undigested further along the digestive system into the hind gut. As starch does not have such a complicated structure as fibre, it can be fermented very rapidly, producing lots of gas, which can then cause the gut to become swollen and painful. Excessive gas production can also be caused by feeding wet, partially fermented grain, or mouldy feed.

Stress is another factor which can interfere with digestion. The muscular process of peristalsis occurs automatically, but any stress that the horse encounters can inhibit this process, thereby reducing the mobility of the digestive tract. Gas can then build up, resulting in the digestive system becoming distended and swollen and the horse will then display colic symptoms. There are obvious situations that can result in the horse becoming stressed, such as travelling, unfamiliarity with show atmosphere, separation from companions and, with youngsters, weaning. In all such circumstances, extra care must be taken when assessing when and how to feed the horse. In simple terms, the safest approach to is feed at times when the horse is most likely to be relatively calm, and to err on the side of caution both with overall quantity and proportion of hard feed. Horses of anxious disposition may become stressed for less obvious reasons than those stated, but some sort of environmental change is often a factor. Such horses should be monitored carefully whenever a discernible change in their circumstances occurs.

It is worth noting that these warnings against sudden changes in diet and circumstances extend to the grazing regime – a factor that might seem innocuous to the less experienced owner. The prime example is suddenly giving a stabled horse ready access to lush spring grass. This is a dangerous practice that invites trouble in various forms; horses should initially be given only brief access to such grazing and, while the grazing period can be gradually increased, extensive periods on such pasture are best avoided. Almost the obverse to this is a situation that can arise during winter. Under some regimes, horses are housed (and thus kept warm) on winter nights, and turned out during the day. Although, during this season, there is little nutrition in the grass, horses will still graze on what is available. If there has been a severe white frost overnight, it is best to wait until the frost has gone from the herbage before turning out, as consumption of frosted grass can lead to compaction in the gut.

The final point to remember about colic is that, because of the horse's physiology, any occurrence should be taken very seriously and a call made to the vet. Pending the vet's arrival, a colicky horse should normally be walked quietly round to prevent it from rolling (which might well exacerbate the condition). However, if the horse is in great pain, reluctant to walk, but not attempting to roll, it need not be forced to walk, but should be watched continually.

Laminitis

Laminitis has traditionally been called 'fever of the feet', because the most obvious sign is severe pain (and, usually, heat) in the feet, associated with damage to the sensitive laminae within the feet. A laminitic horse will be reluctant to move – especially to turn – and will often shift its weight from foot to foot. Laminitis is not, however, simply a form of lameness, but rather a complex disease, which can have a number of causes. That said, in the context of general management, it is a fact that many cases are nutrition-related, being triggered by an overload of soluble carbohydrates derived from cereals or grass. When soluble carbohydrates enter the caecum they are broken down rapidly and the environment becomes very acidic. This results in the death of some of the micro-organisms within the gut and the release of endotoxins which enter the bloodstream. The degree to which this occurs will be related to the degree of carbohydrate overload. For some reason, which is not yet fully understood, the endotoxins in the bloodstream result in blood being shunted away from the laminae in the feet, triggering tissue damage. This, untreated, can have very severe consequences, even to the extent of the pedal bone itself rotating downward, and even cases of moderate severity can have permanent consequences. Therefore, as with colic, suspected laminitis must always be regarded seriously, and veterinary intervention sought at the earliest opportunity.

The risk of nutrition-induced laminitis can be minimized by feeding the concentrate ration in small, frequent meals, and by using corn oil to provide some of the energy so that the total amount of cereals fed can be reduced. Also, the amount being fed must be related to the work being done. In the event of the workload being reduced, the concentrate ration must be reduced pro rata. Also (and related to the point made earlier under Colic) restricting turnout is advised when levels of soluble carbohydrates are likely to be at their highest in the pasture. This occurs on cool, bright days when the light allows photosynthesis to occur, producing sugars that the grass itself doesn't use because it isn't warm enough for it to grow. Instead, the grass stores these extra sugars as soluble carbohydrates, which the grazing horse will ingest. For this reason, it is often best to turn susceptible horses out late at night and bring them in at dawn during peak growing times. This, in fact, may be one reason why working heavy horses in general have perhaps been less prone to laminitis than some other types, since they are often turned out at night after working all day.

Grass Sickness

This is a devastating disease on which much research is still being expended, but as yet with no certain conclusions. Its sad relevance to the heavy horse world is that it was one factor that hastened the demise of the working horse in Scotland. It was and still is extremely common in the Borders, prime young geldings often being the victims.

Although the root cause remains unknown, it is evidenced by paralysis of the gut as a result of degeneration of the nerves that control gut function. The contents of the paralysed gut become hard, dry and impacted, usually causing severe constipation. The stomach becomes distended with fluid that cannot be moved on and gastric contents may reflux from the nostrils. There may also be paralysis of the nostrils.

It will be seen that, in some respects, the signs are similar to those of severe colic – in fact, insofar as colic means 'abdominal pain', a horse with grass sickness does, in effect, have colic. Grass sickness, however, is usually fatal, and any horses that do recover seldom regain their former fitness. Research Institutes tackling this problem deserve our full support.

Strangles

Strangles is a frequent problem in the horse world and major epidemics are constantly occurring. It is caused by the bacterium *Streptococcus equi*. The symptoms classically include high temperature, coughing, thick, pus-like nasal discharge and swollen and abscessed lymph nodes of the head. Sometimes, nasal discharge without glandular swellings may be all that is observed, but the disease can potentially be fatal if the bacterium spreads to other parts of the body. Young horses are particularly susceptible.

Strict isolation of infected animals and good hygiene are essential in controlling strangles. The bacteria are shed from the nose of an infected horse (both as discharge and infective air) and also from draining abscesses, and they may survive in an infected environment (for example, water troughs and contaminated woodwork) for many months.

If a case of strangles is suspected, the horse should be isolated immediately and preferably tended by one person, who should take stringent measures regarding disinfection of clothing, etc. The vet should be called. Caught early, the infection usually responds quite well to treatment based around antibiotics and this may prevent the formation of abscess. If treatment is delayed, however, a different veterinary approach may be necessary, and recovery may be delayed. In all cases, the disease will cause significant debility and the horse will need a prolonged period of rest to aid recovery. The vet may take nasal swabs to monitor the progress of the infection.

Because of its infectious nature and its ability to contaminate the environment, strangles is of particular concern to those involved in breeding and to those who hire out or hire horse transport and stabling (at showgrounds, etc.). Measures for maintaining good hygiene standards for those engaged in these operations are outlined in Transport to and from Stud, in Chapter 7.

Ringworm

This ancient and troublesome condition is a highly contagious skin disease caused by fungal infection. It shows on the skin as circular patches that spread outward from the centre to reach a diameter of an inch (2.5 cm) or so. Although ringworm tends to infect animals in low condition, I have seen it on fit suckler calves turned out to grass and rubbing at a post carrying the fungus. This brings us on to two further points. First, it is not horse-specific and can be a very unpleasant disease in humans. Second, the infective spores can live in isolation from the host for at least a year.

If a case is suspected, isolate the horse and all of its equipment. Do not share any harness, tack, rugs or grooming equipment with other animals. Stop grooming, but remove and burn any affected hair. Consult your vet, who will recommend an appropriate topical anti-fungal cream. Also, take the vet's advice concerning disinfection of equipment, the environment, and your own personal hygiene.

Bone Abnormalities

This is a brief discussion of conditions that may affect the horse's chances in the show ring. In many cases, hereditary factors (perhaps including hereditary predisposition) may be involved, but we have to thank our forebears that the long lists of such disorders which so afflicted the heavy horse a century ago are now absent or rare.

When the book *History with a Future* was compiled in 1988, sidebone was the predominant disease on the Shire Horse Society Inspector's report. Sidebone is an ossification of the lateral cartilages of the foot, which may be triggered or exacerbated by the effects of concussion. The standard set by the Society's Veterinary Inspector, D. F. Oliver, in 1987 was that in *senior* stallions 'the degree of ossification must not exceed the normal natural contour of the lateral cartilage'. Leading Turnout judges do not feel for sidebone, provided the horse is going sound.

In-hand judges feel around the coronets of the forefeet for evidence of ringbone, which, as its name suggests, is a bony enlargement in that region. They also feel on the inside of the lower part of the hocks for evidence of bone spavin, which is arthritic degeneration of the distal tarsal joints, with new bone formation.

These conditions are not acceptable in the show ring as there is a degree of hereditary involvement in their development – for example, although bone spavin is a 'wear and tear' condition, it will be accentuated by poor conformation of the hocks.

Osteochondrosis is a condition in which bone is not formed rapidly enough from the underlying cartilage of the hock to cope with strains and stresses. It is most commonly seen in young horses. It is often mistaken for bog spavin, a distension of the capsule of the true hock joint, which appears as a puffy or 'boggy' swelling on the front of the hock However, Wyn-Jones of Liverpool University claimed that the problem of horses with osteochondrosis lesions in their hocks is comparatively widespread, and that 'swollen hocks' is a condition often accepted by Shire breeders as 'normal'. The practice of draining hocks before showing is becoming all too common, and *History with a Future* recommended that the veterinary profession and the breed societies should give a lead in eliminating this procedure.

The Suffolk Horse Society has now taken active steps to reduce the incidence of osteochondrosis, which is exacerbated by undue growth in young horses, by banning yearling classes.

Although it reiterates advice given at several places throughout this chapter, there is one point regarding equine welfare that bears repeating. Whenever a matter of real concern arises, the first port of call should be your vet. It is far better to call him in earlier rather than later, and prompt consultation may prevent a potentially serious problem from getting worse. Even if your hand shakes a little as you open his bill, you should regard your vet as your, and your horses', friend.

CHAPTER 7

Breeding and Rearing Heavy Horses

This chapter does not presume to add to the knowledge of experienced breeders, but is intended as guidance for those who are considering breeding in a small way. As with many other aspects of equine management, most of the fundamentals apply to heavy horses just as to other breeds and types, and it is recommended that newcomers to breeding read some of the excellent books that cover the subject in detail. The following notes offer general information and highlight points that will require serious consideration and further study if a venture into breeding is to succeed.

Many people are attracted to the idea of breeding their own youngstock, for a wide variety of reasons. Certainly, the idea of continuing a bloodline that has proved successful has obvious attractions, as does the prospect of educating youngstock in one's own preferred way from scratch. However, some of the reasons for breeding are less tenable; for example, the practice of breeding from a mare simply because injury has curtailed its working life has little to commend it; the criteria should be whether or not the mare is likely to prove a good mother and pass on worthwhile characteristics – both physical and temperamental – and these factors will not be engendered simply as a consequence of misfortune. In other words, simply owning a mare is not a good basis for breeding. Unless the mare is free from serious conformation defects, and possesses a basically good temperament, the prospect of breeding worthwhile progeny can be considered a long shot at best.

Two other points should be mentioned. First, many people think that breeding is a way of obtaining stock cheaply. This is rarely the case, and only those who possess a combination of expertise, business acumen and good fortune are likely to make any significant profit from the process. Even then, they will suffer setbacks at times. So far as the individual, occasional, breeder is concerned, while there may be other advantages and a certain satisfaction to be gained from rearing one's own stock, the overall cost of producing a home-bred four-year-old is quite likely to equal or exceed the cost of purchasing a similar animal. 'You can always buy what you want if you have the money, but you can never guarantee to breed what you want', one Shire man observed. His thoughts are echoed by the many who shun breeding their own stock. Fortunately, there are still those for whom the thrill and excitement of breeding something really good outweighs the inevitable hazards and disappointments.

However, to emphasize the point made earlier, breeding and rearing stock successfully requires a good deal of knowledge, and it should not be undertaken on a whim before considerable experience has been acquired in general horse management.

Choice of Stallion

Assuming that the mare is basically suitable for the purpose, and preliminary veterinary examination has found no obvious signs of problems relating to conception or delivery, the next step is to choose a suitable stallion.

The commercial breeder must look ahead, and try to choose a stallion that will sire a foal for which there will be a market in four or five years time. Even if you have no intention of selling the progeny on, it makes sense to adhere to this concept, since the fundamental aim is to produce a desirable animal. However, it is at this very basic level that the gap between ideals and reality can lead to disappointment. This fairly obvious principle has been followed by stockbreeders ever since they first tamed animals from the wild but, despite the good sense that underpins it, it does not always guarantee success. The old maxim 'Breed the best to the best, and hope for the best' serves both as sound counsel and an acknowledgement that the whole business is still very hit-and-miss.

So, proceeding in the spirit of hope, what are the 'best', or at least the desirable qualities to look for in a stallion? For most, especially those for whom heavy horses are a hobby, one major factor is docility. They may not be able to exercise or work their animals as often as is ideal, and they don't want a battle every time they harness up. Why should they? Whatever its other qualities, a temperamental heavy horse is a very dangerous animal, and will make extra demands upon even the most experienced and skilful handler. Yet, since no one admits to owning a doubtful character, and since this may only be evident when there's an in-season mare on the yard, this question of temperament is often the most difficult to assess. This is especially true nowadays, since few modern stallions are tested by either walking or work. Up until the early 1950s, the measured beat of the travelling stallion's massive feet resounded through most lowland areas each spring, the number of miles walked and the number of mares served acting as a guarantee of fitness. In those days, news of nasty or unsound entires soon spread through the countryside's bush telegraph.

For those seeking to evaluate temperament on the basis of superficial observation, the waters may be muddied by various circumstances.

Where it all began: the stallion leader sets off on his rounds. A painting by Joe Godderidge who farms in Norfolk, using mainly horse power.

Don't forget, for example, that feeding can entirely alter a horse's outlook on life, and a dodgy horse kept deliberately on a low level of nutrition may appear quieter than a highly fed one that, although lively, is nice-natured. Bad temperament can also be man-made; that is, it may be induced in an animal that is not congenitally ill tempered. If a stallion has been badly handled at some stage in its career, it does not forget. However, while such an animal may not pass on the acquired defects to its offspring, its own behaviour will hardly serve as an advertisement.

With regard to temperament – and, indeed, other factors – the breeder's best recourse is research and inquiry from those with experience of a particular stallion and its offspring. Some stallions, such as the black Shire, Hainton Jim, gain a reputation for siring quiet stock, which become living recommendations for them. 'If you like a horse,

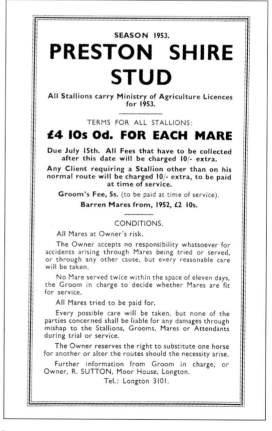

Front cover and inside detail from a stud card of the 1950s.

use its father' was, in fact, the advice given by one of the old stallion's grooms to East Riding horseman Geoff Morton, most of whose Percheron foals now go for riding or ride-and-drive. In the light of this sound counsel, and his own experience, Geoff is naturally very particular indeed about the matter of temperament.

Another factor that will influence choice of stallion is conformation. Desirable characteristics for the individual breeds were discussed in Chapter 1. However, for working horses, some general principles remain the same, no matter which heavy breed you favour. Depth from the withers to the brisket should be similar to that from the brisket to the ground. Overall height should ideally be somewhat over 16 hands and up to or just above 17 hands, with a weight of 16 to 18 cwt. If, however, your aim is to win at the Royal, or to produce a flashy horse for Turnout classes, you may prefer to aim for a giant of 18.2 hands. While it does not carry a guarantee, the stallion's conformation is likely to influence that of the progeny – although the make and shape of the mare must also be considered in this respect.

Economics figure highly in stallion selection, but they must be tinged with good sense. While it may be necessary to rule out a stallion that is too expensive, it is plain folly to use one simply because it is cheap. While you may have the good fortune to discover an inexpensive stallion that suits your purposes, it is the suitability, not the low fee that should be the deciding criterion. Of course, things have a habit of getting complicated, and you may find that the stallion you think would suit your mare and your requirements best is 200 miles away,

Promotional material from a major Percheron stud farm in the heart of Le Perche, Normandy. M. Vallée has some eighty horses on the premises, of which twenty are brood mares.

while a second or third choice is only 20 miles from home. In such circumstances, only you can make the final decision. If the mare travels a long distance and does not hold, you will have much expense for nothing. There again, successful covering may be more likely if a vet is employed to check the mare's receptivity and, while vets are expensive, this may prove the cheaper option in the long run.

In cases where a stallion is home-based, a usual practice is first to 'try', then actually cover the mare, and repeat the process every two days until the mare 'goes off' (comes out of heat), and then try again after a fortnight.

Artificial Insemination

Although artificial insemination (AI) was a well-established practice for cattle and pig breeding by the last years of the twentieth century, it was still in its infancy so far as horses were concerned. There were few in the veterinary profession to whom breeders could turn for advice, results were frequently disappointing and the technique was in danger of falling into disrepute. In the last few years, however, the situation has been transformed. Many veterinary surgeons and stud staff have attended courses and lectures on the subject and there is a network of British Equine Veterinary Association (BEVA) approved practices with a special interest in AI. Techniques of semen preservation and timing of insemination and mare management are being improved all the time and there is now a thriving trade in both the import and export of stallion semen. The BEVA has issued a straightforward Code of Practice regarding AI, designed to ensure parity with other major horse-breeding countries where the technique is controlled by legislation, which is not as yet the case in Great Britain. Key points are that fertility must not be compromised by the use of AI, the spread of infectious diseases must be controlled and the welfare of the animals being used for AI must be safeguarded. However, EC Directives change all the time, and the best course of action for the would-be breeder of heavy horses using AI is to seek specialist veterinary advice. Obviously, considerations such as the stallion's temperament and conformation still apply.

Disease Prevention at Stud

By their nature, studs see a constant throughput of animals, and it is in everyone's interest to ensure that diseases are neither imported to nor transmitted from the stud. The need for precaution is heightened by the fact that there are several equine diseases which are sexually transferred, some of which are also Notifiable, that is to say, there is a legal requirement to report any outbreak to the authorities.

These diseases, and their possible consequences, are well understood by the veterinary profession, and the Horserace Betting Levy Board issues annually reviewed Codes of Practice, which are intended to control and prevent venereal disease in all horses (not just Thoroughbreds). All responsible stud farms will have in place a policy based upon these guidelines, the main diseases covered being contagious equine metritis (CEM), equine viral arteritis (EVA) and equine herpes virus-1 (EHV-1). Although they are not sexually transferred, measures to prevent the introduction of strangles and equine influenza (see Chapter 6) are also likely to be in place.

Details of their own policy on these matters, together with advice on the required veterinary checks and procedures, will be supplied by the stud in advance of the mare travelling there for service, and your own veterinary practice will also be able to give advice. In some cases, breed societies also apply rules related to breeding. For example, the Shire Horse Society requires all registered stallions to be blood tested for EVA before the start of the covering season and unless the test is negative a service book is not issued. All these checks and procedures may seem overwhelming to the newcomer who thinks that covering a mare is a simple act, but they are designed to protect the overall breeding stock from conditions that may have catastrophic consequences.

Transport to and from Stud

If all these precautions are to be taken prior to and during the stud visit, it makes sense to minimize any chance of the mare contracting an infection during transportation. If you possess your own transport, you should be certain that it has not been used just previously to transport a sick horse and, in any case, it is a sensible precaution to disinfect it thoroughly prior to transporting the mare.

If you have to hire transport, it is essential to choose a firm that understands fully the need for cleanliness. At one time, many horseboxes tended to be cleaned out roughly between jobs, but were seldom disinfected thoroughly. All that has now changed. Livestock people became accustomed to submitting to close inspection of vehicles during the 2001 foot-and-mouth epidemic and, although horses do not contract that dread disease, greater movement of stock both in Britain and overseas has greatly increased the appreciation of the risks of spreading disease. Furthermore, the vehicle owner in private transport and the vehicle operator in contracted transport are both legally responsible for cleanliness and hygiene. Operators who regularly transport racehorses have perhaps understood the need for hygiene longer than many and, in this respect, the Horserace Betting Levy Board's transport guidelines that follow may be of interest to owners of heavy horses, regardless of whether their charges are travelling to stud or to a show.

- Clean and disinfect vehicles regularly, preferably with recognized viricidal disinfectants.
- Ensure clean vehicles before horses are loaded.
- Prior vaccination may reduce risk of disease transmission during transport.
- Where mixed loads are unavoidable, consider the categories being transported, e.g. risk of EHV-1 infection to pregnant mares.
- Horses should be healthy and fit to travel: sick animals should not be transported except under veterinary supervision.
- If horses or contacts become ill on, or shortly after, arrival, inform the transport operator at once. The operator should inform other clients with animals on the same load.
- Facilities should be available for cleaning/mucking out of lorries at stops.

Care and Feeding of the Brood Mare

The turn of the year affords a good time to take stock of feeding requirements. At New Year, a mare may be both in-foal and recovering from the last lactation, or may be empty but required to conceive in the coming months. In either case, the mare should be neither too fat nor too thin. A mare out of condition may start ovulating abnormally late in the year, or not at all in extreme cases.

There are many advantages to foaling outside with the grass starting to grow. That usually means March to May according to district, but most owners have their mares served on the first oestrus. Then, if the mare fails to hold, it may be possible to achieve a successful covering on the next oestrus, and still not be too late. However, if the mare starts ovulating unseasonably late, opportunities will be limited if the first service does not hold.

Research shows that a mare in rising condition is more likely to conceive than one losing condition, and this suggests that efforts to improve condition – or certainly to remedy any deficiency in condition – should start some four to six weeks before the service date. This procedure has long been appreciated in the breeding of sheep, although some researchers believe that a general level of good condition, rather than an improvement in it, is the more important factor. Scientists will doubtless debate this for years, but it seems certain that the mare should not be losing condition as the service date approaches.

As stressed in the general chapter on feeding, horses are highly individual, and some are better at converting food than others. If a mare has become significantly overweight and really does need to lose some weight during winter, hay with a high proportion of stem to leaf will help. However, such fodder must on no account be dusty, as dusty hay can cause irreversible lung damage. Such a feeding regime will also call for an appropriate supplementation of minerals and vitamins. This aspect has been well studied in recent years, and the prudent owner should safeguard the present and future health of both mare and foal by providing supplements in the quantities recommended by a vet or equine nutritionist. The mare is the sole source of nutriment for the developing embryo. Tissue formation requires increased levels of protein, minerals and vitamins, and if these are not supplied, the mare's own reserves will become depleted. If this goes on for several seasons, the mare may have a poor foal or cease to breed at all. Old age may then be blamed when in fact feeding and management were at fault.

In all cases, in fact, the mare must receive a correctly balanced diet from the start; the foal may be out of sight for eleven months, but should never, even for a single day, be out of mind. (In this respect, modern research shows that trace elements stored in the foetal liver during pregnancy are utilized by the foal after birth.) The mare's dietary needs may require even more consideration in late pregnancy, when the size and weight of the foetus and placenta are such that they may affect the mare's appetite adversely just at the time when a sufficient intake of nutrients is essential. Feeds suitably formulated to take account of this may be obtained from any reputable supplier and, again, their nutritionist or your vet should be able to give advice as necessary.

Whilst lactating, the mare has a greater demand for nutrients than a horse in hard work. The mare is eating for two – and possibly three if already in foal again ('twelve legs for the price of four' as the auctioneers say). Mare's milk is much richer than that of cows, and contains appreciable amounts of iron, copper and especially zinc, all of which must be replaced by appropriate feedstuff.

The mare's lactation curve rises steeply up to about three weeks after foaling and then more gradually until about the fifth week. It then starts to decline, steadily at first, and then much more steeply from three and a half months onward. From then the foal is eating appreciable amounts of both concentrates and grass, and is becoming less and less dependent on its mother's milk.

Foaling

Foaling is a natural process, but is fraught with hazards, some of which have the potential to be fatal to mare and foal. While most foalings go smoothly, those that do not will require prompt and expert intervention if tragedy is to be avoided. Therefore, to reiterate the point made at the start of this chapter, newcomers to breeding should, well before the event, familiarize themselves with the basic signs and progression of foaling by consulting specialist literature. As minimum precautions, it is well to have a really experienced friend either present, or immediately available, to assist and your vet's phone number should certainly be to hand. Since the vet will be needed, immediately post-foaling, to carry out routine procedures, it may be worthwhile notifying the practice once foaling seems imminent, to put them on stand-by.

The ideal heavy horse foaling takes place in a field which is usually grazed by stock other than horses, and is well sheltered. If a loose box must be used, it should be cleaned and thoroughly disinfected beforehand, with clean bedding. It should also be as large as possible – 18 ft square, or bigger – to allow room for human ingress and general manoeuvring, should any such intervention be necessary. Despite this need for room, if all appears to be well, human interference, and even close presence, should be kept to a minimum. Indeed, some mares delay foaling if they think anyone is watching, so keeping a discreet distance in the open, or making a peephole in the loose box, are advisable in order to keep a watching brief without causing disturbance. Of course, horses have a great aptitude for thwarting human plans, and every year brings its crop of stories about a mare that showed no signs of foaling, so the attendant went in for a cup of tea, only to return to find the foal already on its feet. This, of course, is the sort of foaling everyone hopes for but, if the mare starts to foal and appears to be struggling, call on expert assistance immediately.

Once foaling, however straightforward, is completed, the vet should be called, to check that the whole of the afterbirth or cleansing has come away, since retention leads to severe complications. The vet will also give the foal an initial anti-tetanus vaccination, and advise on any immediate aftercare of mare and foal, as necessary.

Care and Feeding of Foals

Although the new-born foal should be given an anti-tetanus vaccination immediately, the immunity this provides will be short-lived. It should therefore receive a longer-lasting vaccination based on your vet's recommendation. When the foal is vaccinated against tetanus, a course of antibiotics or sulphonamide to guard against the infantile disease of joint-ill may also be suggested. Dressing the navel with iodine reduces the risk of infection gaining entrance and causing joint-ill. Also, ensure that the foal sucks as soon as it is on its feet in order that it receives the particular antibodies found in the mare's colostrum (the especially nutritious first milk).

Worming the Foal

The worming programme for foals will depend on where and when the foal was born. If the dam's droppings are cleared regularly, the worm risk is reduced, but this depends on the environment. Normally two months of age is early enough to start the foal's worming programme. Thereafter, worm every six to eight weeks according to the manufacturer's instructions. Vary the brand of wormer periodically, to prevent the parasites becoming immune to one type, and remember that the correct dosage for wormers is related to the animal's bodyweight, so this will need to be varied in line with the foal's development. The one point about worming that cannot be overstressed is that omitting the procedure in youngstock is a potentially fatal false economy. Some forms of worm damage, especially that to the walls of major blood vessels, can never be repaired retrospectively.

Feed and Development Prior to Weaning

A heavy breed foal can grow at a remarkable rate, but growth can be too fast as well as too slow. Problems tend to occur when rapid growth is stimulated by high-energy diets that are not supported with balanced levels of protein, vitamins and minerals. These nutrients are the building blocks of tissues such as bone, muscle and tendons and if they are not provided in the diet the horse's structure is likely to be weakened.

When development problems are evident in youngstock the trend has been to remove all concentrate feed. This may slow growth temporarily but the body will eventually catch up to reach its genetic potential unless severe malnutrition is prolonged, a process called 'compensatory growth'. Fluctuations in growth often result in weaknesses to tissues that may not become evident until later in life, when the horse is working and its framework is put-to the test. A better approach to the nutritional management of developmental problems is to maintain balanced levels of protein, vitamins and minerals but reduce the energy content of the diet. This ensures that the nutrients required for the formation of tissues are provided but the growth is not forced.

Although milk is the natural diet of the foal, it does not of itself contain all the ideal nutrient levels to support growth and development. As mentioned earlier, the foetus accumulates stores of minerals whilst in the womb to support it after birth and to counteract the lower than ideal levels in the mare's milk. Providing a balanced diet for the mare during pregnancy enables the foal to build up these stores sufficiently.

During the period from birth to around three months, the foal cannot digest forage and grain very efficiently, and thus is dependent on milk. This period is the time of most rapid growth, which requires a lot of energy that should be provided by the milk. However, a mare that is not milking well will not be providing sufficient energy for the foal to grow. In such cases, giving a 'creep feed' to the foal at a stage somewhat earlier than usual is advisable. Such feeds should be milk-based and should have a balance of vitamins and minerals to support growth and development. The term creep feed derives from the procedure often necessary when introducing foals to concentrates while they are still with their dams. Some mares are greedy and have no qualms about eating any feed available, with no thought of sharing it with their foal. In such cases, various means have been devised for ensuring that feed intended for foals is accessible to them only, one method being to construct a robust pen with a low, narrow, opening, into which foals can 'creep', but mares cannot. Where only a single mare and foal are involved other, simpler, methods, such as a separate feed bowl or manger for the foal, with an opening too narrow for the mare's muzzle, may be used but, whatever the construction, the accent must be on safety.

When the mare's lactation starts to drop at about five weeks, there is also a drop in the mineral content of the milk. This is another factor which suggests that feed containing an alternative source of minerals, but with a low energy content, should be provided to support the growing structure.

At three to four months of age the foal starts to digest forage and grain and so the transition from milk-based to cereal-based feeds can begin. Foals that are still receiving sufficient calories from the mare's milk may be more suited to a low calorie feed. As mentioned, there are several feeds available that are low in calories but provide balanced diets and are thus suitable for rapidly growing or overweight individuals. On the other hand, foals that require extra condition should receive a stud feed. Stud rations can be cubes or mixes and have a balance of all the nutrients required for growth and the energy content to encourage weight gain. Stud mixes tend to include oats and so are more likely to result in exuberant behaviour, whereas stud cubes usually contain more digestible, non-heating ingredients.

Weaning

The process of weaning involves not only the foal's dietary independence from its dam, but also a major change in psychological dependence – an aspect that can be stressful for both mare and foal. Prior to weaning, the foal should be consuming the recommended daily quantity of concentrates, to ensure that the stress of weaning does not result in a significant loss of condition. The acceptable age for weaning is considered to be from six months onwards, as the foal no longer relies on milk and the mare can be given time to gain weight and condition before the next foaling, or returning to work. Weaning occurs naturally at around nine months, but if it is left this long the foal may put on a lot of weight and cause the mare to lose condition. The optimum time is therefore between six and eight months.

Further to this issue of age is an observation that relates mainly to breeding for sale. At the autumn sales, a late-born foal may be only four months old, and this is too young for weaning. While an auctioneer might announce that the youngster can return to its mother, if foal and mare are sold many miles apart this does not always happen. Auctioneers and breed societies should combine to try and stop the practice of enforced early weaning.

For the actual weaning, the foal should be placed in a secure loose box, preferably with a companion. Some breeders buy an extra foal just as a pal, or borrow a quiet old pony or even a donkey. Horses are sociable animals, and the trauma of severance from its dam should not be intensified by depriving the foal of all equine company. Furthermore, it is good practice to use the period of confinement to make a fuss of the youngster, and gain its confidence.

The mare should be taken out of earshot if at all possible. If you have only one paddock, try to billet the mare elsewhere for a week. During that time, the condition of the udder should be checked, and a little milk drawn off daily if necessary to relieve any painful pressure, but it should not be completely milked out. After a week or so, both dam and offspring should be accepting the situation. On leaving its box, the foal should have access to a good mixed sward, neither too lush nor too bare.

Growth and Development After Weaning

The amount of feed (in proportion to its bodyweight) necessary to support growth will normally decrease as the foal gets older. This is because the rate of growth slows and so fewer nutrients are required. From this point on, the exact diet will depend on the individual and, to some extent, upon its vocation. For example, if the youngster is to be shown, a certain amount of extra condition may be required. However, it is important to remember that significantly overweight youngsters are at risk from skeletal damage and various other health problems such as poor fertility.

If a youngster is turned out, it is important not to simply forget about its diet (or other aspects of care). Although, since they are very efficient at digesting fibre, good grass is usually sufficient to keep most heavy breed youngsters in good condition, it is not ideal to simply rely on pasture to provide the levels of vitamins and minerals the youngster requires. Analysis of the herbage available, and consultation with an expert, may pay dividends here.

Beyond the age of two, any actual growth (increase in height, girth, etc.) that occurs will be very slow, but this does not mean that a horse of this age is fully developed, or anywhere near it, in terms of skeletal or muscular strength. Generally, the bigger the horse, the longer it will take to develop, and some horses may not be fully mature until six or seven years of age. This is not to say that horses cannot be brought into light work and educated for their vocation at a relatively early age, but the introduction should be gradual and should take account of both physical and mental immaturity.

PART TWO

Vehicles, Harness and Driving

CHAPTER 8

Vehicle Types and Acquisition

Heavy horse exhibitors who wish to show their charges in some form of Turnout class will, unless they have been fortunate enough to have inherited one, need to go in search of an appropriate vehicle. Even now, horse-drawn vehicles are being pulled out of ancient cart sheds where they have rested since the grey Dolly, Boxer the bay or Tommy the black gelding backed them carefully into place for the last time. Inevitably, such treasures are becoming ever rarer – although they are still to be found when a horse farmer retires, a museum closes down or a family leaves after three generations on the same holding.

When such gems can be tracked down, the good news is that our grandparents and great-grandparents built things to last. We benefit from their attitude through these delightful carts and waggons, fashioned a century or more ago, which are often rediscovered in little worse condition than when they were abandoned. Their day seemed to be done, but now there is great interest in them.

Types of Vehicle

At the shows the main types of horse-drawn vehicles are the farm waggon, the farm cart, the tradesman's dray and the rulley. To these can be added the eye-catching hermaphrodite, a combination of cart and waggon. Increasingly, a number of traditional horse-drawn agricultural implements are also seen on display, and we will discuss these in due course. For the moment, however, let us consider the defining characteristics of the main types of vehicle.

Waggons

The waggon is a four-wheeled vehicle designed for transporting bulky products around the farm and further afield. Waggons frequently took sacks of corn to the nearest railway station, perhaps picking up a load of coals for the return journey. With the regional variations in terrain, soil and crop production, it is no surprise that most waggon-building counties in Britain had their own style. For example, the lowland counties, and East Anglia in particular, tended to build huge waggons to cope with the heavy crops associated with fertile, level lowlands. As there was ample grain, the horses were fed accordingly and were big, well-framed animals. However, on arable upland there are often steep banks to contend with, while on the grassy dales the slopes were unavoidable, and a lighter type of vehicle and draught animal were kept. In such areas, the animals were probably not so well fed as their lowland brethren, reducing their power still further, a point that is often overlooked. Significantly, Scotland and much of Wales used the smaller carts, rather than waggons.

There are two main types of waggon, box and bow. The box waggon was built in Yorkshire, the Eastern Counties and the South East. In lowland Wales, English designs followed the coasts and main river valleys, and could be of either bow or box design. The box waggon generally has a deep body, contrasting with the lighter timbering and more elegant curves of the bow waggon. The latter design holds sway along the north banks of the Bristol Channel, across the south Midlands and roughly south to the Isle of Wight and into the south-west peninsula.

Of all designs, the Glamorgan waggon is possibly the most elegant. It is usually a bow waggon, painted blue and salmon, with incredibly intricate and decorative ironwork. C. Fox, in *Antiquity* (1931), described it as possessing 'the seemingly inevitable beauty and fitness of the last days of the sailing ships and other specialized creations which have been perfected by generations of men content to work in one tradition'.

Panelled sides are a feature of the bow waggon, with bowed raves, or

Father and son Martin and Matthew Goymour, of Banham Zoo, in Norfolk, help to promote the heavy horse in many ways. In the first picture, Martin Goymour is driving a pair of Shires to a traditional red and blue double-shafted Norfolk waggon, fitted with racks or gaumers for carrying extra sheaves. The second picture shows the same waggon shafted for a single horse.

rails, over the rear wheels, and a spindled aperture over each end. Frontboards and tailboards lend themselves to painted lettering and chamfering, and anyone who finds a waggon with the original inscriptions still decipherable is lucky indeed. Chamfers are shaved indentations into the various square angles of the bodywork, and were supposedly to lighten overall weight, although some professionals believe they were pure decoration. At the time of writing, a Northamptonshire waggon is undergoing restoration. Although only the turntable and undercarriage of the original vehicle remained, this bodywork has five hundred chamfers in it.

The varying designs of waggons make a fruitful field of study for the heavy horse connoisseur, whether spectator, judge, exhibitor or commentator. The turnout branch of the showing world is blessed with some excellent commentators, whose knowledge enhances our enjoyment of the summer scene.

Carts

The cart is a two-wheeled vehicle, with a wide range of makes, styles and uses. However, despite its basic versatility in traditional uses, it is

A Shire driven to a light Gig. This hitch mirrors the old American practice of ladies driving to visit friends: they often had to use the only horse available, which was frequently a heavy breed, and sometimes a stallion.

designed to be driven at a walk and its appearance in the show ring is generally confined to the Agricultural class. Although it is far better to drive a cart than nothing, its disadvantage as a general driving vehicle is that, at the trot, the shafts bounce up and down in an ungainly and noisy manner, which can also be uncomfortable for the horse. Thus, at this gait, neither horse nor vehicle can be displayed to full advantage. Furthermore, the cart needs loading correctly to maintain balance, a factor that does not apply to four-wheeled vehicles.

Some of these remarks do not, however, apply so readily to the light carts that have long been popular in North America, and which are increasing in popularity in Britain. These vehicles are said to have evolved from the pioneering days, when a rancher's wife might wish to visit a 'neighbour' who was, in fact, some miles away. She, incidentally, would have had to use whatever horse was available, and this would usually be the stallion, since the other horses would be out on range duties.

Yoked to a light cart developed from this era, a horse can show its action much more readily than when yoked to a waggon or a traditional, heavy farm cart. This is one reason why such carts find favour with the Americans and Canadians, who generally put more emphasis on the horse and less on the vehicle than do their British counterparts. These vehicles come from a number of makers, in a wide range of styles, but lightness, and ease of access and egress are characteristic features.

One practical advantage that any form of cart has over a four-wheeled vehicle is that the cart is cheaper and easier to transport, and many a successful exhibitor has started out with some type of single-horse cart. The two-wheel tipping cart may be tipped independently of the shafts, so the horse remains harnessed while the load is tipped. In some makes it can be locked in a semi-tipping position, enabling farmyard manure to be unloaded at desired points, using a long-handled fork.

The various forms of carts have accessories, which may or not be present on individual vehicles. These include sideboards, frontboards and backboards, which slot into metal rings to add to the capacity when carting roots or manure. Shelvings are wooden frameworks resting on the cart body, which greatly augment the carrying capacity for hay, straw and

John Owen's bay Shire driven to a traditional farm cart at the Great Yorkshire Show.

Sally Gray driving her Clydesdale/Shire gelding, Titus, to a bullock cart at the Southsea Heavy Horse Parade. The low loaders of their day, these useful vehicles were often used by dealers to transport stock before the internal combustion engine arrived. This particular cart was built in 1903 and Mr C. W. Vincent used it as a lad to fetch the occasional beast for his father's butcher's shop in Chertsey, Surrey.

sheaves. Neatly painted, all these features enhance the cart's appearance. A great many farm carts were converted from wooden, iron-tyred wheels to pneumatic tyres. While the traditional type is preferable in the show ring, don't let the modern ones put you off. It is far better to show a cart with modern accessories than not show at all.

One of the most pleasing two-wheeled vehicles is the Scotch corn cart. This has racks or ladders extending fore and aft of a comparatively light body, greatly increasing the size of the load of hay or corn carried. British spectators of the 1980s and 1990s will remember Mervyn Ramage's magnificent blue roan Clydesdale, Blueprint, to one of these vehicles.

Other carts have turnip choppers attached, which slice the roots as the horse moves forward. Such devices are put out of gear, or otherwise made safe during public appearances. A bullock cart, with high solid sides and a cranked axle allowing low loading, is a real treasure, and such unusual vehicles do occur at farm and country house sales. All such vehicles add to the perpetual fascination of the heavy horse world.

Hermaphrodites

The hermaphrodite is a most unusual and eye catching vehicle. It is a combination of cart and waggon, the cart being converted into a

One of the late Mervyn Ramage's roan Clydesdales driven to a hermaphrodite: a cart that is converted to a waggon by the addition of a pair of front wheels.

waggon by adding a pair of fore-wheels and fore-carriages. Hermaphrodites were built in the corn-growing counties of England from north Essex to Nottinghamshire, production being centred in the Eastern Counties. For most of the year these vehicles served as carts, but demand for capacious waggons during corn harvest was so great that the conversion was designed. No vehicle is more likely to catch the spectator's or judge's eye than a well restored hermaphrodite.

Drays and Rulleys

Seen in the brilliant Trade Turnout classes, which so enliven the summer scene, the four-wheeled dray is principally a commercial vehicle, often associated with the delivery of beer. The rulley, also called lorry or lurry, is a similar type of vehicle with more agricultural connections, and takes its place in the Agricultural class at shows.

New drays are still being built. The modern craftsmen are every bit as dedicated and skilled as in former days, so the restricting factor in acquiring one is finance. The few built in the latter years of the twentieth century cost around £8,000, so £10,000 may be a conservative estimate today. Old ones also change hands for large sums.

A view emphasizing the range of drays at an English show.

Two unusual and eye-catching vehicles:

Noel Abel's three-abreast to a pantechnicon was a regular showground feature for many years.

The Sampson family's fire engine gives hugely popular working demonstrations at Percheron breed shows throughout Britain.

Examining Vehicles Prior to Purchase

The budding turnout driver may hear of an old vehicle, and go along to inspect it. The rule here is: 'Don't try to be clever on your own'. When buying a new car, most people approach one of the professional associations or take along their own mechanic, yet too many feel that wood is altogether simpler than the inside of an engine, and trust their own knowledge without realizing their limitations. There are, however, all sorts of potential pitfalls and it is far cheaper to engage the help of a reliable professional than to buy something unsuitable or with hidden faults. The points that follow are not offered in contradiction of the advice to enlist expert help, but as examples of the pitfalls that make such help invaluable.

Although the different types of vehicle have design features peculiar to themselves, they also have a number of general features in common. Therefore, while the general points mentioned under Waggons should be borne in mind as appropriate when inspecting other vehicles, specific aspects for checking in Carts, Drays, etc. are addressed separately.

Waggons

Beware of new paint. Why has the vehicle been painted? Does it cover some fault? Plastic wood is marvellous stuff, until it dries and jolts out!

Wooden wheels are subject to a host of shortcomings. They are usually in need of repair, a job beyond the scope of most amateurs, however capable they may be regarding the bodywork. Even the best of timbers will have shrunk or partially rotted with the passing years, for half a century or more has passed since most were in regular use. So be prepared for the expense of having the wheels restored.

Inspection of wheels should start with the bonds, or iron tyres. These may well be loose, which may indicate decayed timber immediately beneath them. The felloes (pronounced 'fellies'), which are the curved wooden sections forming the outside of the wheel, usually made of beech, elm or ash, may also be loose. Each felloe takes two spokes, which are generally made of oak, and heartwood at that. Decayed timber or woodworm may occur where the spokes meet the felloes. Cracks in the paintwork between the felloes are a sign of shrinkage, as are similar signs where the spokes join the hubs or stocks. Movement caused by shrinkage where spokes meet the hub may be detected by rocking the wheel.

Hubs are normally of elm, a tough timber that does not splinter. However, splits in the hub running from front to back may indicate a structurally unsound vehicle; such splits are termed 'shakes', and occur when timber dries out. Although the hub bonds prevent the hub from splitting right through, large splits can retain water and cause rotting later.

In the type of wheel known as the Warner (after its American inventor), all the spokes are in line where they are fitted into the hub. They pass through a metal bond called a cage, which becomes loose if the hub shrinks. If the paint around the edge of the cage is cracking, that is a sign of a shrunken hub. Soaking loose hubs with water does not cure them. It will expand them for a few days (and may therefore be practised by some unscrupulous character when attempting a sale), but after a few days they will be as loose as ever.

If the spokes of a wheel move in the stock, but there is no sign of movement in the joints of the felloes, this means one of two things. Either the hub was not properly seasoned, and has shrunk, or there was not enough joint between the felloes when the bond was fitted. If a new hub is needed, the whole wheel will have to be dismantled in order to fit it.

The box is the metal tube that runs through the hub and slides over the axle, acting as a bearing. It is thus an important part of the hub. Wooden wedges both inside and out hold the box in place and it is important to ensure that these are not loose.

Loose tyres or bonds can be cured, but it is a specialist job. The wheelwright or blacksmith who has the necessary knowledge and also a bonding plate will cut out a section of the bond, re-weld and refit. Experience is also needed to determine how much metal to take out of the tyre, as this determines the amount of dish (angle of spokes from the perpendicular) on the wheel. The smaller the bond, the greater the dish.

The shafts should be examined thoroughly – the principal reason in waggons being to check for woodworm. Waggons are often found with pole or shafts actually missing, and the reason for their demise is that they were often slung over the rafters for safekeeping and to prevent them from being driven over by a tractor. Unfortunately these same rafters are often of softwood, which becomes attacked by woodworm. Once woodworm has entered the shafts themselves, it is usually too late for treatment; the shafts will sooner or later snap under pressure, with potentially damaging if not tragic results. However, while a severe attack makes any timber worthless, a very light infestation, caught early, may be treated with a proprietary killer. Any deposits of fine sawdust usually indicate woodworm; they occur when the grub has bored its way out, particularly in May and June.

If shafts are in place, and not wormy, it is still important to check they are the correct ones for the waggon, or at least suitable replacements. Sometimes a pair from another implement has been used to replace the missing ones. If too light, they are dangerous. The actual material used is also important. English ash is a favourite for shafts, for the good reason that it does not splinter if broken – and splintered shafts are a danger to both horse and man. The old carpenters and wheelwrights knew a thing or two, and to use a substitute such as larch is to invite trouble.

A metal rod running through eyelets is the most common means of joining shafts and body. These eyelets are fitted to the front of the turntable, and take a lot of strain, so much so that the rod running through them may well have become worn at the points where it runs through the eyelets. A new iron rod will be needed, one of the simpler aspects of restoration.

A less common type of fitting allows the shaft side-members to run past the outside of the turntable. The members have holes bored though them to coincide with holes bored through the outside of the turntable. A shaft connecting bar is then threaded through both. This is a very vulnerable point, and besides examining the rod, care should be taken to look out for rot or splits in the timber and enlargement of the holes.

The floor of any cart or waggon is very vulnerable to wear and damage. Floorboards may run either from front to back, or crosswise. More usually they run the length of the vehicle, so that when shovelling out the contents there are no square-on boards to snag the shovel. The boards may be of cheaper softwood, easier to replace, but really should be of hardwood, preferably elm. When laid lengthways, boards are set down between the floor runners. They rest on timbers mortised through runners along the body, called 'keys'. These keys allow the tops of the boards to be level with the tops of the runners. If the keys are rotten or woodwormy at the ends, it is a major task to repair them, entailing virtual dismantling of the whole waggon.

Secondary flooring is often set on top of the runners for longer life. However, water may become trapped between the floors, causing rot in the outside body members. Buyers should beware of body filler used here, as it may indicate structural damage which can be very expensive. Thus, while a second floor fitted above the original and resting on it need not be too detrimental, you should be aware of it and carry out thorough checks.

Replacing side timbers can also be a costly job. This is made more difficult by the fact that, in order to remove the body members, the outside rave or side rail has to be removed, and these components are riveted together. The top member is also riveted to the bottom body member.

The tug, ridger and breeching hooks, points by which the vehicle is connected to the horse in harness, should be examined carefully, both the hooks themselves and their points of attachment requiring careful inspection.

The amount of lock needs some consideration. By this is meant the amount by which the front wheels can swivel before making contact with the body. A waggon may be 'quarter', 'half', 'three-quarters' or 'full lock'. Thus a quarter-lock requires a greater turning circle than a half-lock, while the full-lock can turn tightest of all. It can turn almost in its own length, while the quarter-lock is at a disadvantage in cramped conditions. However, few of the latter are found today.

Carts

When inspecting two-wheeled carts, generally look for the same points on the body as described for waggons. Although cart shafts are an integral part of the conveyance, and are not attached separately as in the case of waggons, they still require careful inspection. They must be checked carefully for signs of decay, and they may also have had pieces spliced onto them, another potential danger point.

Another highly significant point is that, when tractors took over, many a cart had its shafts sawn off and a tractor hitch fitted. Some such are now being converted back again. The first thing to remember here is that the tractor pulled them at a speed for which they were never intended, and the subsequent shaking may have affected their overall life. Also, if shafts have been refitted, they may have been bolted on top of the two stub ends of the original shafts, which not only creates a point of weakness but also alters the point of balance.

The tug, ridger and breeching hooks should be examined even more carefully on a cart than on a waggon. Whereas waggons are usually reserved for specialist jobs such as 'leading' (carting) hay and corn, and load deliveries, carts may be in daily use, so these hooks may be seriously worn to the point of danger.

Drays, Rulleys and Delivery Vans

For general soundness of these vehicles, the checking procedure outlined for carts and waggons should be followed. The seat is a vital part, and its soundness is paramount, otherwise it becomes an obvious hazard. However, no driver is likely to have allowed his seat to deteriorate to that degree.

Since these vehicles are used mainly for roadwork, they are usually sprung. Here is an added complication for the restorer; the condition of the springs often leaves much to be desired. Flakes of rust accumulate between the spring leaves, and bolts through the spring eyelets and spring hangers often become badly rusted and need replacing. Modern high-tensile steel bolts are the answer.

Restoring Paintwork

While major structural restoration is the province of skilled specialists, many amateurs may be inspired to undertake the restoration of paintwork. Here, preparation is at least half the battle when aiming at a professional finish. In today's highly competitive turnout world, nothing less will do, but hours of work are needed.

As we have seen, many of the traditional horse-drawn vehicles have strong regional characteristics, and those engaged in restoration will doubtless wish to keep faith with these. In many cases, paintwork is one such characteristic: although not applicable to all regions, many have a strong tradition of painting waggons and other farm implements in certain colours. Although not exhaustive, the following examples highlight the diversity that appears throughout the English counties. Ochre red dominates in Rutland, with yellow in Shropshire, the Cotswolds and mid-Wales. Although most Dorset waggons are yellow, blue and blue-black is also featured within the county. Overall, blue is the most popular colour. Lincolnshire waggons tend to be dark greenish blue, with those of Devon a lighter shade. Wiltshire, Herefordshire and Suffolk also favour blue, while dark brown is found in Hertfordshire, Surrey, the north-east of Hampshire, and Yorkshire. Craftsmen in Cambridgeshire, east Leicestershire and Huntingdonshire used a lighter shade of orange brown. Whilst yellow, blue and brown are the main colours in Kent and Norfolk, some vehicles from these counties are painted buff, or a stone colour.

So far as the actual restoration process goes, it is well to remember that, in the old days when these vehicles were painted, lead paint was used, and it is highly toxic. When rubbing down the old paintwork, do so outside, unless the building is really well equipped with extractor fans and the like. In all situations, always wear a mask. Remember, also, that lead paint is poisonous to cattle, which nevertheless are attracted to it, so the spoils must be disposed of safely where no animals can reach it.

Various sandpapers are needed, starting with the rough grades, and finishing with fine. Once sanding is completed, the first coat applied should be a very thin one of primer. This will seal absorbent areas and expose parts needing filler. Ask your paint supplier for a suitable filler, as it must complement the paint being used. The filler is usually dry within 12 hours, after which a fairly coarse wet and dry paper is used. This may show up further defects, in which case more filler must be applied. A brush filler (a paint consistency material) should then be given. It is important to achieve a smooth mirror finish with the filler coats before attempting to apply an undercoat. Once the undercoat has been applied, use a very fine wet and dry paper to rub it down lightly. When satisfied with the finish (and not until then), the time has come to apply the top gloss paint. Two undercoats and one gloss coat should suffice. Modern proprietary coach paints do not require a varnish coat to achieve that desired high-gloss finish.

The finishing touch is achieved by lining, to highlight certain features of the vehicle. Lining wheels and lining tapes can be obtained for the purpose if you are determined to do the whole job yourself. However, paint lining is a very specialized trade, with professional results seldom matched by the gifted amateur. If you attempt the task, the main thing is to avoid over-lining. Lining should be used only to highlight the chamfers and the edges of the panels, for too much spoils an otherwise excellent finish.

So far as cleaning paintwork is concerned, spray polish should never be used, as it will leave smears. Clean water and a chamois leather suffice.

Horse-drawn Implements

In addition to the extensive range of vehicles available, a selection of horse-drawn implements with agricultural links is becoming increasingly popular in the show ring. This selection includes implements which prepared the soil for sowing, drilled it, worked in the growing crop and finally harvested it. Painstakingly restored, their display in Agricultural classes offers scope for those chiefly concerned with having fun on show day, rather than being involved in serious competition or depending on a sponsor who will be disappointed if prize tickets are not forthcoming.

The implement that will spring most readily to many minds is the plough, and its use also comes first in the seasonal cycle that follows harvest. Ploughing is universal in the preparation of arable soil, and horse-drawn ploughs were made in every British county. Each had its own style according to the topography and nature of the soil. Devon, in particular, sported a huge number of ploughs designed to cope with steep banks, and any blacksmith-made ones are a prize indeed. A discerning judge in the Horse-drawn Farm Implements class will spot such a model immediately, and it will be of great interest to the many spectators who, in former days, had ties with the soil.

Historically, the advent of the railways and the spread of the banking system caused factory-made ploughs to take over from those produced locally, but there was still a very wide range of styles. Ransomes are one of the best-known manufacturers, especially of match ploughs, but in the show ring the implement is not actually called upon to plough; it simply runs round on its wheels behind a pair of heavy horses with brasses gleaming and manes and tails plaited.

Ploughs suitable for the show ring are not too difficult to come by. Unless you wish to take part in ploughing matches (see Chapter 16) there is no need to try to seek out a match plough with its ultra-long, shining mouldboard; the ordinary wheeled plough being quite capable of show status. If possible, try to obtain one with coulters attached. The standard coulter is a bayonet-like perpendicular fitting that makes the vertical cut, while the skim coulter is a miniature plough that takes out a groove from the stubble, thereby helping to bury the straw and make a neater job.

Other types of plough are the semi-digger and the digger. These have shorter mouldboards, creating much less friction with the soil. They are used on lighter soils, and the semi-digger in particular is fairly readily found. These various forms, except the match plough, are sometimes found with a wooden frame, and since these are now quite rare, they are excellent for demonstrations and shows. At implement sales it is also worthwhile looking out for specialized designs such as ridging ploughs with their double breasts, deep diggers, and 'one way' balance or reversible ploughs. There are also potato-lifting ploughs with tines replacing the plough breasts, and sub-soiling ploughs. All of these may be painted up for the show ring, and the more unusual the better.

Cultivators offer almost as wide a range of designs as ploughs. One model, Martin's general purpose, has a seat, and may be converted into a three-drill grubber or a three-furrow ridger. It is fitted with two depth-regulating levers and a tipping lever.

Horse hoes are also found in virtually infinite form. The steerage horse hoe has shafts, but most models are single row designs of expandable width, with a wheel in front only. Thus they need either a narrow sledge or extra wheels to enable them to travel on grass.

Harrows, too, occur in a wide range of types. Chain harrows are designed for grassland, and thus are suitable for display in most arenas, but other types of tined harrow need mounting on sledges if they are to appear in the show ring.

The most common rollers are of iron construction, in the form of cylinders mounted on a long axle. They are divided into sections to allow easier turning at the headlands. The Cambridge roller has a series of narrow, heavily ribbed rings, while Crosskill rollers have toothed sections. All types are good for outdoor displays.

There is also a whole range of drills to show how our forebears sowed their crops. These make suitable demonstration implements, as they may be jacked up in the transporting position to travel clear of the ground. Corn drills come in varying widths, while root drills for turnips, mangels and sugar beet are usually two-row, sometimes with small rollers to fit the ridges. Northumberland was one region where seed drills were in use by the end of the eighteenth century and, although the twenty-first century exhibitor is unlikely to come across such early models, there are a number around from the period between 1850 and 1950. Anyone painstakingly restoring and painting such models is benefiting future generations as well as present grandstand crowds.

Machines for distributing artificial fertilizers are available in great variety. Some have a centrifugal system, with rapidly revolving horizontal discs, others a cup feed like a corn drill, while there are endless chains carrying scrapers which remove the material from the hopper onto the ground. Liquid manure spreaders comprise tanks mounted on cart frames, with perforated trays or grooved spreaders across the back of the machine. These various fertilizer spreaders do, however, have one grave disadvantage for the collector. The materials they hold are corrosive in the extreme, and it is highly unlikely that many will be found with working parts intact. The farmyard manure spreader is an exception, as modern designs are still being built, and these are yet another addition to this fascinating range.

After ploughing and sowing come reaping and mowing. The self-binder in its side-on transport position is heavy and cumbersome, and seldom seen on the showground, although there are no specific rules against it. The grass reaper is much more common in the ring. This consists of a framework mounted on two wheels, with suitable gearing to transmit the power from the wheels to the cutting apparatus, and a cutter bar containing a reciprocating knife. It is shown with the cutter bar in the vertical position with its guard in place, and when the driver occupies the seat the machine is well balanced.

Although single-horse mowers with shafts are made, the usual arrangement is for a pole with a horse either side. Thus harnessed, the horses can pull forwards and step sideways, but do remember that they cannot back readily as there is no breechings attachment, so try to avoid driving into a corner!

After cutting, the hay crop has to be dried. Numerous designs facilitate this, offering useful scope for the exhibitor. The hayrake with its seat, two large wheels and curved tines is a prime example, and very suitable for the implements class. Before the self-binder evolved, there was a whole range of reapers which cut the crop but then delivered it onto a platform without tying it up. A few still exist, though mostly in museums, but a self-delivery or tip reaper would be a focal point of interest.

When displaying reaping and mowing implements, or any implements with tines, safety is paramount. The cutter bar, for example, must be disconnected from the drive, and the vertical bar covered with its protective wooden shield. Imagine the worst possible scenario of a runaway and a packed crowd. Images of scythe-wheeled chariots spring to mind, and nothing of the sort must infiltrate the modern showground.

CHAPTER 9

Choice, Fitting and Care of Harness

The fundamental choice of harness is dictated by the type of vehicle or implement being driven; the other major consideration being that it must be a correct and comfortable fit for the individual horse, or horses, that will be wearing it. Newcomers to driving heavy horses would be well advised to enlist the help of an expert in choosing and fitting harness, or to put themselves in the hands of a reputable harness maker. (A Harness Makers' Directory is appended to this book.)

The main types of heavy horse harness are:

cart harness – used for shaft work in two-wheeled carts, single-horse four-wheeled vehicles, and four-wheeled, double-shafted vehicles, whether for town or farm purposes.

trace or chain harness – used for work with farm implements, or where the wheelers are on either side of a pole, rather than between shafts, any horses hitched in front of them also being driven in chains or traces. (Also, a 'trace horse' is one that is yoked by traces in

Harness for a double-shafted waggon.

Tandem harness, showing wheeler in shafts and the leader in trace, or chain harness.

Robert Samson ploughing, showing details of plough harness.

front of a shaft horse when extra power is needed; when it is not, the trace horse follows behind, with the stretcher that keeps the chains apart slung over one hame.

plough harness – a variation on trace harness, but significantly different from other forms.

If a horse is sold and warranted 'Quiet in all Gears', this means that it can go between shafts, and stand and back when necessary. A horse 'Broken to Chains' is guaranteed to pull steadily in the harrows or plough team, or to do any job where a cart saddle is not employed. This illustrates the basic difference between cart and trace harness.

Main Components of Harness

The main components of harness are the bridle, the reins, the collar and hames, the saddle or pad, a set of breechings and crupper and, where appropriate, traces or chains.

Bridle and Reins

The main function of the bridle is to hold the bit in the horse's mouth, thereby establishing communication via the reins, between driver and horse. As with riding, a vast range of bits has been designed and tried for driving but, as with riding again, the key to most horses' mouths is correct basic training and good hands. Nowadays, only two types of bit are common in the show ring. The first is the straight bar reversible type, with one face smooth and the other ribbed. The idea behind this dual design is that the smooth side is used on well-schooled horses whose manners are assured, with the ribbed side being an alternative for horses that have less respect for the bit. It is worth noting, however, that the ribbed side is best employed with some discretion, since heavy-handed use of a harsher bit may provoke, rather than reduce, resistance. The second type of bit is known as the Liverpool driving bit. Some patterns of this bit also have a reversible mouthpiece, but its main characteristic is that it is an adjustable curb bit. This means that, depending on how the reins are attached, their use will apply a greater or lesser degree of leverage to the horse's mouth and poll. If the reins are attached directly to the bit rings (a fitting known as 'plain cheek'), their action is mild. However, the further down the slots in the bars (away from the mouth) they are attached, the stronger their action.

The ideal choice of bit will be dependent upon the individual horse and its previous training, and some experimentation may be needed. It might be, for example, that a naturally ongoing type will prove happier in a smooth Liverpool bit on a fairly strong setting rather than in a ribbed straight bar. The fundamental consideration, however, is that the bit must be in good condition and must fit correctly. If a horse is permanently uncomfortable in the mouth, it will never settle properly, regardless of the actual design of the bit. Correct fitting relates not only to the width of the bit, but also to its location in the horse's mouth – that is, it must be neither too high nor too low. On the traditional bridle, the rings of the bit are attached to the rings of the bridle, and adjustments can only be made by altering the length of the head strap. This means that a fairly accurate guess, erring on the side of too loose rather than too tight, must be made prior to the first fitting. On Scottish bridles, however, the bit is attached to the bridle by small, adjustable straps and the London, or trade, bridle also has straps that pass through the rings of the bit, and are then buckled back to the sides of the cheeks, giving scope for adjustment.

Since the reins provide the physical contact between horse and driver, it is essential that they are kept pliable and in good order. There is a high probability that a broken rein will result in a nasty accident. Careful and regular checks should be made, especially at and around the billets or buckles by which the reins are fastened to the bit, since horse's saliva does no favours to leather. It is also important that reins are of correct length for their current purpose; too short, and there is a risk that they might be snatched from the driver's grasp at an awkward moment; too long, and they will be a

A fine pair of Percherons in pair harness, showing Liverpool bits and blinkers.

general nuisance, and may get snagged around the driver's feet. Actual thickness is also significant; ideally, they should be comfortable in the individual driver's hands, in order to maximize sensitivity and control. Over-thick reins induce a feeling of clumsiness, while reins that are too thin become difficult to hold if the horse pulls, or in humid or wet weather. Some reins are made with plaited or otherwise modified hand-pieces to improve handhold in adverse conditions.

The other feature which may, or may not, be present on driving bridles is blinkers, or winkers, which attach to the bridle cheekpieces. Bridles without these features are known as 'open' and do not restrict the horse's field of vision in any direction. The purpose of blinkers is to reduce the field of peripheral vision so that the horse cannot see anything behind it, specifically the vehicle and any activity of driver, passengers, etc. that might cause alarm. The pros and cons of blinkers have been argued by the hour for centuries, with no overall conclusion reached. It may be that the need for them, or otherwise, is dictated largely by the individual horse's temperament and training. However, if they are fitted, they need to be adjusted correctly in order to fulfil their purpose. This means that the widest part should be level with the wide part of the horse's eye; if too high or too low, the horse may contrive to peer under or over them. Furthermore, if a horse has been accustomed to working in blinkers, they should never be removed while it is still put-to the vehicle, since this may cause it to take fright.

Collar and Hames

The collar fits around the horse's neck, accommodating the hames, to which the traces attach. It is by pushing into the collar that a draught horse does its work, and it is essential that the collar is a good fit, in order that it does not pinch and rub the neck and shoulders. If the collar is patently a bad fit, these problems will be magnified, extending to virtually choking the horse (if the collar is too small) and to serious galling (if the collar is too large and loose). The correct fitting, or otherwise, of the collar is one aspect that will always attract the attention of the Turnout judge.

When fitting a collar, the slope of the horse's shoulders and width of chest are basic factors that affect size. As simple guides, the collar should lie flat against the sides of the neck, but without pinching; it should be possible, from the front, to slide a finger between neck and collar on either side. There should also be room to slide four extended fingers between the bottom of the collar and the windpipe when the horse is standing in a normal position. The collar itself is measured by taking its interior height from top to bottom, and its width at the widest part.

Since the fit of the collar relates directly to the size and shape of the horse, it should come as no surprise that one collar may not fit a horse throughout its career. The collar that is comfortable for an unfurnished four-year-old will almost certainly be too tight when it is a muscled-up six-year-old. Furthermore, there may be seasonal variations, when a horse loses flesh or comes into show condition. Where large numbers of horses are kept, it is possible that suitable spare collars may cover such

A view of Northumbrian style harness, with peaked collars less pronounced than those north of the border.

contingencies, but where only one or two horses are kept, second collars are the only answer. Although extra expense is involved, this enables the horses to work in comfort and increases the chance of success in the ring.

Collars are usually put on by turning them upside down, and swinging them round at the highest part of the neck, just behind the ears. However, in some areas, such as the southwest of England, open or split collars are popular. These part at the top sufficiently to enable them to pass over the horse's neck without having to be put over the head. At the other end of the spectrum is the Scottish peaked show collar, which is usually big enough to slide over the horse's head without the need for turning. This is an expensive item, even more labour-intensive to maintain in show condition than the standard English collar, and rather heavy for both man and horse. It is, however, very eye-catching, and its attractions in a show scenario are undeniable.

Every type of collar consists of two main parts, stitched together and padded with rye straw, enclosed in special checked collar cloth, which lies against the neck. Throughout the main age of the horse, attempts were made to cheapen collar production by using other materials, and processes other than laborious hand-stuffing. None proved successful, and it remains a truism that synthetics and livestock do not mix. Horses at work sweat profusely, and nothing seems to absorb sweat better – and thus minimize rubbing – than rye straw in its traditional cloth covering.

The hames are the means of linking the collar to the load. Each collar has its own set of hames and they must fit correctly if the action of the horse pushing into the collar is to be transferred efficiently into the draught. This transfer is effected via the lower hooks or rings on the hames, to which the tug chains are attached. Above these attachments are the rings through which the reins pass.

Hames are commonly made of solid aluminium bronze or half-round steel tubing. The old-fashioned cased hames, which had a wooden core cased in iron and sheet brass, are sometimes seen but no longer manufactured. Brass hames are sometimes favoured for the show ring, but brass lacks strength and is liable to bend or break under pressure.

The hames are linked together at the top by a strap and buckle, and at the bottom by a hook and chain, all of which must be spotless for the show ring. Strictly speaking, the hames should be removed from the collar before this is taken off the horse, and put back in place after the collar has been fitted when harnessing up. Some practical horsemen simply slacken off the top strap and leave the hames on the collar; however, they should never be left strapped tightly to the collar when not in use.

Saddle or Pad

Although heavy horse harness has developed to be as simple as possible, the terminology surrounding it tends to be complicated. Not only do harness styles vary from county to county, but so do the names for the different parts. Thus, while the term 'saddle' is universally known and understood, in many parts of East Anglia it may also be known as the 'pad'. That term, in most regions, is restricted to trace harness, in which the pad merely bears the weight of the chains and provides a conduit for the reins, or 'strings'. There are, of course, no rights or wrongs in these terms, which highlight the regional traditions associated with the heavy horse. However, since saddle is the term more commonly applied to shaft harness, I shall employ it in the following description.

When used for shaft work in a two-wheeled vehicle, the saddle supports not only the weight of the shafts but the load in the cart. This must be balanced properly, otherwise it would press down unduly on the saddle or rise with the shafts pointing upwards.

The cart saddle has a wooden framework known as the 'tree', which is leather-covered. This leather must be bright and clean for show purposes, and often has small brass ornaments and terrets. The saddle is padded on either side of the tree, with a gap between the pads to keep the withers and spine free of pressure from above, allowing the saddle to fit comfortably on the horse's back.

The back of a heavy horse is much flatter than in the case of a riding horse, whose saddle carries the rider and is the subject of endless conjecture. If the heavy horse saddle is well padded, it causes few problems. In working situations, such as delivering coal every day, the cart saddle might well need restuffing every year, but that circumstance does not occur on the show field. The cloth or check retaining the padding should be kept clean and free from wear. Dirt, sweat and hair will accumulate on the padding of collars and saddles, and must be cleaned off, otherwise it will dry into a hard mat, and soon rub sores on the horses' shoulders and backs. Leather facings are easier to clean, requiring little more than a wipe with a damp cloth.

With a four-wheeled shafted vehicle, the saddle carries only the weight of the shafts. For a poled vehicle, a light pad carries the weight of the trace chains, and the furnishings through which the traces run. Yokes with leaders and wheelers have both lead pads and wheel pads; the wheel pad has a centre terret for the lead reins to pass through.

Breeching and Crupper

The function of the breeching is to enable the horse to hold back a load when going downhill, or to back it on the level. The breeching should not be too tight, i.e. it must not rub constantly against the hind legs, but neither should it be so loose as to flop about. Usually, it is joined to the collar by one or two meeter straps, to prevent the saddle from slipping backwards. A word of warning here. The breeching may have a small loop at the back end by which to hang up the harness: beginners have been known to mistake this small loop for the crupper itself, and have tried to force the unfortunate horse's tail through it, which of course is impossible.

The actual crupper is attached to the saddle by a strap or leather loop, and runs along the spine to a point just forward of the tail. Its loop fits around the tail, and stops the saddle from slipping forwards, but is not used for a single horse. From the crupper strap along the spine a loin strap and a hip strap hang from either side, and these may carry suitably small ornamentation. These straps support the breechband, a strong, heavy piece of leather which goes horizontally round the horse's breech. From the front of the breech-band are chains either side, which slip into hooks on the shafts.

Traces or Chains

As mentioned, these are employed on hitches using pole gear rather than shafts, or on those incorporating a trace horse or horses. Where

A pair in pole harness, showing strap attachment of pole to hame ring.

a pole is used, this is supported by a neck strap fastening to the collar but it is via the traces, which also fasten to the collar, that propulsion is transmitted. Traces generally are made of layers of leather stitched securely together, but some used on working horses are made with chain ends, to permit simple adjustment on the trace hooks, or consist mainly of chain, hence the alternative name.

Swingletrees and chains must be not only spotless but also sound. Accidents are caused through worn parts, and there is a suspicion that modern metals are not as good as formerly. Note leaders' reins passing through terrets on wheelers' bridles.

Basic Principles of Yoking or Putting-to

Although the terms used for this procedure – yoking, putting-to, hitching, shutting-in, etc. – vary from area to area, the principles of attaching the horse or horses to vehicle or implement remain the same. Always remember that the possibility exists of something going wrong during the process, and yoking routines have evolved to minimize that risk.

Single Horse

Yoking a single horse to a cart, rulley or dray is normally a one-person job. However, if either the horse or driver is 'green' – or both are – then two people should be employed.

There are two ways of yoking to a cart. The shafts can be either in the air, or on the ground. If the cart is tipped up, the horse, already bridled, and with the reins attached to the bit rings and looped up out of the way, is brought up to it, carefully swung round, and backed into position under the shafts. Using a shaft 'leg' or 'stilt' if necessary, pull the shafts down gently until the already affixed back-chain or ridger

Yoking or putting-to a cart or single-shafted vehicle.

Bring the horse up to the shafts.

Turn it quietly so that it is in line with the shafts.

If the shafts are to be raised, back the horse under them.

Lower the shafts so that the back-chain slips into the saddle channel.

Note that the reins are already attached to the bit and threaded through the hame rings.

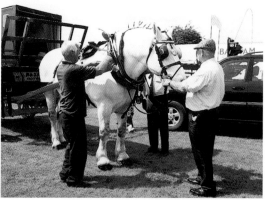

Hame chains are attached on either side...

...then the breeching chains.

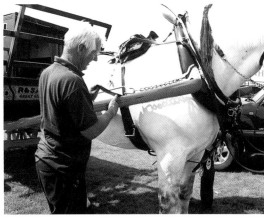

The belly-band is now attached.

The length of the back-chain is adjusted if necessary...

...so that the breech-band is parallel to the shafts.

Adjusting the loin straps on the breeching.

Checking the breeching for tightness; that's about right.

No finger marks allowed!

Yoked up, but the reins are still looped tidily round the near hame.

Now they are taken down ready for mounting.

Clambering aboard. This is a farm vehicle, with racks fore and aft to carry more bulky material such as hay or sheaves of corn. A trade vehicle would have a step.

Driving position, two or three feet from the front, with reins taken up in the left hand, and any slack in the right. The driver is smartly dressed in typical country attire.

slides into the saddle channel. Slip on the near side shoulder chain, then go round the horse's head, speaking to it as you go, because if it is wearing blinkers it will not see you approach. Fit the off side shoulder chain and then the off side breeching chain. Return to the near side, and fit the breeching chain on that side, and then the belly-band, which stops the shafts rising.

If you start with the shafts on the floor, the belly-band will be in place, but the back-chain will not. Bring up the horse gently as before, and swing round so that it is backed between the shafts. Do this carefully, because big horses have been known to stamp on a shaft, and break it. If there are two of you, lift a shaft apiece, then the person on the off side passes the back-chain over, via the saddle channel, to the near side partner, who fixes the appropriate link into the hook. The shafts should be pointing very slightly upwards. The shoulder chains are then attached, and finally the breeching chains. The reins should be unlooped – from around the hames if the shafts have been lowered, or from the crupper if the shafts have been raised. They are placed within reach of the driver, but are never tied to the cart. You are then ready to mount and drive away, but never let the horse move off before you say so.

If working alone, back the horse between the lowered shafts, go to the off side and, after lifting the shafts, attach the shoulder chain to its hame hook. The height of the shaft enables the back-band to be set in the channel and it can then be reached on going to the near side, where it is attached to its hook, and the shoulder chain linked to its hame hook.

There is one cart operation in which two persons are definitely better than one. This is when the load has been left standing, with its legs taking the weight, and the horse taken out for a break. The wheels are chocked so that the cart cannot swing sideways. When re-yoking, the breeching is then slung over the saddle so as not to catch, and one person steadies the shafts while the second backs the horse carefully between them, ensuring that nothing catches during the process. This is usually a working rather than a showing operation.

When yoking to a rulley or single-horse dray, the shafts are often held up by a short chain between them and the vehicle. The horse is backed in carefully, and the chains linked on in the same order as for a cart.

Pair

Two people are needed to yoke a pair, except in the case of a tandem, when the second horse is tied on behind until needed. When yoking the pair, the pole has limited movement, and the horses are brought into position on either side. They soon learn their place. One person stands at their heads, and the other slips on first the near side pole chain, and then the off side. Even with this simple operation there are differing views. One is to attach the inside trace chains first; they have been hooked either onto the crupper ring or the breeching, and can be attached without going between the horses. The outside trace chains are then hooked on, turning the hooks to the outside. The alternative method is to hook the outside trace chains on first, which is done to prevent an uneasy horse from swinging outwards.

The reins are buckled together, a good tip being to use a bit of lace on them to hook onto your little finger. This prevents them from slipping down behind the horses' legs. Note that the length of the reins may be adjusted according to the size of the horses. Sometimes one of 18 hands has to partner one of 17 hands.

When unyoking, loosing out or unhitching, the reins should be accessible but not tied to the vehicle. The trace chains are hooked on to the big ring at the end of the crupper.

Harnessing a unicorn hitch to a trade vehicle.

Above: *Attaching the breeching strap to the ring of the trace chains.*

Left: *The Percheron's hard blue hoofs are smartened still further.*

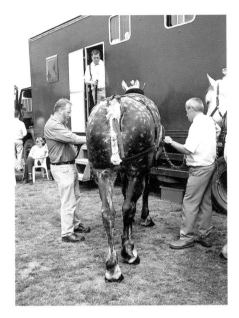

Above left: *Harnessing is made easier if there is one person on either side.*

Above right: *One method of hanging the breeching chain before yoking.*

Above left: *Owen Garner, the driver of this Percheron unicorn hitch, takes the reins before mounting. He is wearing the apron and the smart hat and gloves expected in Trade classes.*

Above right: *He mounts by the step, still holding the reins.*

Notes on Other Hitches

In the unicorn hitch, the leader's reins go through the rings on its saddle, and then through the terrets on the wheelers' bridles, the reins of which run outside. The driver thus has four reins in his hand.

Reining principles for the four-horse team are similar to those of the unicorn. For a six-horse team, the middle or 'swing' pair are coupled together. British and American styles differ; Americans tend to drive double-handed, whereas in Britain all four reins are held in one hand. Double-handed driving is becoming more popular in Britain, but it is not considered correct. The standard British way, developed over a century ago, and described by such authorities as the Duke of Beaufort and Captain Morley Knight, was used by men driving coaches for eight or ten hours a day, because it was the most practical. It most certainly is not an affectation. The precise manner of holding the reins in these larger hitches is explained in the drawings on page 198.

Harnessing a team.

These Hollesley Bay Suffolks leave their transport and are tied alongside by their headcollars. They receive a final strapping before harnessing, using a body brush in conjunction with a light curry comb for cleaning it. (Note: most grooms require a stool to brush heavies effectively!)

Tails are plaited before harnessing.

Above: *The headcollar shank is released and the collar put over the head. Usually the collar must be turned from the upside down position at this point, but with these big show collars that is unnecessary.*

Right: *The collar is lifted back to fit snugly onto the shoulders.*

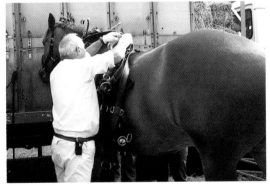

The pad is then lifted on, and secured by meeter straps to the collar.

The breeching is then lifted on . . .

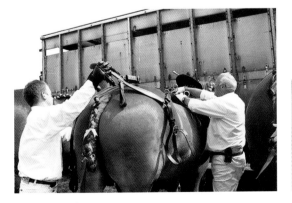

...and spread out.

The crupper is placed over the tail and. . .

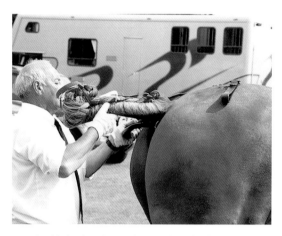

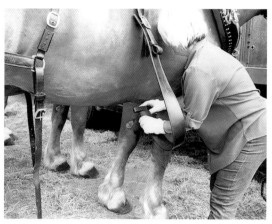

...unbuckled, placed round it, and buckled up again.

The martingale strap is threaded over the girth strap. The martingale carries a series of brasses, and is attached to the collar at the other end.

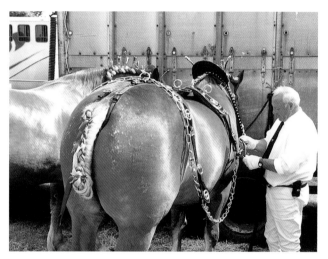

Traces are attached to the hame hooks, and to the pad by a large strap, then hooked into the big ring surmounting the crupper.

The throat strap is fastened; on all these straps there is usually a groove in the leather showing which hole is normally used. The curb chain dangling down must be turned until flat, and then hooked on.

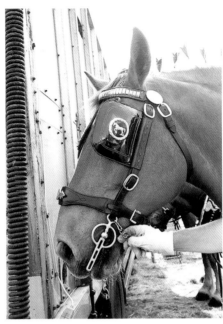

The noseband is buckled on.

The curb chain is hooked in place. When the reins are pulled, it tightens against the jaw, affording extra leverage. The fingers should easily pass between it and the jaw. The Liverpool bit clearly shows four positions for the reins; the bit ring is the mildest, and is the one used for coupling reins. The bit cheek itself has three positions for attaching the reins, the lowest being the most severe.

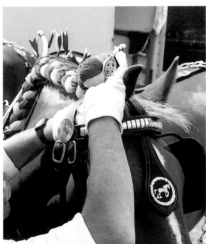

The leaders' reins are attached, using the middle setting on this occasion, but varying with the individual animal.

The forelock is tidied; everything is done to make the horse as comfortable as possible.

A ribbon lends the finishing touch to the forelock.

One person per horse is needed for the four-horse team, and all horses are brought out together. The wheelers are swung into position first.

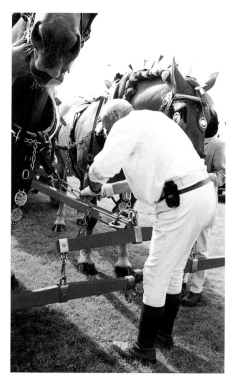

The pole is attached to the collars. Swingletrees for the leaders are clearly shown.

The wheelers' reins are attached, and looped round the hames.

Above: *Their trace chains are attached to the vehicle by wrapping them round 'mushrooms' on the splinter bar.*

Right: *The coupling rein and method of cross-reining the leaders is clearly shown.*

The driver sorts out his reins and...

...away we go!

Plough Harness

Plough harness is substantially different from other trace harness. It consists of bridle, bearing rein, collar and hames, back-band and crupper. The back-band has a ring on the outside, i.e. on the near side for the near side horse and on the off side for the off side horse. The reins, often called strings in ploughing parlance, run from the bit rings, through a spare link on the trace chains where the latter are attached to the hames, then through the back-band rings and finally through a strap dropping from the crupper, the object being to have the strings in a direct line between bit and ploughman's hands, without any risk of them dropping to where they might entangle the horse's legs. They do not pass through the hame rings, which are too high for this purpose.

Storage and Care of Harness

Since the turnout horse is no use without its harness, the harness room might be described as the fulcrum of the heavy horse establishment. Besides harness, it is often used to store such items as first aid materials and grooming tools.

Features of the Harness Room

While there is scope for much individuality in a harness room, and while many may not be purpose-built, there are certain principles that need to be observed, the main ones being security, handiness, and suitability for the job in hand. Sadly, harness – and heavy horse harness in particular – is high on the thief's list. Items such as collars can make big money, a remark which – for those inclined to enter the new ridden classes – applies also to saddles. For this reason a room of the house itself may be considered for harness storage, or (subject to obtaining planning permission) one may be added on specifically for the purpose. This latter course of action may not prove as expensive as one might think, especially since niceties such as external windows are not particularly desirable from the security point of view and a simple (preferably insulated) concrete floor will suffice. However, if the harness is to be stored in the house, this means that the house needs to be near the stabled horses, which may not be the case. If, as an alternative, an outbuilding is considered, this should be as burglar-proof as possible – a remark that extends to matters such as roofing materials and the manner in which security devices are fixed. There is no point in buying heavy-duty padlocks, hasps and staples, then fixing them to suspect timber with one-inch screws!

Another defining characteristic of the harness room – wherever it is located – is that it must be dry, but kept at a moderate temperature. Dampness will prevent leather from drying and predispose it to attack from mould but, if the temperature is high, it will dry out too quickly, and crack. In some hunter establishments a through draught is preferred, to help dry the harness fairly quickly without the use of heat. However, especially in winter, this is incompatible with human comfort if the cleaning is carried out in the same room as the storage. In principle, there is a strong case for following the tradition of the larger, old-time establishments, of having two rooms – one for harness storage and another warm, snug room where cleaning was done. This second room often became a centre of the establishment, redolent of smells of leather, harness oil and horses, conducive to good chat and the careful work necessary to keep harness in top condition. In real terms, such idyllic arrangements may not always be practical, in which case low wattage tubular heaters, set just above floor level, give an even level of heat, sufficient to ward away damp, and take the chill off, thus avoiding cracks in leather and hypothermia in humans.

So far as layout and storage are concerned, one requirement is a reasonable height from roof or ceiling. Given a height of 10 feet, the bridles hang from a top row of pegs, which are preferably semicircular in design to keep the bridles in better shape. Below them will be a row of pegs for the collars. Sometimes the collar peg also takes the breechings and cart saddle, but in such cases, the collar pegs must be high enough to ensure that the breechings hang clear of the ground. Since harness – especially bridles and collars – is tailored to individual horses, each peg should be marked clearly with the horse's name, and care should be taken that equipment is stored correctly and not left casually on the nearest peg.

One essential feature of the room used for cleaning harness is good lighting, whether natural or artificial. Overhead lights are recommended. The light should show up any slipshod work; it is disheartening to arrive in the collecting ring and then find some dull or dirty place on the harness that the lights at home had not shown up up. However, strong artificial light should be turned off when not required, since prolonged exposure to such lighting may contribute to the drying out of leather.

Cleaning and Care of Harness

If good quality harness is looked after, it will last for a long time, but regular maintenance is the watchword, both in terms of safety and the horses' comfort. All harness must, of course, be cleaned to perfection prior to a show, but it is also the case that, immediately it is stripped off the horses, it should be washed clean. Transporters may be equipped with harness hooks to facilitate this cleaning at the showground. A soft, damp cloth or sponge is usually employed, together with mild soap or saddle soap. The harness is then left to dry, which takes about half an hour in benign conditions. In practice, the first lot is usually dry by the time the last lot has been washed, especially with team harness.

Once dry, metal parts such as buckles are coated with a metal polish such as Brasso. It is essential this is dry before boot polish is applied to the leatherwork, or the metal polish will run onto the black boot polish. Patent leather harness is wiped clean, then sprayed with a proprietary cleaner manufactured for the purpose. Since it scratches and dents easily, it should be stored with care.

The actual order of cleaning is a matter of personal choice, but most grooms start with the more straightforward parts and finish with the breeching seats, which are the most difficult. The main point is that there are no short cuts – if there were, they would have been discovered years ago – and one person can easily spend two days cleaning a set of team harness thoroughly. Indeed, each pair set can take a whole tin of polish.

Most trade collars have brown leather facings where the collars meet the shoulders. This makes them easier to clean, using brown boot polish. Agricultural collars may have cloth linings, and these must be sponged to remove sweat, dirt and hair, using just enough water to do the job without soaking them. The same applies to the underside of cart saddles, if these are faced with cloth where they meet the skin. (Leather or cloth facings are equally correct.)

At least once a year, and more often if it is in regular use, the harness must be completely taken apart and every piece minutely inspected for cracks, wearing thin, buckling or fraying, as appropriate. If only done on a yearly basis, this should be at the end of the show season – to ensure time for replacement or repair – and not a few days before the first show of the year.

CHAPTER 10

Turnout Driving

The essence of Turnout classes (called Hitch classes elsewhere) is that the horses haul a vehicle. The number of horses per vehicle can range from one (single harness) through two to six or, very occasionally, eight. In most cases, the number and formation of horses eligible for a particular class will be designated in the class description, for example 'Pair of Heavy Horses', 'Team of Four'. At some smaller shows, three- and four-horse teams may be combined in one class, although a recent exciting increase in numbers has resulted in separate classes at the bigger shows.

Two horses are usually driven side by side (as a pair) but in an alternative formation, known as tandem, one leads the other. The tandem is spectacular but difficult; much depends on a good leader. Horses are gregarious animals and, while two perform happily side by side, one out in front on its own may be less sure of itself and is less easy to control.

The same applies to the 'threes'. Here, the formation is generally 'unicorn', with one leader and two at the wheel, either in shafts or with a pole between them. The alternative formation is the 'pick axe', with two horses in front and one between the shafts. Three abreast or 'trandem' is another hitch, used during the 1980s and early 1990s by Noel Abel's pantechnicon for furniture haulage and by Mervyn Ramage's three light roan Clydesdales. It is also possible to yoke three horses in line, known as a 'randem'. This hitch is really spectacular, calling for horsemanship of the highest order, and a leader that responds readily to voice commands.

The four-horse team is usually hitched two and two, although four in line is dramatic in its effect. The 'six' is the pinnacle of North American horsemanship. To see those massive six-horse teams swooping through the narrow arch of the Toronto Winter Fair at a fast trot makes crossing the Atlantic worthwhile for that alone. Just as the heavy horse revival spread from North America to Britain, so the 'six' is becoming a major part of our summer scene. All these big turnouts are expensive in terms of transport and manpower, yet they are such crowd-pullers that shows offer grants to help exhibitors compete in what would otherwise be an exercise beyond most private pockets.

In all Turnout classes, the vehicles must be immaculate. The horses are neatly decorated and braided, and many exhibitors will also enter separate classes that emphasize this aspect, such as the Decorated Harness class (see Chapter 14).

The choice of turnout and formation driven will be decided by a number of factors, of which personal preference is clearly one. There are, however, a number of pragmatic considerations and constraints, including finance, availability and suitability of horses and, of course, driving skill. It can take some time to become truly efficient at handling a single heavy horse in harness and, until a fair degree of proficiency has been attained, it would be folly to attempt to control two or more animals, especially in some of the more demanding formations.

Principles of Single Harness

Since this is the form most suitable for a novice, it makes sense to consider here some of the principles of breaking a horse to harness, and basic driving technique. Prior to that, however, it is worth reiterating that the choice of horse is important, not only in terms of temperament and tractability, but also in terms of type.

Naturally, classes for single harness horses tend to attract more entries than those for either the pairs or teams. Of course, anyone may enter and enjoy the class, but in order to win you must have a really big, eye-catching horse. The single-harness Shire should make 17.3 to 18.1 hands, and fill the shafts as it moves; it should be really beefy and have a mature weight of 18 to 19 cwt. Such a horse was Woldsman, so successful for Billy Cammidge some years ago, while Young's Brewery have had some magnificent single-harness horses in their favourite colour, black with four white socks. They use geldings exclusively, as do most Shire people, but there is now a distinct move to introduce mares into the Turnout classes of the Percheron and Suffolk worlds.

For Turnout classes a horse should be at least four years old, and some shows specifically bar younger animals from these classes. This is eminently sensible, since heavy horses are late maturing and most will be at least five or six before reaching their best. However, winning ways begin long before that.

Preparing the Horse for Work in Harness

The first step in this process is 'mouthing'; getting the horse accustomed to accepting the bit, as a precursor to teaching correct responses to it. This is a vitally important but frequently neglected part of breaking, or training in the modern term. Too often it is not well done. Some horses have mouths like iron, or respond more to one rein than the other. These are signs of bad mouthing, and are likely to backfire on the driver. If you are to have nearly a ton of horse at the other end of the reins, it is a distinct advantage if that horse accepts, and responds to, the action of the bit.

Mouthing usually begins when the horse is three years old. The youngster should be fitted with a bridle that includes a mouthing bit, which is thicker (and thus milder) than a normal bit and has 'keys' dangling from the mouthpiece, which encourage the horse to play with them and thus salivate. A little treacle smeared on the bit is an additional aid. A roller and crupper are added, which allow the attachment of side reins. These should not be fitted tightly, but should be adjusted in such a way as to produce a light rein contact when the horse's head is in its natural position. The horse is then backed into a stall, and 'pillar reined' by attaching a rein on either side from the bit to the end of the standing. Twenty minutes a day suffices for a start, but stay within sight in the early stages, just in case the horse gets upset.

This process continues for three weeks at least. Horses vary so much that no specific time schedule can be laid down. Also, don't forget that at three years of age the horse's mouth is not 'made'; that is to say it is still gaining extra teeth and these may make the mouth tender as they push through. So far as is possible, it is best to arrange the mouthing process around teething, or even to abandon it temporarily if teeth start erupting while the horse is being mouthed. If this is not done, the horse may associate the bit, rather than the teething, with discomfort, and this may set the stage for long-term resistances. Once the horse has become accustomed to the mouthing bit, a standard bit of your choice – preferably a mild pattern, at least to begin with – can be introduced.

Once you are fairly satisfied with the horse's acceptance of the bit, harness may be added carefully. The horse is then left in a loose box with breechings and dangling chains, to accustom it to the rattle. This process generally needs about a week to ensure that the horse has accepted the harness fully.

The youngster is then ready to be driven from the ground in long reins. At first an assistant may be needed to lead the horse by the bridle and to help, as necessary, with stopping and backing, but soon the driver should be able to manage alone. During all this time the horse must be encouraged to get its head up. An open bridle (one without blinkers) is fitted and the roller and crupper are in place to allow the addition of an overcheck. This is a type of bearing rein designed to keep the horse's head up. It is used regularly in Hackney classes, but for heavy horses it is simply a training aid, designed to encourage a good head carriage and to keep the horse looking where it is going, rather than peeping about. Thin rope, like old-fashioned window cord, is best for forming the overcheck. This is attached to both bit rings by spring clips and runs along the cheeks, through rings clipped on either side of the bridle, and thence to join and be fixed on the top of the roller.

Whilst long reining, walk, walk, walk is the watchword. One and a half to two hours daily are really needed, and allowed for in a professional stable, this time being split up into two, or preferably three, sessions and built up to longer overall. The amateur may not be able to adhere to quite such a rigorous daily routine, but should not be discouraged, for many of today's exhibitors are in the same position. The key points, with young horses, are consistency and repetition. Adhering to these, albeit with some reduction of time, will serve you better than an erratic regime in which the horse is overworked on some days, and not worked at all on others.

These pictures from a long reining obstacle competition, organized by the Heavy Horse Riding Club, highlight the training that can be achieved with this technique.

Periodically, the horse must be made to stop. For this, the voice command is 'Whoa!' and then 'Stand Still!' This is combined with steady pressure on the reins, not snatching or sawing at them. The horse should feel this pressure at the same time as it hears the command. If it doesn't, it will simply keep going. This is where an assistant with a lead rope may be useful. So long as the horse is used to leading and stopping in-hand (see Training at Home in Chapter 11), an astute assistant can help it to associate the voice command and rein pressure with the requirement to stop. Whether or not such assistance is needed, it is important not to stop in the same place each time, or else the horse might begin to associate stopping with a particular spot, rather than with the signals.

Once the horse will stop consistently upon command, and walk on freely again, it must then be taught to back. This is an important part of preparation for the show ring, since some judges ask for a demonstration, and classes have been lost because a horse refused to back properly for the judge. Backing is not, however merely a show ring exercise, but an essential requirement of the working horse. Indeed, in the days when stalls rather than loose boxes were the norm, each horse had to back out of its standing before anything else could be done. During work, farm horses were usually backed from the ground, since they were working on uneven surfaces. Town horses had to back as part of daily routine, perhaps into narrow alleys and round tight corners. To assist them a good horseman would take up the breeching chains perhaps two or three links, but that technique is not used in the show ring.

To introduce the horse to backing in the long reins, after stopping, it should be reined in, through steadily increased pressure on the reins, while the command 'Back!' is given. If your assistant simultaneously pushes his thumb into the horse's breastbone, at the tender spot just where the bottom of the collar fits, this may help considerably. However, the long-term aim is to get the horse to respond primarily to the voice command; first, because an assistant may not always be to hand, and second, because you do not want to rely too much on heavy rein pressure, since this is not good for the horse and it risks teaching him to run backwards out of control.

A horse that has progressed to working in shafts may be taught to back by holding the bridle in the left hand, and the shaft end with the right. On the command 'Back!' push the shaft back at the same time as applying pressure to the bridle. Once this lesson has been learned, the horse may be backed from the driving seat by applying slight pressure on the reins and giving the command. While backing a cart is fairly straightforward, a four-wheeler quickly shows up any deficiencies in training; if the horse or pair does not go straight back, the pole or shafts soon turn the turntable to an acute angle. Therefore, thorough home preparation and practice is the answer, with backing as with so much else.

Voice commands play an important part in turning to the left and right, the commands 'Harve' and 'Gee Back' respectively being used most commonly. However, these do vary in different parts of the country so, when buying a horse from another area, be sure to ask what commands it has been used to, and write them down! Whatever voice commands are used, they are accompanied by an increased bit pressure on the side to which the turn is being made, and a slight slackening of the rein on the opposite side. Neither the increase nor the slackening should be overdone and the commands should be given in good time. The horse should not be expected to make unnecessarily sharp turns, and should not be hurried whilst turning. Draught horses, especially those that are to be driven in pairs or teams, need time to learn to cross their legs whilst turning, otherwise, with two or more abreast in chain gear, there is a danger that they will swing their legs out and catch their neighbour's coronet. In fact, if horses can be taught to creep round when turning in such gear, so much the better.

Once the stopping, starting and directional controls are established, some trotting can be introduced. Again, at this stage, the presence of an assistant may be desirable, and whoever is doing the long reining should be agile and well shod. The usual command, from walk, is 'Trot on', with a click of the tongue. To return to walk, say 'Steady' and 'Walk on', at the same time slightly increasing a steady and equal pressure on both reins.

Long reining goes on for weeks. It is absolutely essential that the horse knows what is expected of it, and that you know it will comply. This is a matter of safety as well as of winning prizes. One aspect of this is that, when you come to mount your vehicles, your horse must stand. You have to climb aboard, gain the dickey seat, and fasten your safety belt. During this time, you must not be in the position of wondering whether the horse will move off before you are ready. This discipline is instilled during long reining, time and time and time again, by increasing the period in which the horse is expected to stand after being brought to a halt.

If these early stages have been carried out carefully, and the horse is accustomed to harness, the process of shafting, also known as shutting-in or putting-to, should not be too difficult. If blinkers are to be worn, then the horse should become accustomed to them during the long reining process; do not fit them for the first time when first putting-to. The general procedure for putting-to was discussed in the previous chapter, but in terms of the horse's early introduction, the following points should be borne in mind. To begin with, the horse must first be brought opposite to and square with the shafts. Then, by pressure on the hame rein and the voice command 'Back', it can be made to step backwards between the shafts. The ridger, or back-chain, which is usually permanently attached to the off side ridger bar, must lie clear, so that the horse does not step on it. If the vehicle is a cart, it will need a belly-band to prevent it from tipping backwards when it is tail-heavy. If this is permanently fixed to both shafts, the horse will have to step over it. If, as sometimes happens, the heel of one of the shoes catches on the belly-band, then the horse must be drawn forwards and the process begun again. This should not be a problem once the horse is experienced in being put-to but, in the early stages, it is better to ensure that it is unnecessary. That said, a two-wheeled cart is still better than a dray or rulley for breaking. If the horse starts to run back with a cart, there is less likelihood of damage to horse, vehicle or driver. In the same circumstances, a rulley or similar vehicle may jack-knife, and could overturn or throw the driver off the seat.

Driving a vehicle is first done at the walk, again for a total of an hour and a half to two hours a day, with a trot for the last ten minutes. The horse must be made to answer either rein by driving in a figure of eight, and to stand stock still as it would in front of the judges.

With this continual work, the horse will become muscled up. This is essential. Sometimes the show ring going will be heavy and, if your horse is not fit, 'the light goes out', as turnout people say. Your outfit falters while the top drivers keep going. The training principle is the same as for human athletes.

Throughout all this time, the horse must be encouraged to flex its hocks and keep its head up. To help achieve this, some trainers long rein their horses over a succession of telegraph poles laid on the ground, in much the same way that trainers of ridden horses use ground poles or cavalletti. Following on from the other lessons on the long reins, the horse must learn to back the vehicle a yard or two and, as previously mentioned, must be relied on to stand when you dismount, hang the reins on the hames, and stand a yard or two away. (Under no circumstances should you tie the reins to the vehicle. If you do, and the horse sets off and then breaks shaft, pole or harness, it could pull its mouth to pieces.) Furthermore, the horse must not move when you put your foot on the step to remount; an animal that starts to move off as soon as it feels the foot on the step is a danger to itself, its driver and other competitors. This is still an all-too-common fault.

The Driver

Breaking a horse to harness and driving correctly make demands on the driver, as well as the horse. During the preliminary work and practice sessions the reins must be held correctly. Using the left hand, take the near side rein between finger and thumb, and the off side rein between the third and fourth fingers. Some prefer the off side rein between the second and third finger but in either case the wrist is held vertically and tilted in that plane to give leverage either way as desired. The right hand is for holding the whip, and for pulling the reins through the left hand. Thus the right hand is positioned behind the left when this is done.

Hold the whip almost, but not quite, upright; five or ten to twelve o'clock is the angle. The whip is used as a signal, extending it horizontally left or right to indicate a turn in the given direction. However, if you have to make a sudden stop, the whip is shot up straight, at arm's length, with the driver bolt upright. Although this meaning may be unclear to other road users nowadays, it may be given in emergency by exhibitors when circling the ring, and is an important signal; therefore be prepared to use it or react to it as necessary.

The driver's smartness is all-important, and is helped by adopting a

Peter Tribe driving for Cyril Knowles. Everything about the driver's appearance must be smart; hat, clothes, gloves, footwear and apron – which is an essential heavy turnout accoutrement. The safety belt strapping in the driver must also be clean.

Roger Buglass of Morpeth, Northumberland is a stalwart of the heavy horse scene, and one of many exhibitors who drive for the sheer fun of it. This does not mean that the turnout of horse, driver or vehicle is any less than immaculate.

Ken Taylor's Shire gelding, Brigadier, being driven at the Shire Horse Show by Peter Riseborough, one of the 'greats'.

half-standing position on the seat, the object being to allow your legs to be in a straight line. A sloping cushion helps, strapped to the dickey seat. Make this about four inches high at the back, sloping down to about two inches, and you will find it is a good aid. Your knees should be fairly straight, with feet braced against the footrest. Although good training should render the horse tractable, it is a fact that, in some circumstances, even a single horse can take every muscle in your body to hold; it cannot possibly be controlled by the arms alone, and some horses would pull you right off the seat were it not for the safety belt, if you did not position yourself correctly.

Driving a Pair

If choice of horse is important for success in single harness, it becomes even more so where pairs are concerned. For real success at pair driving, matching is essential. Note the great winners of the 1990s: John Peacock's dark bay Shires, Young's Brewery's blacks with four white socks, Whitbread's and Tetley's grey Shires, Tom Brewster's bright bay Clydesdales, Vaux's and Jim Young's grey Percherons, and Clarks' bright chesnut Suffolks. Modern competition is so strong that judges can often only assess a class by looking for faults, and a non-matching pair is immediately noticeable. An example of this – an extreme one, if you will – is that one horse of a grey pair may go lighter with age more quickly than the other, so it may become necessary to change the pair. However, this also serves to illustrate the opposite point: it is far better to put two heavy horses together and drive them as a pair, even if they don't match, than be put off by potential competition from others with more facilities and money. Perfection takes time and, if you drive an oddly assorted pair, someone is sure to come along and say 'I've just the horse for you!' In the meantime, practice makes perfect in other areas.

In respect of the (probably gradual) path towards perfection, a fundamental tenet is that the pair should match as nearly as possible for height, and also action. This is a tall order, often made taller by circumstances. It is by no means a rare occurrence that two horses appear a perfect match to the human eye, and then refuse to work together.

Much time is spent outside the show season trying to find horses that 'click', trial and error being the only method. One point for consideration is that some horses go better on one side than on the other. In a well-run stable, bringing on its own horses, every animal should be taught to drive on either side, reducing the chances of a mismatch. This is a policy of perfection, and even the best stable will sometimes find that it is short of a really good horse to match an established favourite. If horses are otherwise compatible, but one is somewhat bigger or showier than its mate, it is a common ploy to put the bigger or showier animal on the off side, i.e. nearer the judge. The crowd then sees the slightly less attractive side, which is a pity, but they are not placing the turnouts! The successful Coalite pair of Vincent and Viking was

John Walker driving a splendidly matched pair of bays from a great Shire enthusiast. Bay comes in a range of shades, and is especially attractive against four white legs.

always driven with the exceptionally showy Vincent on the off side.

Having decided on your pair as nearly as may be, the introductory routine is as described for the single horse. Each individual to have lots and lots of long reining: walk, walk, walk to get the muscles built up; 'Whoa' and 'Back'; 'Gee Back' and 'Harve', or whatever the local commands may be.

A start with four- or five-year-olds is ideal; your three-year-old is too immature. However, a youngster's training will doubtless benefit from a spell alongside a steady horse in the pole gear used for pairs harness, but only after it has been broken to shafts. The reason for introducing shafts before pole work is that there is more chance of something going wrong at the pole. For one thing, if a wheel drops into a pothole, the pole may shoot up and alarm the trainee, that doesn't appreciate what is happening. However, when Leeds brewers Tetley's are training young harness horses, they drive them round and round an enclosure that has a number of 'sleeping policemen' which really send the pole up in the air. When the youngster can cope with that, it can cope with most things.

Pair Harness

Even if both horses are naturally straight movers, they can only go correctly if they are harnessed correctly. The animals are on either side of a pole attached to the vehicle's splinter bar. The cross-piece on the front of the pole is termed a crab. To it a chain or strap is fixed, which joins it to each collar at the bottom of the hames. These straps serve to control the pole and guide the vehicle, and in the absence of a handbrake can take the vehicle's weight downhill. They also serve to back the vehicle. The movement of either horse will affect the other as it turns. Leather or chain traces run from the hames to the splinter bar.

Coupling reins are used in pair driving. These short, inside reins cross from one horse's bit through a ring on the other horse's hames, and then through a similar terret ring on its pad. They are then joined to the outside reins. These coupling reins have from 12 to 14 buckles, which enable their length to be altered. It is necessary to understand how and why to alter them. If, for example, the off side horse is turning its head in, and perhaps the near side one turning its head out, the coupling reins must be adjusted to make both straight. In order to do this, someone must first stand in front of the moving pair to assess the situation. This person must not become so absorbed in his task that the horses run him down! It has happened, and to top-class horsemen.

Pair Driving Technique

The reins are held in exactly the same way for pair driving as for driving a single horse. You still have just two reins in your hand: pull them through as described for single driving. There used to be a practice contraption consisting of strings (light rope reins) attached to weights over a series of pulleys, useful for strengthening wrist and hand muscles, but this is not easy to find these days. Modern technology could surely invent a practical version. Some pre-show practice in

A fine example of the turnout driver's seat. David Coffen driving Bass Brewery's pair of Shires.

Tetley's pair of grey Shires in action at the National Shire Horse Show: another fine example of driving style by Dudley Parker.

Mike Millington driving Gale's Brewery's pair of Shires: note the correct details of driving apron, gloves, whip and hat.

handling pair reins is highly advisable: if your hands are not sufficiently strong, then by the time two big horses have taken you six times round the ring, you will have lost the necessary grip and power.

In all respects, even when you have decided on your pair and have them going fairly well, hours and hours of practice at home will still be needed. Ideally, your horses should move like machines, each leg a matching piston. When meeting an onlooker (especially the judge), the forelegs should be moving straight, not dishing to the side, and the hind legs, flexed at the hocks, should be following the forelegs.

The whip is as much a part of the driver's equipment as his hat or apron, and is more likely to be needed when driving a pair. If one horse goes slower than the other, a touch of the whip often suffices to bring it into line.

If you get into any real trouble, put the whip away. At other times, however, dexterity with it is an added accomplishment noted by a competent judge, and certainly clumsy handling will count against you. One way of practising with the whip is to draw the vehicle, without horses, front first up to a wall and park it before clambering on to the dickey seat. Then practise flicking the whip at certain points on the wall until you become proficient in your placings.

Tandem Driving

Of all forms of driving, tandem is arguably the most difficult. The object of the tandem is to have a spare horse to give extra power when needed, usually up a slope or over very rough ground. The tandem leader should not give the appearance of pulling the shaft horse along. The leader's chains should be tight but not taut. This is all very well in theory, but it is far easier in practice to have a real mix-up, with the leader facing round towards the driver! Such incidents seem to run through the historical fabric of tandem driving: one of the classic situations highlighted in an old *Punch* magazine was when an ardent suitor tried to show off his light horse tandem to his swain, and the leader finished up turned around facing the wheeler.

Today's heavy horse tandem driver is equally open to being a victim of such circumstances, which is one reason why this yoke is so seldom attempted. Prerequisites for undertaking this formation are, perhaps,

Young's Brewery's tandem, driven by Kevin Flynn.

highly developed driving skills and a robust sense of humour in adversity. That said, with a skilled driver and a good leader, few turnouts look better. Kevin Flynn, head horse keeper for Young's Brewery, is one of the younger horsemen to drive a show tandem, backed by Mr John Young's encouragement and knowledge. Furthermore, Elspeth Walker (née Ross) won her first tandem class at the East of England Show in 1997, having not previously attempted the yoke competitively.

The main difficulty at the root of tandem driving, that needs to be addressed by anyone attempting this yoke, is that few horses are natural leaders. Some can be trained to accept this role, but others never make it. Experienced horsemen will not waste time on the last group. The horse is a herd animal, not relishing being alone, and even an experienced driver feels grateful for a competent leader, rather than being frustrated by a non-starter. One point to note, in searching for leader material, is that a good single harness horse may well make a better leader than one used to going as a pair. When a horse shows promise in the role, its potential is brought out by schooling, driving, and walking ad infinitum.

For tandem driving the reins are all in one hand as in pair driving but the leader must not be allowed to stretch out. It must start when the wheeler does, but after that must be kept back so that the traces are just tight; neither taut nor swinging about like a skipping rope.

Three-horse Yokes

There are four different ways of hitching a team of three horses: trandem (three abreast), unicorn (one leader and two wheelers), pick axe (two leaders, and one wheeler in the shafts) and random (three in a line). The variety of yokes adds to the fascination and glamour of the show ring, and the way in which they have developed and been incorporated into the modern show circuit is a fascinating tale in itself.

During the 1960s the chief turnout exhibitors were the breweries, or a few firms with adequate resources, who usually entered a single, a pair or a team of four. Then came the 'great revival' of the 1970s, when heavy horses emerged from the dark years of near extinction, and more and more individuals turned to them either as a hobby or for business. Only when private individuals entered the fray did the 'three' become more popular. This was partly on the grounds of expense and availability of horses, and partly through the mistaken belief that three were easier to drive than four!

The number of horses involved reflects the natural progression of the amateur enthusiast. Starting with a single, the turnout bug soon bites, and the jolly camaraderie of the show circuit encourages a move to a pair. That accomplished, the desire to drive three or four becomes the next ambition, but the move from one to two is a far smaller one than the jump from two to three or four. A bigger transporter, more staff, extra fodder, extra harness to clean and more time spent grooming and exercising are among the factors that must be considered before that leap is made.

A good example of individual progression is that of Percheron driver Robert Blake. He was a leading scurry driver and, having achieved success in that field, decided that the intense competition and split-second timing of that spectacular sport should be replaced by something easier. As a regular showman he had observed the 'heavy boys' sitting around shirt-sleeved in the sun, drinking beer. 'That's the life for me!' decided Robert, and bought a Percheron, which he showed in single harness, thoroughly enjoying the experience. In fact, he enjoyed it so much that he moved on to a pair. Then, the next season, he had to have a 'three', which gave rise to ambitions to field a team. The result is that Robert Blake spends every waking moment of his life during the show season catering for his handsome Percherons and their tack and vehicle. Beware! When the heavy horse showing bug really bites, it does not let go. However, assuming that it has bitten, or is about to do so, let us consider the possible options involving three horses.

Trandem

This is the three abreast. It is a spectacular hitch, brought into prominence in recent years by Noel Abel's Shires driven to a pantechnicon and representing the family haulage business. Mervyn Ramage also drove his light roan Clydesdales three abreast to a Wolds waggon, and proved difficult to beat in Agricultural classes. Driving a trandem is easier than a tandem, and certainly easier than the random or three-in-line.

SINGLE AND PAIR (SAME)

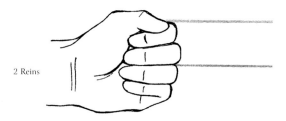

2 Reins

FOUR HORSE TEAM AND TANDEM

4 Reins

Leader

Leader   Between
                          same
Wheeler   fingers

Wheeler

Coaching

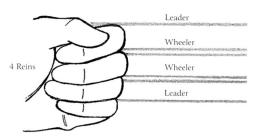

4 Reins

Leader

Wheeler

Wheeler

Leader

Style adopted by most heavy horse drivers especially the breweries

SIX HORSE TEAM AND RANDOM

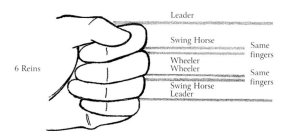

6 Reins

Leader

Swing Horse   Same
                    fingers
Wheeler
Wheeler   Same
Swing Horse   fingers
Leader

EIGHT HORSE TEAM AND QUADREM

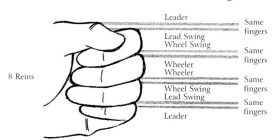

8 Reins

Leader   Same
                     fingers
Lead Swing
Wheel Swing   Same
                     fingers
Wheeler
Wheeler   Same
                     fingers
Wheel Swing
Lead Swing   Same
                     fingers
Leader

As teams get bigger, all aspects of hitching and harness become more complex. This series of drawings, showing how the reins can be held for various hitches, is based on sketches kindly provided by top driver Kevin Flynn, of Young's Brewery. Kevin comments: 'Reins are always held in the left hand and you assist with your right hand (which should also be holding the whip). In the drawings the blue reins are near side and the red reins off side. The coaching style for the four-horse team is recognized as being the more correct. The six- and eight-horse styles are my own personal preferences; I am sure that other people will have their own opinions.'

Mervyn Ramage, a man whose obvious delight in his horses always lifted the crowd, driving his distinctive Clydesdales in a trandem hitch. Often, his team were all roans, but here the middle horse is a black. The vehicle is a Wolds waggon, fitted with shafts with a trace horse on either side, instead of the usual pole gear.

There is no lead horse, all have a companion, and the centre one has a mate on either side. For that reason the trandem may be used as a training hitch, with the newcomer in the middle.

The third horse is accommodated by means of a postillion pole fitted to the under-carriage. The driver steers by reins to his outside horses only, the centre one being controlled by cross-reins from the main two.

Unicorn and Pick Axe

The unicorn is comparable with the tandem in that a good leader is essential. With two horses behind it, the leader cannot turn quite as far round quite so easily as a tandem leader, but there is still ample opportunity for error. Despite this, the standard of unicorn driving in the heavy horse world is remark-

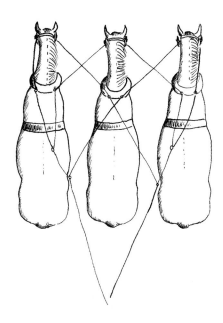

Method of reining for trandem, or three-abreast, drawn by Roger Clark.

Alan Tillier getting the best from the Brookfield Shires. This alert and stylish leader is a boon in a unicorn hitch.

Another enthusiast bitten by the heavy horse bug. David Lambert took up driving to advertise his fodder business: having begun with a single, he moved on to a pair and then to a three-horse hitch.

ably high, reflected in the special classes for teams of three at such shows as the Royal Highland and East of England.

These teams are all likely to be unicorns, for the pick axe is seldom seen, despite the fact that it is easier to drive, in that there is no need for a leader that will readily go out on its own. In pick axe, the two in front are coupled and driven just like the leaders in a 'four'.

When the pick axe was used on the land in sticky conditions, reins were used only on the leaders, according to Norfolk master horseman Jack Juby. With two in front, the shaft horse had no option but to follow. At shows, however, the shaft horse would be reined in the interests of safety.

Random

This is the three-horses-in-line hitch. It is spectacular, but calls for quite exceptional horses and horsemanship. As an exhibition hitch it has much to commend it, especially when the practical aspect is remembered. Its purpose was to prevent paddling the unploughed land, hence the horses worked in single file, keeping in the furrow when ploughing – and of course that operation is always done at walk. One Northamptonshire farm had soil so strong – almost pure clay – that five horses were yoked in line to a single furrow. It was essential to plough such land early to give the frosts a chance to break it down, otherwise it was completely unworkable.

The latest exciting development in showing is a variation on the random that acknowledges such practicalities of the past – a four-in-line hitch called the quadrem. This was pioneered by the Young's Brewery team at the 2003 National Shire Horse Show at Peterborough. Highlighting the need for great rapport between driver and horses with such a hitch, Young's Kevin Flynn said:

These black Shires are on regular beer deliveries in London traffic. The leader is fourteen-year-old Wandle Harry, a brave, confident horse, who knows his name. The wheeler, Wandle Mascot, is twelve. It is vital that they have absolute confidence in me, and I in them. All the horses will stop instantly to voice command, without using the reins, and stand still. These are the two most important factors in team driving.

The talented Kevin Flynn, driving for Young's Brewery, makes the tricky random hitch look a good deal easier than it is.

Kevin Flynn driving four of Young's Brewery's black Shires in line from the box seat. This is a tremendous feat of horsemanship, the basis of which is that every horse knows its name, will stop immediately on command and await further orders. Complete two-way trust between horses and driver is required.

Teams of Four or More

Traditionally, in Britain, a team of more than four horses was an unusual sight, but in recent years larger teams have become more numerous. Some showing enthusiasts in the United Kingdom are following the American pattern, where the 'six' has become the apex. Such big teams are very spectacular and are to be encouraged, with the proviso that due allowance must be made for the extra costs involved. A big team really needs one attendant per horse, and staff and horses all have to be fed and housed. Attending a long show with such a team entails a great deal of forward planning and the means to pay for everything. Yet the crowds really appreciate the sight of six or eight arched necks straining to the creak of the harness, and the bigger the team, the better the chance of photographs appearing in the local, national and equine Press. Another point, from the show organizer's perspective is that, if entries by large teams are to be encouraged, safety must be paramount, and gunnery or aerial displays must not be scheduled to start while the teams are in the collecting ring.

Driving Large Teams

Before anyone essays to exhibit a team of four or more horses, driving skills should be honed to a high level, and it is essential to have worked out the most efficient system of yoking and reining. Generally, with a

An eye-catching team of four moving in unison.

Black Shires with four white legs are becoming scare these days, but here is Radford Farm's team of four driven by Colin Horler. Note the immaculate turnout of driver and grooms.

Hugh Ramsay's relaxed driving style brings out the best in his often-changing teams.

team of four, the driver has four reins, to the outside bits of both wheelers and both leaders. In a team of six, the middle pair is known as the 'swing' pair, and in the United Kingdom the practice is to pass the leaders' reins through hame or terret rings on the swing pair, which are cross-coupled to their partner's inside hame or terret ring. North American practice, however, is usually to have six reins, threaded through the outside rings to the driver's hands, a method preferred by some British drivers.

With big teams, one particularly important aspect to sort out before the showing season is the position of each horse in the team. This point was mentioned in respect of pairs but, with just two horses, it is usually fairly obvious if one prefers and shows better on one side than on the other. Decisions are much more difficult in the case of three or four

The 'six' is the apex of the North American hitch, and is now seen more often in Britain. Whitbreads' six grey Shires are also used on State occasions.

Young's Brewery's spectacular eight-horse hitch at Windsor.

Something very unusual and rather different from traditional hitches – a twelve-horse Percheron hitch, with equalizing device.

horses – let alone six or eight! In a perfect world, each exhibitor would have a stable full of massive geldings, each suitable for the lead or the wheel, and able to go happily on either side. In the real world, few can afford such a luxury, nor might they be able to find sufficient really big horses if they could. Thus, in practice, days, weeks and months are spent in trying to find the best arrangement of the animals available.

As a general principle, if there is a range of sizes, the tallest horses go at the wheel, tapering down to the smallest in the lead, in fours, sixes or even eight-horse hitches. Then there is the matter of matching colour. While large commercial exhibitors may have the funds to maintain a matching team, the private exhibitor may establish such a team, and then lose one horse and be unable to find or afford a suitable replacement. In such circumstances it is worth remembering that, in the old coaching days, a grey leader among blacks or bays was fashionable, and for a practical reason – it was easier to see in the dark. Again, as mentioned in respect of pairs, if a team is not fully matching, it may pay to yoke the horses that are more eye-catching in looks or action on the off side, so as to catch the judge's eye. And this brings us back to another point – that the true enthusiast's place is inside the show ring, even if the team being driven is not yet the ideal one.

PART THREE

Planning and Preparation

CHAPTER 11

Preparing for the Show Ring

Winter is the time to prepare for the show season. Horses are schooled, taught their manners, made fit. Driving round and round in January and February can be cold, wet and horrible, but that is when the summer cups are won.

No sooner does one show season end than the next begins, and the exhibitor must be aware of this in terms of overall organization as well as in horse management. The dates of autumn foal sales should be carefully noted by those looking for youngstock to bring on; youngsters seen with their dams at these sales will be next season's yearlings, and future competitors. Most foal fixtures fall in September or October, though in Scotland they continue until nearly Christmas.

Some newcomers to showing start with a foal bought at one of these sales, in which case the next step is to join the breed society concerned. Animals cannot be shown in-hand at major events unless they are registered, and membership and registration help to strengthen the society and promote the breed. On the practical side, each society issues lists of shows with classes for its breed, and this brings us on to the planning side of showing.

Planning and Paperwork

While newcomers may feel their way into the showing scene, perhaps entering just two or three local shows in their first season, experienced exhibitors will need to do a considerable amount of pre-planning, especially where long journeys and large teams are involved. There are many factors to be taken into account; availability of grooms and the support team, overnight accommodation, transport, perhaps arrangements with sponsors, to name but a few, and these things do not organize themselves. Indeed, even the one-horse newcomer would be well advised to plan ahead prudently, to ensure that the entry form does not remain unposted on the kitchen mantelpiece and that the local horse transport has not been pre-booked by another client. Occasional exhibitors with their own transport would be well advised to carry out basic checks on a regular basis – and certainly just before the show dates – to ensure that they do not rise at 4 a.m. on the crucial morning to find that the box is out of diesel, or has a flat tyre or battery.

Entries for the Shire 'Spring Show' go in early, but the only other major English event with a closing date before April is the Nottinghamshire County at Newark. This was formerly the Newark and Notts, a name still often used. Despite the apparent lack of need for urgency, show secretaries have exacting jobs. Try to help them by entering in good time, thereby avoiding the situation of claiming that the form was held up in the post and that therefore the late entry should be accepted. More and more societies have strict deadlines, and with modern communication methods there is less excuse for lateness. At one time, a certain society assistant put a few entry forms to one side for those she knew always entered but were always late! Those days have now gone.

Once you have entered a particular show, schedules for that show are usually sent to you automatically the next year. However, the newcomer must obviously apply for them in the first instance, and even seasoned exhibitors must check that the expected schedules have, in fact, arrived.

Entry forms are usually clear enough. For In-hand classes, they will seek the name and sex of the horse and its pedigree number, and probably those of its parents. If a gelding, its dam may not matter in all cases, though it must generally be by a registered stallion of the breed concerned. The year of birth must be notified for catalogue inclusion, to be listed after the entry in the case of mature stock, or to indicate the appropriate class for its year. Most shows stage separate classes for yearlings and for two- and three-year-olds, and differentiate between the sexes. The exhibitor must read the schedule carefully on this point; smaller shows may combine fillies and geldings, while the bigger ones may have four-year-old classes, especially for stallions. In the case of a foal, precise date of birth must be given. The foal may be excused a name, but its sire's name must be given. It will be linked to its dam, which will either be appearing in the same class (if Mare and Foal) or else, usually, in the preceding or following class.

Entries for Young Handler classes differ somewhat from other In-hand classes in that it is usually the handler's name and age, rather than the horse's details, which appear on the form – although stallions are not usually permitted. Commonly, these classes are open to youngsters over 13 and less than 18 years of age, who are expected to prepare their charges as well as exhibiting them in the ring.

So far as Turnout classes are concerned, different shows may have different class definitions and specifications. Differences between Trade classes and Farmer's, or Agricultural, classes (the latter two being more or less synonymous) are sometimes vague, so check what you are entering. For example, some shows accept certain farm implements in the latter bracket, while others confine them to carts and waggons. So far as horses are concerned, less detail is required for Turnout classes than for In-hand. Obviously, you have to enter with the correct number of horses – a pair, team of four, etc. – but specifics such as horses' names have their snags and, if a horse goes lame between the entry date and the show date, it is quite permissible to bring in a substitute. Thus 'pair of bay geldings' will usually suffice on the entry form. However, if specific names are given, and a late substitution is made, the secretary and steward should be informed, as should the commentator if the opportunity arises.

A plea here to both entrants and secretaries. Contemporary newspaper and magazine practice insists on Christian names of exhibitors and judges. If they can be catalogued, it is of enormous help to the Press, to whom the showing world is looking for publicity. If a reporter covers one particular class of stock for some years, these names do become familiar, but at a local show a general reporter may be deputed to cover all the livestock, and is highly unlikely to know the

Christian names of all involved or, indeed, have time to seek them out. At the larger shows, a journalist specializing in Arabs and showjumping will be all at sea among the varying spellings of the Alans, Dereks and Sydneys of the heavy horse world.

One final point regarding paperwork is a reminder that some shows, or showgrounds, require all exhibits to have up-to-date equine flu vaccinations, and the documents to prove it. In this respect, forward planning is essential. In certain cases, other documents, such as EVA certificates, may also be required. The fundamental rule relating to such matters is that, if you intend going to a new show, or entering a new class for the first time, check the rules on the schedule minutely, and if you have any doubts about anything, ask the show organizers or breed society as appropriate. In that way, you will avoid the frustration of preparing for weeks, travelling for hours and then being unable to exhibit.

Vehicles, Harness and Equipment

Showing is a team effort, and nowhere is this more evident than in care and preparation of the vehicles for Turnout classes. The driver could never take to the ring without back-up from staff, family and friends. While off-season is the prime time for any major maintenance, repairs or refurbishing, the vehicle will need constant monitoring and, especially, constant cleaning, throughout the show season. To have any chance of success, the vehicle must be spotless all over. This applies to the underneath as well as to the obvious places. For example, ledges must be clean; some older vehicles have an unbelievable number of ledges carved into the framework, often with the idea of reducing weight, but not strength.

Past feedback from judges can help in ensuring that points of detail are correct. Turnout judges are usually enthusiasts and experts with regard to the history and traditions of the different vehicles and any observations they make should be seized upon, not dismissed as pedantry.

Harness, too, must be both spotless and in good order. As mentioned in the chapters on Choice and Care of Harness and Turnout Driving,

Showing heavy horses is often a family venture. Terry and Jean Pleavin-Edge and helpers at Wembley.

it is imperative that it should fit each individual horse properly. It is also essential that every horse is fully familiarized with any harness or equipment that it is to be shown in, of which more shortly.

For In-hand classes, male horses are shown in leather headgear. Geldings usually wear a sound, smart headcollar, whereas stallions are shown in a special stallion bridle with a bit attached. These are cleaned in the same way as any other leather tack. However, extra care should be taken to clean and check a stallion's bridle properly. A 12.2 hands grey Welsh pony stallion once broke loose at a major show when the rein on the bit ring snapped because the buckle had been buffed over rather than unfastened, cleaned properly and checked. The little stallion then ran amok among a class of hunter mares and foals, checking every one most thoroughly and eliciting comments from the hunter exhibitors quite impossible to reproduce here.

Mares and fillies are shown in white halters, which lend a more feminine appearance than leather. Bedfords' mare, Landcliffe Laura, came alive as soon as a show halter was fitted, and won the Shire Horse of the Year Championship four times. Since the white halters are made of rope or hemp, they are best put through the washing machine – no amount of soaking and scrubbing can match a thorough mechanical wash.

Decorations

In addition to checking and cleaning major items of equipment, winter – especially in the long evenings – is the time to start preparing the necessary sets of 'standards' or 'flights' that will adorn the manes in the show ring, or checking that those that have been bought are clean and bright. Basically, these consist of shaped, decorative heads made of various fabrics such as woollen yarn, silk, raffia, etc., mounted on copper wire stems that are inserted into the braided mane and twisted around themselves so that they stand upright. Traditionally, five standards are used on Turnout horses, and seven for In-hand exhibits, although some people vary these numbers. These decorations can make or mar the look of a horse and the photo sequence on pages 232–238 shows how the former effect can be achieved. There is no bar on materials used, and although the beginner may well play safe and buy them, there is scope for artistic members of the family to do something really eye-catching. Christmas decorations have sometimes provided inspiration in this respect! Home-made standards have the advantage that they can be individualistic and made to really match the horse; those purchased may be perfectly adequate, but you seldom gain an edge with them, and such details count in today's highly competitive heavy horse show scene. Once made or checked for condition, they should be hung up carefully and not left jumbled in a box.

The 'jug handles' or 'sprigs' used to decorate Shires' tails are another decorative necessity for exhibitors of this breed and this is a good time to check that tail ribbons, mane plaits and mares' neck ribbons are on hand, and to order them if this is not so. The old cotton ribbons are now difficult to find, and synthetics must often suffice. All such ribbons should be hung up on the wall after each class, otherwise they will be creased and crinkled next time you want them.

For those who exhibit in Decorated classes, this time may also be one for much experimentation with new colour schemes, and for the acquisition of new brasses and other accoutrements. Most heavy horse people realize that they are continuing a tradition, but all these decorations evolve, and adjustments are continually made to enhance the beauty of the horse.

Conditioning and Preparation of Horses

There are two basic aspects to preparing horses for the show season. The first entails bringing them into good physical show condition and 'prettying them up', the second entails educating them for the task in hand. Obviously, much of this is carried out in parallel and some work, such as the preparatory walking in harness, serves both purposes. However, for simplicity, we can consider these two aspects separately.

Conditioning and Tidying

As we saw in earlier chapters, heavy horses are much better wintered out. Two Yorkshire exhibitors, Ted Cumbor and Geoff Morton, say that 'the worst place for a horse is a stable!' Volumes have been written about stable design, floor covering, drainage and ventilation, but a field shelter and high hedges circumvent all such expensive expedients where the soil allows, and the horses are the better for it. Tramping about in snow is excellent for feet and feather.

Of course, it is not always possible to pursue this policy. The grazing may be windswept and treeless, on very heavy land, or simply unavailable in winter. Turnout teams may have to earn their winter keep by delivering goods, and an urban stable seldom has the chance either to remove shoes or to turn out on sheltered pasture. Such stables have to guard against itchy feet and the subsequent rubbing that ensues.

Further to this, even when horses are turned out, their feet must be examined and dressed when necessary throughout the winter, and any cracks checked. Grass will work into a crack and make it bigger, and then the condition known as gravel occurs, and the horse goes lame. A neglected crack will eventually spoil the hoof. All this attention takes much time, which is difficult to find in a busy life, yet it must be done. Some owners keep the hooves short, but others dress the foot at each trimming to match the shoe that will eventually be applied to it. Delousing is also carried out; there's no point in growing a thick coat and then letting the horse rub it off!

It is important to keep the feather in reasonable condition. This is where the clean-legged breeds, the Percheron and Suffolk, score, but feather is an essential feature of the Shire and even more so of the Clydesdale. The feather should be oiled regularly, as described in

Chapter 4, the principle being to waterproof and clean the hair. A clean field without too much mud or droppings from other stock is a boon, but where this is not possible the oil dressings help the mud and muck to slide off. Feather is never washed during this period.

Show horses that have wintered out are brought in a few days before their first event, and the worst of any mud on the coats is brushed off. It is pointless to make the feather spotless and then brush a lot of muck on to it from the body.

If it is the practice to wash horses, the first washing of the show season is usually done only a day or so before the event – although some exhibitors prefer to give a preliminary wash ten days beforehand to check that the situation is under control. Too much washing can cause a horse to 'strip out' and lose its hair, though a Clydesdale colt bred on both sides to Ayton Perfection grew more hair the more it was washed. 'Treat each animal as an individual' is the moral here.

Feeding

One factor that impacts upon both the physical conditioning of horses and their likely behaviour in the show ring is feeding. We have already discussed this in Chapter 2 and it will suffice to say here that feeding horses to optimum effect is both a science and an art, which takes a great deal of practice and an intimate knowledge of the individual animals.

Enthusiastic newcomers to showing will naturally do as much research as possible, and may seek to emulate the top exhibitors in many respects, including feeding. However, the top exhibitors are, by definition, top handlers who can cope with animals that are raring to go, or even showing signs of temperamental behaviour. These experts' feeding regimes, applied to the horses of novice handlers, may be a recipe for disaster – especially if the horses, too, are novices, unused to the electric show atmosphere.

Therefore, in the build-up to the show season, the less experienced handler – particularly of turnout horses – must be very careful not to over-feed concentrates. The main aim for the newcomer is to get the horse in and out of the ring safely; winning a ribbon being less important at this stage. Moreover, a horse that is playing up through over-excitement and too rich a diet is only likely to attract the judge's attention for the wrong reasons. Therefore, by all means feed the horses so that they look well and have the energy for the job in hand but, certainly in the early days, err on the side of caution so far as feed is concerned.

Prohibited Substances

Another point to bear in mind in connection with show ring preparation and nutrition is the thorny one of prohibited substances. Most breed societies have rules on this matter similar to those of the Shire Horse Society, which state:

It is an offence under the Society's regulations to exhibit an animal which is under the influence of any prohibited substance at a Shire Horse Show or Sale. Horses may not take part in any competition or exhibition while under the influence of any stimulating or calming drugs in any shape or form.

It is the responsibility of the owner to ensure that his horse is exhibited only when free from abnormal substances. The security and integrity of the animals under his care is the responsibility of the exhibitor.

The term 'Prohibited Substance' shall apply to any unnatural chemical or drug which could affect the performance, appearance or behaviour of a horse, and include:

(a) Analgesics (pain-relieving substances, including steroids and non-steroidal anti-inflammatory drugs).

(b) Stimulants.

(c) Depressants and sedatives.

The Society reserves the right to detain a horse at any time during a Show or Sale for the purpose of taking urine and blood samples by a Veterinary Surgeon for analysis at an Approved Laboratory, in accordance with the International Equestrian Medication Control Programme of the International Equestrian Federation...In the event of a sample being found to contain a prohibited substance, the exhibitor of the horse shall be automatically disqualified from the Class and the Show, and all prize money shall become forfeit. As a result, the Society may impose on the owner/exhibitor a penalty which in its view is appropriate to the offence.

Patently, no sensible person of integrity would deliberately enter a show knowing that they were in breach of such rules, but it is possible, in certain circumstances, for an unintentional breach to occur. In this respect, if it is necessary to medicate a horse in the period leading up to a show, veterinary advice should be sought regarding whether the medication is (or contains) a 'prohibited substance' and, if so, for how long a residue may be expected to remain in the horse's system.

The other consideration concerns feedstuff. One problem that occurred in the early years of compound feeds was that manufacturers would often use the same equipment to produce feeds for different types of stock, and the cleaning processes did not always guarantee that residues from one feed were completely absent from another. Thus minute amounts of a substance that might, for instance, be a legitimate constituent of cattle feed, could find their way into a horse feed, in which they were prohibited under various competition rules. Although the industry seems far more aware of this nowadays, accidents can happen and, while reputable compound feeds have certain advantages (as described in Chapter 2), it may be the traditional feeders of oats, bran, hay and chop who rest easiest if their animal is detained for sampling. However, the main lesson to learn from this is the inadvisability of mixing into a horse's ration feed designed for other stock. More than one heavy horse competitor has run into testing problems after mixing a few pig or calf nuts into the horse's ration, and this is simply asking for trouble. Apart from the likelihood of failing a test, these feedstuffs are not formulated with the horse's physiology or digestive system in mind, and should be avoided.

Training at Home

The aspiring newcomer will note how experienced exhibitors handle their horses in the ring, and so become familiar with the routine. However, it is important to realize that the rapport between these exhibitors and their charges does not just happen; it is the product of countless hours of training and practice at home. If you want to win the trust of your charge, or charges, and establish a seemingly effortless authority, then you and they must do the homework, throughout the weeks, months, even years that lead up to your appearance in the show ring.

We have already discussed the education of youngstock in respect of such matters as making a fuss of them during weaning, and teaching them to pick their feet up for the farrier, but the importance of early handling cannot be overstressed. A horse that becomes accustomed to being handled at an early age, and learns to accept human company and direction, is likely to be more tractable in all aspects of its education than one that has been ignored or, worse still, treated inconsiderately or roughly.

In order for a horse to be led, and tied up safely, it must first be fitted with and accustomed to a halter or headcollar. In this respect, it is good practice to fit a 'foal slip', made of soft leather, to the youngster when it is just a few days old. It is important that this is in good condition and fits correctly; a breakage or slipped collar at this point must be avoided at all costs since, if it escapes at this stage, the foal will remember it for the rest of its life. If, on the other hand, there is no such drama, the foal will soon get used to the idea of wearing such a contrivance, and it is then just a case of ensuring correct adjustment and comfortable fit of the headgear that supersedes it.

With leather headcollars, it is important that they are clean and neither too tight nor too loose, in order that they do not rub or chafe. Regarding the white halter for mares and fillies, there are two types – the slip type with shank and headpiece all of the same material, and the type with the flat hemp headpiece. The slip halter gives slightly better control, but must be put on correctly, with the rope running under the chin to the near side of the face.

A common mistake with nosebands is to have them either too high on the face, or too low. The noseband should clear the nostrils by about four inches; if too low it will affect breathing and cause the horse to blow, and if too high on the head the horse cannot be controlled properly.

Once the youngster is accustomed to wearing a halter or headcollar, a basic requirement that can be addressed from an early age is teaching it to lead. Obedience in this respect is necessary for such basic processes as turning out and bringing in, let alone future acts such as loading onto transport or negotiating a crowded showground.

The foal should first be taught to walk calmly but actively on the lead rope, in obedience to voice commands. A competent helper will be needed, to lead the dam. From the beginning, to introduce the voice commands, stand level with the foal's shoulder, with a few inches of slack lead rope between your right hand and the headcollar. Give the command 'Walk on' (for both foal and dam) and step forwards yourself; don't look at the foal and don't make any significant effort to drag it forwards. Assuming that it walks with you – and most animals accompanied by their dam and familiar with their handler will do so – give verbal praise and encouragement. Once mare and foal are walking freely, the command 'Whoa', which the mare will understand, can be given. At this point, stop and brace yourself somewhat, but do not haul back on the youngster's lead rope. Since the foal will be close to its dam, it will probably copy her but, if necessary, lean into it gently but firmly with your right shoulder.

Once the foal will walk on and halt in close proximity to the mare, the distance between mare and foal should be gradually and occasionally increased. However, be mindful of the individual's temperament

Jim and Sue Yates' filly foal, Cowerslane Charlotte at the Newark Show. The owners are regular exhibitors in Mare and Foal classes, and here their foal takes a keen interest while mum is trotted out.

and wait for signs of increasing confidence and understanding on the youngster's part. If you hurry this process and ask too much too soon, the foal may become nervous and panicky and it is then less likely to pay attention to you and your commands, which is the object of the exercise and an important part of the rapport you are trying to build up. It may also try to run or 'scuttle' after its dam, which is not a good basis for establishing a correct walk.

While this work is important, it should be emphasized that foal training must not be overdone. As with training a puppy, it is not just a case of not *demanding* too much at once, but also of not *doing* too much at once, since young animals cannot concentrate for long. Also, with a view to the show ring, while good behaviour is desirable, the youngster should look fresh and should not lose its 'foalness'.

Given a good start at a young age, further refinements and developments in leading in-hand should, in due course, be fairly straightforward. However, not all animals benefit from such an early education and it is possible to acquire a young horse that has only the vaguest notion of what is required.

If a horse shows any reluctance to walk forward on command, a light tap on the flank from a long whip carried low in your left hand, accompanied by a fresh verbal command, should help it to get the picture. However, any whip aids should be kept light, and to the absolute minimum necessary; you don't want to become reliant on the whip, let alone get the horse scared of it, or you may end up with a horse that wavers when run out in-hand in the ring.

It is only once such a horse is really walking out in-hand that it is worth practising actual halting (as opposed to the occasional stop when opening a gate, etc.). Say 'Whoa' in a calm tone, stop and brace yourself somewhat; actions that should cause the horse to stop. However, just as some horses may not have been taught to walk out properly, so others may be ill-mannered and try to barge onward, in which case it may be necessary at first to lean your right shoulder against the horse's front, in a far more forceful manner than described for educating foals.

Once the horse is walking and halting obediently, you can begin trotting in-hand. From an active walk, say 'Trot', or 'Trot On' and do so yourself, again without trying to drag the horse forwards. Since the horse has now got into the habit of following your actions, it should trot quite readily but, if it is a little lazy, you can give a click with your tongue and, if absolutely necessary, a light touch with the whip. Again, when you wish to return to walk, you say 'Waaalk' in the same calm, protracted tone as for 'Whoa', and walk yourself.

With the horse leading obediently, there are three things you can do to enhance its education. First, if it is to have a future in harness, it may be useful to lead it in turns to the left and right, introducing the voice commands that you intend to use when it is driven (see Chapter 10 Turnout Driving.) Second, you can begin to introduce it judiciously to various new sights and sounds. What you can achieve in this respect will depend a great deal on your location, but it is inevitably better if the young horse has seen something of the world beyond its immediate boundaries before being thrust into the sights, sounds and atmosphere of the show ring. The third thing you can start to look at, with experienced assistance, is how the horse moves naturally in walk and trot, with a long-term view of showing it to best advantage in the ring. With the younger horse, however, it is probably best not to try to make too many adjustments to its natural movement too soon, since this may confuse and unbalance the horse and make matters worse. Another point to remember here is that the action of many horses improves naturally as they mature and muscle up. Therefore, refining and perfecting the running out in-hand can be considered a long-term task.

When displayed for inspection, whether in the line-up or elsewhere, a draught horse should be stood up squarely. The hind shanks should be parallel, with the hocks together naturally and the forelegs directly under the horse. The hind legs are at a slight angle to the perpendicular, but nothing like so much as is fashionable in some of the lighter breeds, which stand with their hind legs stretched way out behind them. The forelegs should be straight, well under the body and slightly apart, so that the horse is nice and level. There are photographs showing good examples of correct posture in Chapter 1 and in the In-hand section of Chapter 13. Some horses stand well naturally, while others need a lot of training. You may get an early clue about this by how a youngster stands when brought to halt after leading in-hand. If it naturally stands up well, giving praise will do no harm. Teaching a horse that does not naturally stand squarely to do so may entail much patience and persistence, and perhaps initially the help of an assistant. Pressure as necessary on the horse's shoulder and head should persuade it to alter its balance and taps with a show stick will encourage it to adjust its feet. As with most matters pertaining to the training of horses, steady progress is the best way forward, with generous praise for any sign of improvement, and admonishment kept to a minimum. Also, especially with youngsters, training sessions should be kept short and stopped at a point when progress has been made; if this is not done, the horse's short attention span is likely to cause fidgeting and frayed tempers, and thus unravel anything that had previously been achieved. Never forget that the long-term aim is to produce a horse that will remain set-up for quite some time, and this will not happen if it has been made anxious and fidgety by hurried attempts at training.

In Chapter 10 Turnout Driving, we have already looked at the basics of breaking a horse to harness, one aspect of this being mouthing the horse. This procedure will also be necessary for any stallion that is to be shown in-hand in a bit – a precaution that aids control. Although not unknown, it is a very dangerous practice to put a bit in a stallion's mouth without any prior preparation, simply because you fear fractious behaviour in the ring. Indeed, there is every likelihood that such a decision will backfire in spectacular fashion. It is no wonder that a stallion may misbehave if it has an unaccustomed bit thrust suddenly into its mouth, with a chain under the chin, and all the fresh sights and sounds of the ring to contend with, and one consequence of this may be permanent damage to its mouth. Therefore, as with any horse, a stallion must be mouthed properly and carefully, the benefit being that it is then more likely to respect and respond to the bit at crucial moments.

The other parallel between home training for harness horses and in-hand stallions is that the stallion can be introduced to its show harness in much the same way as the harness horse is introduced to breechings. This harness, the main purpose of which is to maintain control, consists of a roller, a crupper, a side check-rein on the off side to hinder eating or biting, and a bearing rein through a loop on the roller. It is best to ensure that the stallion is completely used to having a bit in its mouth before introducing the rein elements of the harness.

Travelling to the Show

As noted earlier, transport must be booked early if you do not have your own. Hauliers are in great demand, especially in the summer. When booking transport to a show, be mindful of the hygiene considerations mentioned in connection with transporting a mare to stud (see Chapter 7); it is important that neither your exhibit nor anyone else's at the show contracts any infection. In this respect, if you are using your own transport, you should ensure that this is in a suitably hygienic condition.

When booking transport, check that its size and the arrangement of the partitions are suitable for your horse or horses. To bring a horse to the foot of the ramp and then start wondering where to put it, and whether it will fit, is quite futile. These details *must* be worked out in advance. Also, if two horses are particular friends, try to place them side by side; if they don't get on, then avoid doing so. Further to this, if a stallion is being transported in company, try to stand it next to an animal that is more likely to placate rather than upset it – and certainly don't transport it with a mare.

Although it may require some deviation from your normal schedule, a feed should be given before departure, at a time that allows digestion to begin before the loading process. On journeys of any length, hay nets should be provided and, if a horse is a bad traveller, it is a good idea to give it a small net to pick at, even if you are just going a few miles up the road.

If you are going to a major show that requires staying overnight then, to some extent, you can time the journey at your own convenience, but you should always take adverse weather conditions into consideration. If you are forewarned of foggy or icy conditions, try to avoid travelling at night, and certainly allow a good deal of extra time. In the summer, however, one overriding principle is to avoid travelling during the heat of the day. During a hot, humid spell, late evening or very early morning is preferable. While modern racehorse and showjumper transporters have air conditioning, they cost a fortune to buy and to hire and are seldom available to the heavy horse fraternity. More traditional horseboxes, without such mod. cons., quickly become as hot as an oven if they get held up in a traffic jam in the heat of the day and, although horses are not as susceptible as pigs are to heatstroke, they can really get in trouble in such circumstances and will do their showing prospects no good.

For a one-day show, your journey must be timed to arrive at the showground at least two hours before your first curtain call. This requires calculating the journey from the time that the transport *leaves* your premises, not when it arrives. Don't forget that traffic queues to enter the showground must be allowed for and, if it is your first visit to a certain show, find out about facilities and ease of access from a regular exhibitor. Half an hour lost early on show day is never regained, and top exhibitors are seldom late, keeping everything in apple pie order throughout.

As mentioned, prompt departure will be facilitated by a planned and organized loading process. Apart from sorting out beforehand which horse is to go where, this presupposes that the horses are accustomed to loading and have been trained to load calmly and quietly.

Whereas light horses, particularly showjumpers, travel swathed in masses of leg protection, there is seldom need for this in the heavy horse world, the main purpose of bandages being to keep the feather clean. If feather becomes stained on a journey, it is difficult to clean again at the show. When they are used, bandages should be fastened on the outside of the leg. If fastened on the inside, there is a bigger danger of the knot or clip catching against the opposite leg and the bandage unravelling. Knots should not be tied on the front of the leg, where they may press on the bone, or at the back, where they may press on the tendon.

The other matter that ensures a prompt departure is having all the necessary equipment and stores checked and packed neatly before-hand. A last-minute panic because you can't remember whether you've packed the curry comb, or don't know where it was left, will help neither your blood pressure nor your time schedule. Individuals will have to make their own checklists as appropriate, but the following may serve as a basis:

Water buckets, separate ones for drinking and washing, and a large screw-top container full of fresh water (in case of severe delays en route and as a back up if showground arrangements are unsatisfactory)

Sawdust bucket
Sawdust and wood flour for drying feather
Oil cloths
Tack box incorporating full range of grooming equipment and 'soft soap'
Smocks
Whips
Halters
Scissors
Mane combs
Needle and thread for plaiting
Adhesive tapes
Spare headcollar and lead shanks
Twitch (just in case)
Leather spats or bandages to protect feather
Set of stallion bluffs – a leather or canvas blindfold
Farriery tackle including hammer, nails, etc. (For running repairs, but remember that it is illegal for anyone who is not a registered farrier to shoe a horse, even their own. At bigger shows, there will be a farrier on duty – probably surprisingly busy!)
Veterinary kit (checked and stocked up as appropriate)

On the human side, camp beds, flasks of drink, food and a camping stove are basics. Add maps, sunglasses and a watch. There should be also be a first aid box, the location of which must be known to all.

Also, be sure to carry a fire extinguisher. Check that it is in working order, and that you and your team know how to use it. Its position in the horsebox must be obvious, and known to everyone.

Another important point, both when travelling to the show and at the showground, is to have enough back up. With more than one horse, a team of helpers is essential; it is quite impossible for one individual to do everything in the time available. However, even if you have only one entry, two pairs of hands are far better than one. This means someone responsible; it is no good if your 'helper' has wandered off to watch another class at the crucial moment. More seriously, there are matters such the possibility of injury to consider – if a heavy horse treads on your foot, will you be able to drive the box home? Also, if the box breaks down en route to the show, it is undesirable to have to walk off in search of a phone box and leave the horses unattended. In this respect, the advent of mobile phones has greatly eased the lot of the livestock haulier, whether amateur or professional, and if you have one, it is another item that should go on your checklist. A radio in the cab is also very useful, since it can be tuned to local radio stations in the event of, or as forewarning about, traffic problems.

On arrival at the show, the gatemen will direct you to the appropriate place and the final preparations begin. The first things to find are the lavatory and the secretary's tent (probably in that order), and also the nearest water tap. If you have booked overnight stabling, an early inspection is advisable; indeed, if you are unfamiliar with the showground, it may be prudent to make a discreet inquiry as to the form this takes at the time of booking. When it is necessary to make use of the temporary stabling provided at many shows, it can be advisable to take some extra boards with you, especially if you are showing a stallion. This is because few of the temporary boxes provided are really big enough for a heavy breed stallion. The extra boards may allow you to modify the temporary box and/or prevent any touching of noses between a stallion and adjacent horses. However, so far as possible, try to box a stallion so that it is not directly adjoining another horse – especially another stallion – whether at the sides or back. If no boards are available, tarpaulins may be brought into play, but these are less satisfactory since they can be torn. (At one time, adjacent boxes were used as sleeping quarters by grooms, and these made a useful barrier. However, today's grooms tend to prefer the relative luxury of sleeping quarters in modern transport!)

Unloading the horses is a process that must be carried out with due care. With further reference to stallions, they should not be unloaded using the halter alone. A leather bridle with a bit is ideal, and this should be fitted before leading the stallion down the ramp. If there is any likelihood that a stallion will prove fractious on arrival at the show, it may also be prudent to fit a bluff or blindfold which, since it reduces the stallion's field of vision, generally has a calming effect.

When a number of horses are travelled together, it is important to ensure that one is never left alone in the horsebox. That is when accidents happen. The horse, already unsettled by the journey, now loses its companions, and starts to pull at its halter, kicks the walls or tries to break down the partition. At the very least it will dung and urinate, leaving stains that take still more work to remove. If it is not possible to leave the horse with an equine companion, then someone from the team of helpers must stay with it.

Showground Preparation

At a one-day show, the unloaded horses should be fed as soon as possible on arrival. A horse will be more amenable in the ring if its stomach is full enough for contentment. However, this presupposes that you have planned correctly and arrived in good time, since you cannot feed the horse and then rush it straight into the ring. After feeding, the horses will be given a final wash or brush over before preparation for their class begins in earnest. At shows requiring overnight residence, the normal feeding and grooming routine is followed each morning, the latter leading into final preparation for the show ring at the appropriate time.

Washing, Plaiting and Decorating
WASHING THE FEATHER
Other than for the clean-legged breeds, one of the key factors in preparing for the ring is the thorough washing and drying of the feather. Before washing this hair, it is essential to clean the feet out thoroughly with a hoof pick. Amazingly, this is not always done, and the horse sets off for the ring with each upturned hoof showing neglect.

The twin essentials for washing the feather are ample warm water and 'soft soap'. In the initial wash, at least one bucketful of water per foot will be needed. (Although horses are not generally hosed down all over in the manner of cattle, the face should be washed, again using warm water and soft soap – but not the water that has just been used to clean the legs.)

'Soft soap' is bought in containers, and varies in quality. It is based on coconut oil, and on removing the lid the top should be firm enough to prevent the finger from pushing through easily. Reject a watery sample. Shampoos are available, but seldom give the same lather. The feather is wetted and the soap worked in, a little at a time. Working with the fingers should be done downward; if the soap is worked in with an upward motion there is a danger of breaking some of the hair. At this stage you can generally see the muck running out. It is essential to work the fingers right down to the roots of the hair, and the job is best done by a team of two, one giving a thorough preliminary wash and the other following on with more clean, warm water.

The hair should now come up a beautiful colour. A hose may be used at this stage to wash out all the soap before drying. Check particularly around the heel: if the hair there is at all tacky, it means that not all the soap has been removed, and it will stick to the sawdust used for drying. Not all exhibitors make a really good job of cleaning the feather, some leave dirt around the hair roots, which counts against them in presentation.

This imaginative shot highlights the fact that Black Shires with white legs are a striking sight – but only when absolutely clean. This Young's Brewery team is spotless.

For drying, Shire people tend to use wood flour, but this must be washed out carefully after the class, or it becomes a sticky mess. Clydesdale exhibitors, in general even fussier about fine feather than their Shire counterparts, more often use white sawdust. This may be expensive and require miles of travelling to obtain it, but the true devotee ignores such considerations. Red sawdust is plentiful, cheap, but useless. It stains the lovely white hair, and is to be avoided.

After washing and drying, some exhibitors bandage the feather. Others believe this to be unnecessary if the washing has been thorough, and certainly if the bandages are too tight they leave unsightly rings.

At one time, a type of resin was used to stiffen the 'spat' hair – the hair covering the hoof itself – but this resin is now unobtainable. Applying a ring of soft soap under the spat hair does help to keep the shape, but if oils are used on the cannon bone, ensure that they don't run down on to the spats. Proprietary brands of baby powder are much favoured for lending that final whiteness to the feather.

SOAPING UP

For early shows 'soaping up' of the coats is generally allowed (for Shires, strictly in foal classes only) but it is not allowed at later shows, when the animals are in their summer coats. (Check this point with the show organizers, if need be.) Soaping up consists of rubbing up the coat into a series of little waves or ripples, using a small ball of soft soap in one hand. The effect is to add width to the animal, making it appear more substantial. However, not all coats are suitable for this process at any time of year. A horse with a fine, glossy coat cannot be 'soaped'. If in doubt, try a bit on the flank before doing the whole coat, but never do the top of the rump, since this may make the horse's rear end appear too high, thus spoiling the topline. The late John Brewster was an expert at this technique, and would frequently step back from his horse to ensure that the process was even on both sides. It is not a job to be rushed; at least fifteen minutes must be allowed. Above all, do not soap if rain threatens; that is the ultimate disaster!

PREPARATIONS FOR PLAITING

Preparing the horse for plaiting, or braiding, is very important. The first step is to comb out all knots and rough edges whilst the mane is dry. This must be done really thoroughly. To neglect it means a less than perfect job, and only makes extra work later when time is at a premium. This should be done before washing, and the mane should be washed thoroughly on the day prior to the class, never on show day. Use cattle shampoo in lukewarm water, damping the mane with a wet sponge, and laying it flat and in place. Treat the tail similarly. Rinse out well. This is essential, since any soap left on the horse will encourage scurf.

After plaiting, manes and tails may be sprayed with a modern hypo-allergenic highlighter, in the case of the former, taking care to avoid the

Youngsters that have been prepared by being 'soaped up'. David Worthington's Walton Royal Sovereign, Champion Foal at the Lancashire Show, and Geoff Robinson's grey, Metheringham Upton Baron, winning at Lincoln.

eyes. These modern products are there to be used; there is no virtue in sticking to age-old substances for their own sakes; your fellow competitors certainly won't!

Preparing Individual Breeds

The are various conventions relating to show ring presentation that apply to certain individual breeds.

SHIRES

The general preparation for Shires is as just described, and the plaiting process is explained by the photographs that follow and the accompanying captions.

Walter Bedford demonstrates how to plait up a Shire for the show ring.

Approaching the horse with the necessary materials: the bass (raffia) and ribbons are slung round the groom's neck, with the flights held in one hand.

The flights will be needed as work progresses, so are kept handy in a pocket.

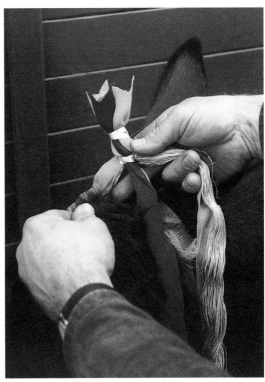

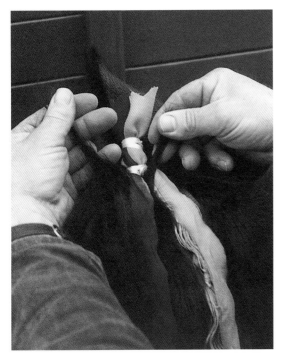

Above left: *How to hold the plait to prevent tangling. A full plait, as shown, is used for In-hand classes; a 'half-rig' is used for Turnout classes, to allow for the collar. The plait is divided into three, with two yellow strands and one blue in this case. Although any colour combination is permissible, generally one dark strand and two light strands are used.*

Above: *The plait is laid across the horse's neck, so that the central ribbon has one strand over the neck and two on the horse's off side, nearer the groom.*

Left: *Two fingers of hair are selected; each the thickness of a pencil and dainty enough to tie in a neat knot.*

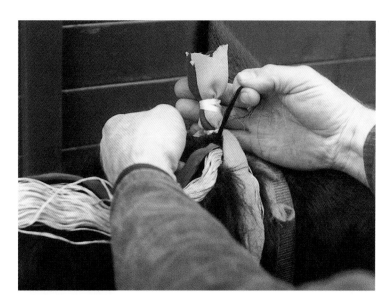

A reef knot is tied tightly round the central strand of the plait. This is done at the back of the headcollar, as high up the neck as possible.

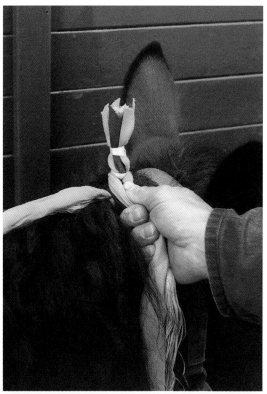

Starting to plait: the two strands of the plait are criss-crossed around the central piece from one side to the other, picking up the third strand each time.

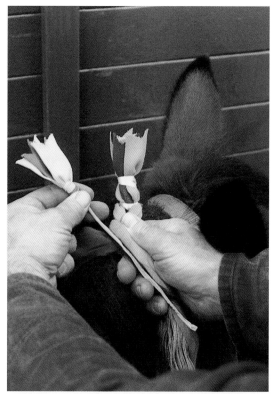

Placing the first flight at the very top of the plait.

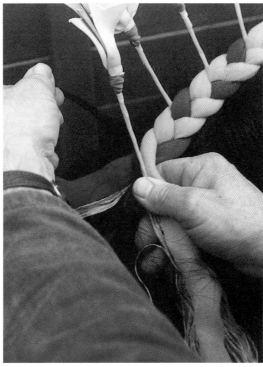

Above left: *To secure the plait at every crossover, a strand of hair must be picked up from the mane, pulling it through from the near side to the off side with every wrap of the plait.*

Above: *Following on from the initial flight, one is inserted after every two wraps, right to the very end. Each flight is placed under the ribbon, so that the end is plaited in. Although the flight stems are all the same length, less stem is exposed at the start, rising up to an arch – see top photo page 237. Judging this process to maximum effect is a major part of the art of plaiting.*

Left: *At all times whilst plaiting, the plait must be kept tight. If tension is lost, the plait will be spoilt. Therefore, it is essential to complete the plait in one session.*

At the end, one ribbon will always be longer than the others. To finish, this longest ribbon is wrapped once around the whole plait and threaded under to form a half reef knot. Ribbons should then be cut off to finish the same length.

The end result.

Note how the flights have formed an arch. Early efforts may not match this level of presentation: Walter Bedford has been honing his skills for many years.

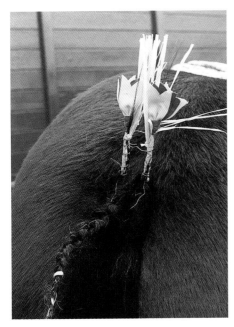

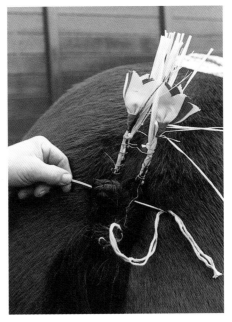

Left: *For the Shire tail, two flights are used. Each will need four strands of raffia about 18 inches (45 cm) long, to be plaited with a four-strand plait. Two strands of tail hair are then separated in the middle and the raffia, doubled into eight strands, is criss-crossed between them to make about five inches (13 cm) of plait, and the rest of the tail is fanned out.*

Right: *The tail flights are similar in principle to mane flights, but longer, with very flexible wire stems. Each flight is laid against the four-strand plait, and the wire stem wrapped round it, starting at the base, with the top wire out of sight and the other end laid down the tail.*

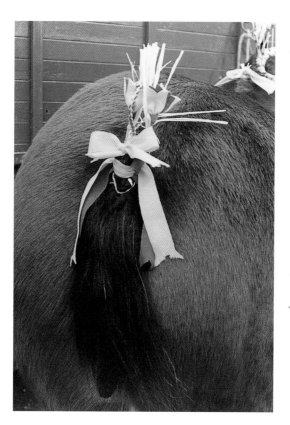

Left: *The tail ring or 'jug handle' is fashioned from coloured flex wire with a sharp point at the base, and placed in position after the bun has been formed (see text). The point is inserted into the top of the bun then three 30 inch (76 cm) lengths of ribbon, matching the mane plait, are added. First, the dark ribbon is wrapped round the tail bun and secured at its centre with a reef knot, leaving the ends to hang down neatly and evenly either side of the tail. This is repeated with one of the light ribbons, then the other light ribbon is placed on the base of the tail ring and fashioned into a neat bow, facing outwards.*

CLYDESDALES

Foals are soaped, or 'larded', more frequently in this breed, the object being to enhance the width of the animal. The coat is 'soaped' into little ripples but, as mentioned earlier, don't do it if rain threatens! The skilled operator stands back frequently from the foal to assess balanced progress.

Young Clydesdales, up to and including two-year-olds, are shown with long tails (i.e. unclipped tails). On three-year-olds and upwards, the tail hair is plaited, preferably by two people working together. Plaiting the tail is done by starting from near the dock end of the tail, and using three lots of hair with the plait threaded through. This plait is of raffia, bonded with fuse wire. Stiff standards are pushed into the plait at either side, and there is a wide choice of these. Tail peaks are flag-like pieces standing out from the bob, and these decorations are best made out of season, to be ready for the big day. Another method of tail decoration is to cut off the tail square, and have the top plaited

Shire aficionados will instantly recognize this plait on Shire stallion Landcliffe Tomahawk as the handiwork of the skilful Walter Bedford.

into a small bun, decorated by dangling ribbons.

North of the Border the mane may be left unplaited for In-hand classes. The Shire method of mane plaiting is acceptable, but Clydesdale people have their own styles, one of which involves two strands of ribbon, one of each colour. By crossing the plait with small bunches of hair, a chequred appearance is formed.

Clydesdale mares do not, in any case, have their manes plaited, but the mane should all be brushed to one side. A little pig oil helps to keep an unruly mane in place. An old practice is to rub a foal's mane down the correct side (its off side) as soon as it born. When combing the mane, it is important to divide it from the forelock at the correct place. This is easily found in practice, but both forelock and mane can be spoilt through carelessness here.

PERCHERONS

Percherons should not be washed above the knee and hock. The Percheron has the most attractive head, finer than Shire or Clydesdale, through the Arab influence. Because of this, some tidying of chin, whiskers and ears is done. This is something of an exception to the general practice of the heavy horse world, which is to leave the tactile hairs of the lips, nostrils and eyes alone. The heels also should be clean and tidy

The Percheron's mane plait is similar to the Shire's. It may be decorated with wool, ribbon, flights and plumes, but not with pom-poms, which are exclusive to the Suffolk. Red and blue are favoured colours for decoration. The Percheron is exhibited with all hair on the tail fully used, never shaved, and a well-dressed Percheron tail adds greatly to the horse's attraction. The plaited dock gives the impression of a high-set tail and rounded croup, which helps the look of the quarters.

The show bridle with bit is worn with or without a noseband, according to which best suits the horse. Mares and youngstock wear white hemp halters. So far as stallion harness is concerned, the roller pad, browband if worn, and flights are all in the same colours.

SUFFOLKS

Whiskers and chins on Suffolks are not trimmed at all and, while the breed is officially 'clean-legged', any hair that does appear on the legs or feet is not meant to be trimmed in any way. The hooves are oiled.

The Suffolk's entire mane is plaited in, and concealed by the raffia or braid. This is similar to light horse dressing, except that there is one continuous running plait edged by the raffia. Woollen pom-poms are allowed in Suffolk classes, or flights or bows of ribbon and braid may be used. Ornaments are added after the plait has been completed; green and gold are favourite colours.

The mane is prepared in the following fashion. The top-knot should stand up just behind the ears. Then take a piece of mane in the left hand, and plait it in with the braid so that the braid is on top of the crest. The coloured plait should stretch the length of the off side and top of the crest. Once the withers are reached (or the front of the collar, for a harness class), continue plaiting the hair and braid together until all the hair is plaited in. The plait is secured by stitching with very strong mane thread or fine string, and finished with the braid threaded into and knotted around it. The ends hang down three or four inches (8 to 10 cm). The forelock is not plaited, but is fastened by a ribbon or braid bow tied at the front of the browband.

The Suffolk has its own style of tail plaiting, and a very attractive one it is. The whole of the tail hair is plaited in, absolving the practitioner of the shaven tail criticism so often levelled at the Shire. The Suffolk tail is plaited conventionally, with three lengths of braid running down the centre to the end of the tail and secured. The tail is then rolled up into a bun, which is then secured and decorated. Ribbons are tied in at intervals down the tail and trimmed, usually into arrowhead formation.

Final Preparation

Once all the detailed preparations have been completed, just before leaving for the ring, or just before the harness goes on in a Turnout

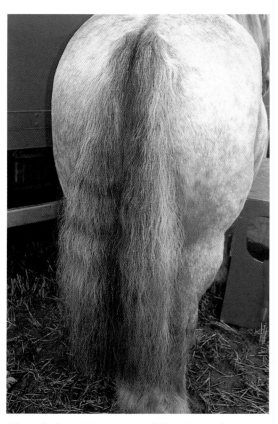

The tail of an Ardennes, seen full and plaited.

class, the horse is given a light grooming all over with the body brush, and a cloth is used to clean around the eyes, mouth and nostrils. A separate sponge should be kept for the dock. This is an item that may be needed after the horse has entered the ring, as horses are sometimes prompted to dung because of the unaccustomed clamour. If fresh dung from an in-hand horse cannot be removed immediately, the animal should be moved clear of the droppings to avoid its treading in them. In a turnout team, fresh dung may drop onto the breechings, which must then be wiped clean.

PART FOUR

Showing

CHAPTER 12

The Judge's and Steward's Role

In this chapter, we will consider the judge's and steward's role in assessing the main types of In-hand and Turnout classes in the show ring. Classes such as Young Handler, Trade or Agricultural require similar basic protocol to these main events, with judging criteria being modified in line with the requirements of the particular class. Judging a Decorated class has much to do with personal choice and aesthetics – so long as it is remembered that it is the *decoration* that is being judged. Ridden classes are judged on performance and obedience, or as dressage tests, depending upon the nature of the class, and are thus rather different from traditional heavy horse classes. The criteria applied to judging Obstacle Driving and Ploughing Matches are explained in the Chapters devoted to those topics.

Obviously, an appreciation of the judge's role will be of value to exhibitors, as well as to aspiring judges and stewards.

Becoming a Judge

While the different breed societies have different rules about judging in-hand, the Shire Horse Society's procedure regarding selection of judges serves as a general pattern. The aspiring judge must be at least twenty-five years old, have at least five years practical experience with heavy horses, and be proposed to the Probationer Judges Panel by two Council members. Having the time and enthusiasm to attend shows during the season is, of course, an essential prerequisite. It will also be

Judging young stallions at the Shire Spring Show, depicted by Malcolm Coward. His painting skills make judges Messrs Cecil Burton and Herbert Sutton readily identifiable.

stressed to the would-be judge at this stage that one does not become a probationer to learn about *horses*, but to learn about *judging*. Further to this, the nominee is instilled with the fact that he is very much in the public eye as the breed society representative. He must be seen to be fair. He has a duty to the gate-paying public, and to all competitors, including those at the bottom of the line who have paid their entry fees and deserve to be looked at, even though they have no chance of a place, since the show would be the poorer for their absence.

If accepted by the Council, the nominee becomes a probationer. He then approaches an established judge (who must have been officiating for at least three seasons since his own probationer days) to take him on at a particular show and, if that is agreed, the probationer must then approach the show society involved for permission. The Shire Horse Society issues a list of shows that accept probationers, from which Wembley qualifiers are excluded. The probationer must repeat this process with at least six respected judges before applying for full judging status. He will then appear before the Assessment Panel of four members, of whom one is chairman, with one replaced every year to try to ensure a democratic process.

At meetings of the Assessment Panel, staged at various points around the country, applicants are given four horses to assess. They are expected to spot such faults as enlarged hocks, cracks in the foot, and other partially hidden blemishes. On the turnout side, a pair is displayed, with six deliberate faults. These are usually minor, such as a strap turned the wrong way, but candidates must find them all, and the Panel of Judges must be unanimous in their conclusions. No majority decisions are allowed.

If accepted onto the Probationer Judges panel, the candidate must then await invitations. (Judging invitations may come a year or so before the event, and show societies do tend to ask earlier and earlier, to try to get the best judges.) Having received an invitation, the Probationer Judge must bear all his own expenses for travel, accommodation and meals, including meals at the show. At the show itself, like senior judges, he must wear a bowler hat, and preferably a dark suit, or riding kit for Ridden classes. The main point here is that judges must be instantly recognisable as such, and set apart from other individuals.

At the end of his three years as a probationer, the aspiring judge may then be elected to the official Panel of Judges. At this point he is able to claim expenses, but these vary widely among different show societies. At even the smaller county shows, the number of judges required for pigeons, pigs, Percherons and a plethora of other classes can become very large indeed. Judges and their partners will be dined on the day, but actual expenses are a matter for negotiation. This issue must be agreed upon beforehand. Judging heavy horses should be fun, but it

Intense concentration from probationer judge, Mr Neil Wright, accompanying Mr Brian Winn at Wisbech Foal Show.

Showing may be serious business, but also fun. Judges of vast experience, Harry Ranson (left) and Patrick Flood, enjoy their stint at the Spring Show.

can only be done from a secure financial base. (Local firms and hotels may sponsor judges' expenses in return for free catalogue publicity, an angle which all show secretaries should explore in times of ever-mounting expenses. Some societies set down a fixed expenses fee for the trip, leaving the judge to decide between a five-star hotel and farmhouse bed and breakfast. If a society cannot afford to cover the judge's costs, they should say so at the start, and then it is up to him to accept or otherwise. *But if he stays with friends, they must not be exhibiting under him the next day.*)

Once all these negotiations have been finalized, the judge will receive tickets and a timetable for the show. When the great day comes, he must never be late. He must present himself at the appointed time in the judges' room (or secretary's tent or members' enclosure in the case of smaller shows). There he will meet his steward, and there he must familiarize himself with the number of classes and the time allowed for each. He must also bear in mind the special awards to be determined at the end of the main judging. In some cases, these special awards have become extensive and complicated; horses by the same sire or one particular sire, best horse bred by exhibitor, best hair (feather), are only part of a growing list. However, such prizes have been donated by enthusiasts who wish to be remembered, and they must receive due consideration.

Judging In-hand

After such studies, and refreshment, the judge is ready for the fray. The first class may be already awaiting him in the ring, but more usually he will see them enter. A good judge lets the horses walk around the perimeter two or three times, making an initial assessment on freedom of movement and presence. He must always remember that he is judging draught animals whose natural working gait is the walk, so free movement here is vital. He will probably stand at a corner so that he can watch horses meeting him and leaving him, alert for any tendency towards 'dishing' (outward sweeping) or a pigeon-toed (inward pointing) gait.

The judge will then ask the steward to bring the horses into line. This initial line-up is usually for inspection only, and may bear no relation to final placings. The judge may ask for one animal to be moved alongside another, but that also is for comparative purposes, and is no indication of the outcome.

On beginning his inspection, the judge says 'Good morning' to each exhibitor in turn, and their standard reply should be 'Good morning, sir'. The exhibitor should volunteer no information, unless asked about a particular point. He certainly *should not* say: 'This filly won a class of twenty at Bakewell last month!' Such observations do occur, and if those making them were immediately ordered from the ring, the practice would stop.

The judge must feel for the things he cannot see. He may examine mouths, but usually only if the head conformation suggests some deformity such as a 'parrot mouth'. In the case of exhibits up to four years old, he may check mouths to ascertain their ages, but that normally happens only if there is a suspicion that an animal has been entered in the wrong age group. (At one show, a three-year-old entered among the two-year-olds was recognized by the judge as one he had seen as a two-year-old the previous summer! His examination confirmed the true age, to which the exhibitor had to admit.) 'Mouthing' a horse correctly is a facet of basic horsemanship with which the judge should be completely familiar.

The other places where touch is vital are the hooves and feet. In most heavy breeds, these will be hidden by a wealth of feather, which in the case of Clydesdales will be neatly combed to the last hair! The fault most likely to be found will be ringbone, located around the top of the coronet. Heavy horses with upright and relatively short pasterns are more disposed to this defect than are blood horses with long and springy pasterns. The other hidden condition is sidebone, felt by the thumb around the top of the heel. This is an ossification of the lateral cartilage, normally elastic and compressible, and assumes the form of bony growth on the side of the foot. (Refer to Chapter 6 for more information about ringbone and sidebone.) The judge is perfectly entitled to ask for a veterinary opinion on these conditions. A lot of money may be at stake for the horse's owner, and a wrong diagnosis by a man who is a competent horseman but not a qualified vet could lead to a costly and damaging dispute.

Besides checking for these specific conditions, the judge may wish to carry out further examination of the feet. There may, for instance, be a slight crack on the hoof, and the judge will want to see how far it goes. He also needs to determine the quality of the frog, and the general soundness of the hoof.

The other area in which the judge may take a 'hands on' approach is in assessing the quality of bone (i.e. the cannons). Quality of bone is a most important aspect: it should be flat and firm, not round and spongy, and there should also be sufficient bone to carry the animal's weight.

With regard to handling, the judge should approach every exhibit from the near side, as it is accustomed to being treated at home. Any horse being shown should pick its feet up without question. (If an animal is not completely trustworthy to handle, the exhibitor should warn the judge accordingly; this is one exception to the rule of not speaking unless spoken to.)

Most faults other than those mentioned should be visibly apparent, with no need for feeling. This applies to bumps on the hock (see Bone Abnormalities in Chapter 6) and to most other blemishes; if they can't be seen by the naked eye, they aren't worthy of note. (It may be said here that a Turnout judge has less need for such detailed examination of the horses. If they are moving soundly, that should suffice.)

The In-hand judge looks for a size of head in proportion to the body, with – particularly in the Shire and Clydesdale breeds – a slightly Roman nose. (Percherons, with their early influx of Arab blood, may be more dish-faced). There should be a bold carriage of the head. The way the horse holds its head determines its presence; head steady, eyes alert, ears pricked. The character of the horse can be judged partially at least from its eye; the acid test is the way it responds to being handled. The neck should taper neatly into the head and the throat should be clean-cut and lean.

The heavy horse's shoulders should look as though they are made to fit the collar. A certain amount of slope is desirable, but not so much as with a riding horse. The back should be short, strong and muscular (although rather longer in the case of a mare, to give foal-carrying capacity). There must be plenty of heart room, and draught horse breeders seek height through the chest rather than the leg.

The hind leg is a vitally important part. Hindquarters should have plenty of sweep, with the hocks set underneath the horse, not trailing behind. The hocks should be sound and broad, but not too straight. A horse must be able to bend at the hock, and cannot do so if the hind leg is too straight. If the hocks are set too high, all sorts of problems arise.

Having assessed such points in the stationary horse, the judge will then want to see it move at both walk and trot. The groom will first walk the animal in the direction indicated, turning either at the end of the enclosure or at some other point indicated and returning to 'meet' the judge. The walk is the heavy horse's natural gait and should be assessed as such, with the judge looking for correct movement. As the horse is walked away from him, he notes the closeness of the hocks. For most judges, the hocks should be fairly close together, although in Scotland this closeness has almost become a fetish. (Vets believe that hocks that are very close together set the hind toes pointing outwards, and this is not conducive to maximum power.) Where hocks are wide apart, this width often begins higher up the legs. This is not usually regarded as a fault, but judges may differ on such points. The judge will also watch to see that the horse moves straight, neither pin- nor pigeon-toed (turning the feet in), nor 'winging' (turning them out), and that there is no sign of lameness.

Some horses can walk better than they trot, or vice versa, and this is an area in which handlers may try to use ringcraft. If, for example, a handler knows that his horse is not a really good walker, he may try to keep it at the jog. Although this is not a common occurrence, it is a legitimate example of showmanship, for it is the handler's job to show the animal to best advantage, and the judge's to spot such ploys.

When the horse is trotted, the more natural the movement, the better. Welsh handlers tend to trot their Shires more quickly than the English – anyone who has ever had the joy of seeing the stallions on Welsh Cob Day at the Royal Welsh Show will understand the reason for this! Overall, astute handlers will keep their charges moving in the manner at which they look most free and comfortable. When watching the individual display, an interesting point to note is that horses with white knees appear to bend the knee more. This is only an optical illusion, but it is very showy.

Having assessed the exhibits on an individual basis, the judge will have the steward send them off round the ring while he makes his final decision (which, at this stage, a good judge will do promptly). He will then ask the steward to call them into the final line-up, in preparation for the awards.

Judging Turnouts

It is very difficult to appreciate what goes into preparing a turnout for the ring, unless you have actually done it. For that reason, In-hand judges sometimes prove quite unsatisfactory if called on to assess harness classes. At smaller shows, one person may be asked to officiate in both categories on grounds of expense, so the following observations may help them.

In the first place, it is terribly important to have time to look at the finer points of turnout, both inside and outside the main ring. So, although it may not apply to smaller shows with few entries, with a big class of fifteen or twenty turnouts, some pre-judging is essential. There are two reasons for this. First, if all such examination were carried out in the main ring, the crowd would become bored as they would be too far from the judge to be able to see and understand what was being done. Second, shows must run to schedule, and the time allowed in the main ring precludes leaving all examination to that final stage.

If properly scheduled, pre-judging can be more leisurely than that which takes place in the main ring. However, the same standards apply. The judge must be respected, and should have no friends and no enemies on the day. As with other forms of judging, the judge should always acknowledge competitors, but this should simply take the form of a mutual 'Good morning' and tipping of hats. Most certainly, judges and exhibitors should never address each other by their Christian names, even though both may have been in the same line-up the previous week.

Both when pre-judging and in the main ring, the judge must give every exhibitor a reasonable amount of time. Although some turnouts may be so far below the general standard as to have no chance, their connections should, nevertheless, be encouraged rather than discouraged. The main thing is that they are there, and part of the summer scene. Given encouragement, they can slowly improve. (In this respect, seminars can be helpful, especially concerning points of detail. A good tutor can explain about harness and harnessing, the different types of buckles available, and the role and placement of decorations. These seminars can be as valuable for judges as for competitors, for there is a shortage of really capable Turnout judges, which will be with us for some time.)

The next point to be emphasized is that the whole turnout is being judged, not just the horses. Using a points system, the horses would not constitute more than 50 per cent of the total. Yet some judges treat them as they would an in-hand horse, feeling their legs while disregarding the vehicle. The experienced Turnout judge, however, rarely bends his back, and this applies particularly to pairs, unicorns and teams. Any harness horse of seven or eight years old is bound to have some blemishes, but is no less a horse for that. If the Turnout judge cannot see any blemishes, there is no point in looking for them. Although hocks should be clean, their condition can be seen well enough without feeling them. In the Shire and Clydesdale, the long feather covers the foot. This is a breed characteristic and in a Turnout class it is silly to go poking about trying to find faults underneath the feather. What matters is that the horse should go sound.

Once the exhibits enter the main ring, the judge should give the horses a moment or two to settle. There's little point in watching their entrance; they may have been standing for some time and become either cold or hotted up.

As the teams settle into a trot, their size is noted, among other things. We are dealing with draught horses, which need weight to move weight. Heavy breeds are not built for speed; we don't want to see them running fast, particularly with noses poking out.

The first impression should be of horses going with power, chins on collars, and collected. They pull an unloaded vehicle, which should be no great effort for them. A horse flattens out when in heavy draught; it cannot then show itself to full advantage. The leaders should not be really pulling. They are there to help if and when necessary. They certainly should not be pulling more than the wheelers, or dragging them along. Under normal show conditions the wheelers do eighty per cent of the work.

The judge should not overdo the horses. After one good circuit of the ring he should have seen most of what he wants to see. Endless trotting round and round is pointless. A change to walk is desirable, for that is the draught horse's normal working gait.

At some point the judge *must* get in front of the horses. Here, he notes whether they are leaning on the pole, or shying away from it. An In-hand judge watches as horses leave him and meet him; with turnouts this frontal view is even more important. The judge picks his spot for optimum viewing, possibly in front of the grandstand. At an unfamiliar showground he reconnoitres beforehand, and chooses his place. He watches all teams over the same bit of ground, and stands firm. Any judge wandering round and round in circles doesn't know what he is looking for. It is important to see both off and near side horses, and for this reason some judges favour a figure of eight for the teams' route. Although it is time-consuming, this certainly shows both sides.

Once the judge has made his first assessment, the entries are brought in for the initial line-up. This should be done smartly and, as mentioned, the judge and steward should have already discussed who is to give the signals. Usually, this will be the steward's job, under the judge's orders. When signifying who is to come in, the judge should give the exhibitor's number, not his name, in order to reinforce his aura of impartiality. The turnouts are brought into a provisional line abreast, usually with the top teams on the judge's left as he stands with his back to the grandstand. The judge can now look for faults (some of which work may have been done during pre-judging, as mentioned.) Among the faults he should never find but too often does are wrongly positioned buckles. All should buckle from the outside, readily accessible. Adjustment on pair harness girths should never be on the inside. The near side is the side on which the driver approaches the horses after leaving them for any reason, and grooms should approach from that side as they leap down to go to the horses' heads.

Turnout showing is based on attention to detail, and much of this detail concerns the harness. Every spot of rust must be removed and every bit of brass shining, including the tongues of the buckles. Some competitors are so keen on their brasses that they neglect the leather. Edges of straps should be cleaned, polished and blackened equally with the faces, which should be supple.

However clean the harness, it is of fundamental importance that it should be correctly adjusted. Nevertheless, there is so much badly adjusted harness nowadays, and this criticism applies to all classes. An extra couple of holes taken up, or a very few links in the chains, could make all the difference. If exhibitors had to work their teams on deliveries every day, they would harness them differently.

One point is that collars are often too big. This causes more sore shoulders than collars that are too small. The collar should lie flat on the shoulders, and at the same angle as the shoulders. This is very important to avoid soreness. The hames should be adjusted so as to fit the *whole* of the collar, not just here and there.

It seems to be stating the obvious that horses' bridles should fit, yet many horses have to look either under or over their blinkers. Blinkers are there for a purpose, to prevent the horse from being distracted by movements behind and to the side, so they must be level with the eyes. Also, the edges of the blinkers should be clean and black; standards in some Turnout classes are so high that placings may rest on such minute points.

Bits should also be correctly adjusted. The bit should lie flat across the bars of the mouth, just puckering the outside of the mouth. The throatlash is one piece of harness that should not be too tight. When the horse is relaxing, you should be able to get hand and arm between lash and throat.

When assessing final placings, the turnout and competence of driver and grooms are likely to be factors – competence, especially, for obvious reasons. The driver should be correctly attired and should always wear a hat. He should also be able to use his whip. It is a functional piece of equipment, and should really be carried all the time and not stuck in its holder. Having to put the whip in its holder because both hands are needed for the reins can cost a place. However, if the driver feels he must put his whip down to have both hands free to control his team, he should do so. No one looks pretty with a runaway team!

In brewery teams, one or more grooms or 'trouncers' assist the driver, watching unobtrusively for signals from the steward, and ensuring that there is no danger of collision with other turnouts. They should stand smartly to attention, one hand behind the back. The left hand should be behind the back if standing on the vehicle's left or near side, and the right hand if on the off side. If the grooms' outfits match the driver's, as is often the case with sponsored turnouts, so much the better. However, judges should be mindful that such factors add considerably to the cost of exhibiting, and should be diplomatic if this issue is raised in post-class discussion.

After the detailed inspection comes the individual show. The judge may then require all the entries, or those short-listed for placing, to circle the ring again. At this point, he will ask the steward to bring them in for what should usually be his final placing. Once satisfied with his placings, he will indicate the fact either by approaching the winner or by conveying a message to the commentator, and the presentations can begin. While the judge may do so himself, it is more common for rosettes and awards to be presented by the sponsor of the class, or his representative.

Although no such discussions should take place while a class is in progress, after it has finished, a competitor has a perfect right to ask the judge where he went wrong. Any judge worth his salt will give a constructive answer, and this can have beneficial and lasting results. When Patrick Flood was once placed down the line by Arthur Lewis, he

Judge Mr Nigel Blakey interviewed by Sarah Rowse at the Staffordshire County Show. Judges expressing their thoughts publicly has become an interesting feature of the modern heavy horse scene, and we are fortunate in having skilled and knowledgeable commentators.

asked the reason. 'You had no candles in your lamps', said the judge. Never again in his long career did Patrick Flood enter a ring without candles.

The Steward's Role

The standard of stewarding can make or mar any show. Although the judge is king for the day, he can only operate effectively if exhibits are presented to him in correct order and on time. Good stewarding oils the wheels in unobtrusive fashion: bad stewarding brings disgruntled exhibitors in its train. The job is certainly not the sinecure that it appears to be in some people's eyes! Although there are no official qualifications required of stewards, familiarity with the class of stock in the ring, organizational ability and an authoritative bearing, tempered with politeness and the right degree of tact, are invaluable assets.

The steward wears his badge of office on his lapel. While this is not readily seen from the ringside, his bowler hat is. This is his other mark of office, setting him aside from spectators and exhibitors. While this attire should distinguish him from other personnel, it is also the case that there should there be no confusion as to who is the steward and who is the judge. Although they must liaise at all times, they should not be continually in a huddle, or it will appear from the ringside that the judge is asking the steward's opinions on placings, and that he must never do.

Badges of office aside, neatness and practicality should dominate choice of clothing. The steward should wear a suit (possibly a kilt in Scotland!). The suit should be on the dark side, and he should wear a tie. If the weather is inclement, a neat and well-made waterproof coat is perfectly acceptable, but not a sloppy anorak or duffel coat. Heavy shoes or boots are in order, but it matters not whether they are black or brown, nor is there any objection to wellingtons at a really wet show. The bowler, as already mentioned, is however a 'must', and should not be supplanted by other headgear, whatever the conditions.

At the start of a showing day, judges and stewards are asked to report to a named centre by a certain time. In addition to ensuring their presence, this gives them the chance of a cup of coffee and allows them some time to become acquainted with each other.

At this point, the steward's duties have begun. He must ensure that the judge is familiar with the programme, and how much time is allowed for each class. He should discuss with the judge such matters as who is to draw competitors into line, and who presents the rosettes. He must also check with the show secretary to ensure that those rosettes and the accompanying silverware will be in the correct place at the correct time.

After these preliminaries, the steward makes for the horse lines, be they boxes, or transporters with heavy breeds tied up alongside. He must ascertain the number actually forward for each class, which may be very different from the number entered. Failure to make this check can result in time wasting: it is by no means unknown for a class to be held up waiting for an exhibit that is not at the show. Such occurrences are exasperating for the judge, other exhibitors, and the paying public, without whose support the show could not continue.

At the same time as checking numbers, the steward checks that entries are actually in the correct classes, that each is wearing their correct number, and that there are no mistakes in the catalogue. Incorrect classification is most likely to happen in the youngstock classes, particularly between two- and three-year-olds.

It is while making such checks that the queries begin. Someone misses the Three-Year-Old Filly class, and asks if their animal may join the Barren Mares, four years old and upwards. There is only one answer to that one: a firm refusal. If prize money is won by the unscheduled entry, it is not fair on the other competitors who have correctly entered and presented their exhibits. On the other hand, there are sometimes genuine catalogue mistakes, perhaps with a three-year-old gelding listed among the seniors. The steward must be aware of this, and any transfers made known to all other competitors in those classes. This is the steward's task, not the judge's. Also, the steward must be aware of how the rules apply in unusual circumstances. For example, a mare that has lost a foal can still compete in the Brood Mare class (being, as a matter of fact, a brood mare, albeit bereaved) but it is the steward and not the judge who must inform all others in the class about what is being done.

Once in the ring, the steward must respectfully ensure that the judge is aware of just how long he has to place the class. This should be done courteously but briefly; it cannot be over-stressed that continued prolonged consultation between judge and steward gives a very poor impression, yet it is seen all too often. At a big show there may be both a main ring steward and a collecting ring steward, the latter controlling entry into the main ring. Once one class has entered the ring, the collecting ring steward cannot stand around watching – he must ensure that the next class is heading for or is already present in the collecting ring, maintaining a smooth flow.

With entries circling in the main ring (usually, unless they are North Country Clydesdales, in a clockwise direction) the judging begins. Once the horses have circled the ring for a few minutes, they are brought into line. This initial line-up is not final, but it is important, and must be done smartly and properly. As previously mentioned, judge and steward between them should have already decided who makes the actual signals. If the judge wants to do this himself, that is his prerogative. More usually it falls upon the steward – under the judge's orders, of course. The judge should indicate the number and not the name of the exhibitor to be drawn in, thereby retaining that aura of impartiality. The bowler hat now really comes into play. It is used at the end of the steward's straight, extended arm in clear and positive fashion, so that the exhibitor has no doubt that he is being signalled to move into line.

He should need no second bidding! Those on board a six-horse turnout have enough to think about without wondering whether the steward really means them or someone else. Simply waving arms around vaguely will not do. The steward's directions should be clear without being too officious or overbearing. Once the turnouts are lined up, the steward accompanies the judge as he makes his individual examination.

Following individual inspection comes the individual show. Entries placed as they appealed to the judge during the preliminary circling are now subject to individual scrutiny and then display, at which point the steward is called upon again. He must ensure that each entry in turn is ready to give its individual show. He must then see that the next in line is ready, and that the one just displayed passes round the rear of the line and back to its appointed place. An aspect sometimes neglected is to insist that no animal or turnout takes the stage until its predecessor

The presentation: Jim Yates's Alan's Starlight Blaize winning at the East of England.

has been scrutinized to the judge's satisfaction. This is not too difficult in Breed or In-hand classes, but when turnouts are circling the ring it is no easy task to ensure that one team of flashy Suffolks or Percherons does not start to show its paces while the judge is still assessing the previous team from behind.

After static examination and individual show, the judge may order the entries, or some of them, to circle the ring again. He will then order them to be brought in for what is virtually his final placing, and the steward must be really on his toes and make sure he interprets the judge's decisions clearly.

The judge then indicates that he is satisfied with his placings, either by approaching the winner or by telling the commentator, who relays the news to the assembled company, and presentations begin. At this point, the steward will usually stand aside while the rosettes are being presented either by the sponsor, the sponsor's wife, or the judge. However, although the steward does not, as a rule, place rosettes on winning bridles, he still has a vital role to play. He must check that the awards sheet is filled in correctly, and that appropriate names and numbers correspond. Inaccuracies here cause havoc right down the line: the results board will be wrong, and the Press results wrong, as will prize money dispatched later.

(Although the steward is available in case of any mix-up in the presentation, he should not be responsible for the silver cups. Such items belong to the show society, which must keep them firmly under its wing until they are presented, often during the final event of the day. In this respect, their insurance should be covered by the society.)

Regardless of final placing, or other appointments, no exhibitor should be allowed to leave the ring before the presentation except by permission of the judge, as relayed by the steward, unless there is a genuine emergency. In a large class, however, unplaced entries may be

Mr Philip Moss (right) signs his judging sheet for the ring steward at the East of England Show: after signing, these sheets are put on public display in the results tent.

directed to leave before the winners make their lap of triumph. In a Turnout class, the winner is generally granted a lap of honour alone. Even if classes are running late, this should be allowed. However, stewards have been known to become over-officious at this stage, and direct the class winner out of the ring with the rest. This is unfair, both to the driver and his sponsor, if he has one. Sponsors pay to have their name displayed, and they are a vital part of show economics. They must be encouraged, not dissuaded. Roger Clark, having brilliantly won the Interbreeds Team Class at the Royal with his four Suffolks, threatened to run down an over-zealous official who tried to divert his lap of honour, to the huge delight of the heavy horse contingent in a nearby grandstand!

CHAPTER 13

In the Show Ring

Appearing in the show ring is the culmination of all the hard work and preparation that has gone on beforehand. Even if you are a first-time newcomer to showing, there for the day out and the experience, you will want to show your horse and/or vehicle to best advantage. If you are an experienced exhibitor, out to win, you will be looking for legitimate ways of attracting the judge's attention and gaining an 'edge' over your rivals. Of course, the main ways of catching the judge's eye are to have an outstanding horse, or a beautiful turnout, expertly driven, but the details of presentation are also important, and this is where ringcraft comes in. For the novice, ringcraft will operate at the basic level of knowing what is required of you and carrying it out competently and safely, showing courtesy and respect to other exhibitors and the judge. With experience, these skills will be refined to the level of clockwork: an almost telepathic response to the steward's instructions; smooth, instantaneous changes of gait; the ability to hide imperfections in a horse's movement; a magical ability to make enough room to be seen, and to have one's horse or turnout going at its best when passing the judge.

While some aspects of ringcraft can be garnered by watching experienced exhibitors, the key is a full understanding of what the judge is looking for; the idea is to show him what he wants to see. For this reason, exhibitors should study the previous chapter carefully, since they, and the judges, are two sides of the same coin.

Showing In-hand

Having attended to all aspects of the horse's preparation, be sure that you, too, are neat, clean and properly attired before entering the ring. Common sense, personal pride, and self-interest, rather than rigid rules govern this situation. However, as guidance, a suit, or a good jacket and trousers, with a tie for gentlemen, is acceptable wear. In wet weather, a smart topcoat or waxed jacket may be worn. Stout, waterproof walking shoes or similar, with a sole that affords some grip, will assist when running up in-hand. A show stick completes the ensemble.

On entering the ring, the usual course is to walk round in a clockwise direction. However, Clydesdales in the north are often shown anti-clockwise, and it is imperative for the new exhibitor, or anyone exhibiting out of their usual area, to ascertain what is expected before-hand. You do not want to meet the others head-on halfway round! As we will see shortly, another local variation concerns the way in which horses are turned during the individual run-out. Inquiry in respect of these details can be made in advance to the collecting ring steward, or judge's steward, as appropriate. Such queries should not be addressed directly to the judge.

When showing in-hand, alertness is essential. This applies to both horse and handler, for a groom walking in a slipshod fashion is very often accompanied by a drooping horse. Such sloppiness is at odds with the blend of economy and efficiency of movement that is sought-after in the draught horse. These qualities are evident in a long stride, covering some ground. Plenty of 'snap' in the action, with joints that flex so that each foot is lifted cleanly off the ground, indicates a willing-ness to work. The feet should hit the ground with the frog and not the toe or heel taking the impact. Movement should be straight, with hocks reasonably close – very close in the case of Clydesdales – or they may spread when pulling a serious load.

Therefore, walk smartly, pay attention to the job in hand, do not wave at or chat with friends in the crowd which, to the keen exhibitor, should be a mere blur. Above all, do not smoke!

The ability to walk at a reasonable speed is, to some extent, governed by the horses in front. Therefore, try to avoid getting behind a horse, or group of horses, that is dawdling. On the other hand, if yours tends to walk idly, getting behind a horse that is walking out smartly may help to sharpen it up. In all cases, however, try to keep two or three horse's lengths between yours and the one in front. There are two reasons for this; first, safety and second, to enable the judge to see your horse properly. If you find that you are gaining on the one in front, move outwards; never cut in. In the tense show ring atmosphere, especially when championships are at stake, it seems natural for exhibitors, perhaps unconsciously, to continually edge in towards the coveted top position.

The aspiring exhibitor will have noted how experienced grooms handle their horses in the ring, and will have practised the routine at home. Leading the horse in-hand, running it up, and teaching it to stand correctly will also have been practised, as an extension of teaching basic good manners. Even so, a youngster may forget its lessons when confronted by the electric atmosphere and strange sights, sounds and smells of the show ring, and 'play up' to some extent. Typically, if the horse has a good basic temperament but is somewhat overwhelmed by the occasion, this may take the form of 'jigging' at the walk. The horse may walk perfectly at home, but the excitement of the crowds and the other horses unsettles it into this semi-prancing, and often crooked, movement between a walk and a trot. Hopefully, the horse may be snapped out of this behaviour immediately, by a jerk-and-release action on the halter shank, accompanied by a verbal reprimand. Following this by talking to the horse in soothing tones may have a calming effect, but if this does not resolve the problem, other remedies may have to be tried, since it is important that the horse does not learn that prancing about is acceptable behaviour in the ring. To this end, it is worth remembering that, when jigging about, a horse actually covers less ground than when walking properly, so a determined effort to get the horse really walking out strongly may have a settling effect. Other than this, it may be worth halting him every time he jigs about, and then getting him to walk on again. If these corrective measures – especially the latter – are attempted, it is imperative to keep your eyes out for other exhibitors and avoid any action that might endanger or inconvenience them. In cases of extreme difficulty, where behaviour crosses the line from excitable to unmanageable, you should heed the advice given in the *American Draft Horse Journal*:

Even with thorough preparation you can wind up with an unmanage-able horse, usually with stallions or young horses on their first trip from home. There is only one thing to do, excuse yourself from the class and take the horse back to its stall. To present a horse that is out of control is unfair to the horse, yourself and every other competitor in the ring.

The point about excusing yourself relates to two basic pieces of show ring etiquette. First, if a competitor feels it necessary to leave the ring for any reason (whether personal illness, the horse's lameness, or misbehav-iour), the judge's permission should be sought and second, that all communication with the judge should be through the steward. Leaving the arena without informing the judge is considered a serious misdemeanour. However, observing this protocol should not entail a protracted wrestling match with a fractious animal. Any steward worth his salt will soon spot an exhibitor in difficulties and a raised hat or hand will quickly secure his, and the judge's attention. Similar signals or nods then will convey permission to leave the ring, which should be done with dignity and without disturbance to other exhibitors.

Assuming that no such traumas arise, in normal circumstances, you should walk at the horse's side, level with its front legs, a position that should be maintained both in preliminary circling and individual showing. The right arm should be extended in such a manner as to keep the horse's head well up at all times. Not only does this look smarter, but a horse that is constantly jerking its head down may well pull out the mane plaits.

The halter shank should be rolled up so that the horse can be shown with one hand only, but the shank must never be wrapped tightly round the hand. One man who neglected this precaution lost a finger. At the

Walking out in-hand: a clean, active walk, head steady, and ready to respond.

walk, the right hand holds the shank close to the horse's mouth, but at the trot the animal is given more freedom by lowering the grip on the shank by some nine inches to a foot (22–30 cm). However, with a difficult or headstrong horse this may not apply; common sense must be used throughout.

The judge begins his duties by standing near the centre of the ring. He can then see every horse side on. He should then move outside the circle so that he can see the exhibits from the other side. During this procedure, the handler's aim is to keep the horse calm and straight.

After this comes the pulling-in stage, for which there are different practices. The English and Welsh fashion is usually for the horses to circle, and then be drawn into provisional order before being examined at close quarters. In Scotland and Ireland the exhibits are usually lined up in the order of their appearance in the ring. The steward does the calling in under the judge's instructions, so keep at least half an eye on the steward throughout these preliminaries.

When coming into line, remember that you are putting your animal alongside horses that are strangers to it. Don't crowd your neighbours. If you must move your horse while in line, back it all the way out so as not to knock against horses next to it. This need to allow plenty of space is especially important in classes for stallions, or for mares with foals.

Once the horse is halted in line in its allotted place, the halter shank should be dropped to the ground, in perpendicular and tidy fashion. The horse is then 'stood up'. It should be standing squarely on all four legs, not three, in the correct stance that has been taught at home. It is important to get the hocks together and the forelegs directly under the horse. If it is necessary to move feet in the stationary position, use the show stick, with pressure on the shoulder, the head, and the horse's balance. Do not follow the lead of those handlers who kick at the pasterns to move the front feet. Once the horse looks as good as you can reasonably expect, you should stop fussing, but you must keep alert to ensure that the horse remains set up while the judge is walking up and down the line. 'Many's the time I never see what's in the class against me, because I've always been watching my own horse', said Ted Cumbor. 'Keep your horse alert, even if you haven't won the red ticket. This is your showcase, when potential customers look on. But use common sense – don't be too strict all the time, or your horse will get fed up with it.'

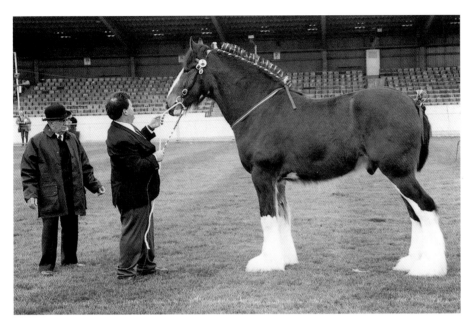

Alan Tillier is best known for his driving skills, but he can also deliver the goods in-hand. Here, he is standing up two-year-old Shire gelding Montague Merlin for inspection by judge Mr Billy Cammidge. The young horse is standing to perfection, and Alan is keeping his hands and arms well clear so as not to impair the judge's view of the horse.

Young handler Adam Claridge with his Suffolk charge standing up nicely at the Royal Norfolk Show.

These handlers are keeping their Percherons relaxed, yet standing correctly.

This practical exhibitor's advice modifies that often given in showing manuals to 'always keep your animals at attention' – advice which, followed to the letter in large classes, risks souring the horse. It is also a reminder of another function of showing: it is the exhibitor's shop window, and a potential buyer may have come to the ringside just to seek the very sort of horse you have on display.

Once they are in line, the judge goes round each entry in turn. On arriving at your horse he may say 'Good morning', to which the only response should be 'Good morning, sir'. The judge may be an old family friend, but this is an occasion for a certain formal aloofness, not for chit-chat. The essential strict impartiality should be evident to spectators as well as to fellow competitors. Any questions about the horse's age and so on should be answered fully and politely, but no further information should be volunteered. The only exception to this rule of not speaking unless spoken to concerns the horse's behaviour. The judge may feel legs for ringbone or other faults, and he will expect the horse to be quiet. If it is not completely trustworthy, you should warn the judge accordingly if he has not already asked; this is simply having due regard for another's safety. While telling the judge that your horse might kick may not advance your placing, not telling him, and having the horse lash out, can have far more serious repercussions.

In general, be conscious of the judge, and when he is viewing your horse, move aside as appropriate to allow him to do so: make it easy for him to do his job.

Once they have been inspected in line, each horse then gives an individual display or 'stand show' in turn. On the judge's command the exhibitor must walk his horse away in a straight line, turn, and head straight back to the judge. The display is then repeated at the trot. Exhibitors are expected to know this basic procedure. There may be a steward to mark the end of the walk, or the handler may have to use his own judgement. In either case, the trot requires about double the distance of the walk to give a proper display, as the horse may be well down the track before settling into the correct action.

Turning at the ends brings a problem as breeds spread into new geographical locations. In England and Wales, Shires, Percherons and Suffolks are turned clockwise or right-handed, so that the handler walks around the horse. In Scottish and north of England Clydesdale classes, the horses are turned anti-clockwise or left-handed, turning round the groom, who remains more or less stationary. When Clydesdales are shown in southern England, where the breed may be less common, local judges may frown if the traditional northern practice is followed, which is unfair on the competitor. However, as mentioned earlier, if you are unsure of the method required, try to find out in advance by inquiry through the steward.

During the individual display, the judge will be assessing the horse's movement and action. The qualities desired in the walk have already been mentioned; in this respect, the judge will simply have the opportunity to examine each exhibit in greater detail than before. So far as the trot is concerned, the first point that will

This rear view shows that a good, straight walk is propelled by powerful haunches; although a draught horse 'pushes' into the collar, the main propulsion should originate, not from the shoulders, but from the rear end.

A stallion in show harness. This is an excellent example of a horse being run out in-hand to good effect – an active, powerful trot, balanced and controlled.

impress the judge is the horse moving promptly into an active trot in response to the command 'Trot', or 'Trot On'. Further vocal encouragement is quite acceptable and, indeed, top handlers talk to their charges as much as possible throughout the show.

Good action at the trot is important in the potential draught horse. It is also more revealing than the walk, as deficiencies become more evident. Faults are 'spraddling', or going too wide at the hocks; 'interfering' or going too close; 'paddling', or throwing the forefeet either in or out; 'rolling', or excess shoulder movement through the legs being placed too wide. Most faulty movement stems from faults of conformation. For instance, horses that are toe in or toe out, stand wide at the hocks, or have short, stubby pasterns or straight hocks will show these faults when on the move. However, temperament also plays a part in movement: the lethargic horse will display an inactive, unimpressive trot, while an excitable temperament will tend to exaggerate faulty action.

As mentioned earlier, part of ringcraft is showing your horse to best advantage, and this means being aware of its strengths and weaknesses and practising ways of showing off the former and concealing the latter. Know your horse, in other words. The *American Draft Horse Journal*, edited by Maurice Telleen, has this to say on the subject:

Some horses look better at a very collected trot, others at a more extended trot. A horse that wings [dishes, or throws its feet out] will generally accentuate this fault the faster it goes. Give your horse enough slack so that it can keep its head straight ahead, but not so much as to allow it to get the jump on you if something should startle it. When turning your horse, do so in a relatively small circle. Hold it back slightly as you make the turn. After making the turn, straighten the horse out at a walk, and get it balanced and settled down before putting into a trot. Always go straight away and straight back to the judge.

Another factor that can influence the way a horse moves in the run-out is the show stick or whip. For example, Shire exhibitors hold a whip in their left hand. By the time the horse is ready for the show ring, this should be purely decorative, and is certainly not there for regular use, or else a horse may come to fear it, and be watching for the whip when it should be walking or trotting straight ahead. A wavy run is often caused by a horse looking at the whip. A long driving whip is unsightly in In-hand classes, and should not be used. If the horse is the sort that needs touching up, this training should be done at home with a second groom following behind.

On returning after the trot, the judge may ask for the horse to be backed. Again, if this has been taught at home, it should not prove difficult. In fact past masters of the show ring could back a horse in such fashion that a slight unsoundness did not show.

After assessing the horses individually in the line-up, the judge will have the steward send them off round the ring while he makes his final decision. At this stage, it is important to have your horse walking out every bit as well as during the earlier stages. Although a good judge will, at this stage, make his decisions promptly, he just might be deliberating between your horse and another exhibit, and the better yours is going at this stage, the better your chances!

Showing Stallions

At this juncture we should give special consideration to showing stallions in-hand. This can bring you into a different ball game, since you are dealing with a stronger and probably more temperamental animal than a mare. At one time, professional grooms handled most of the show stallions, but amateurs are now more usually in charge.

Because showing a stallion makes extra demands of the handler, it is advisable to have plenty of experience of showing other animals before this is attempted. The other all-encompassing point to consider is that, since an excitable 18 hand stallion cannot be controlled by force, it is very important to build up a real rapport with the animal before venturing into a show environment. While rapport with any working

A young stallion set up to great effect. Sladesbrook Sensation, as a three-year-old, winning his class at Derby. The judge that day was the late Tom Gardner, a wonderful and universally popular judge of both light and heavy horses.

John Richardson's first major winner, the Shire stallion Toc Hill Sir Alfred, seen here as four-year-old champion at the Shire Horse Show.

or show animal is important, it must be considered an absolute necessity with a stallion but, once achieved, the bond can be very rewarding.

We have already noted several points about handling stallions in passing: the need to teach them to accept a bit and harness at home; the need to check that everything is in a good state of repair, and procedures for travelling, unloading and stabling on site. Following on from these precautions, assuming that the stallion is in a temporary stable, carry out your pre-class preparations there, not standing in the alleyway as a potential source of trouble. Even if you are not making use of showground stabling, the same principle applies; prepare in as secure a location as possible, do not stand in the open, with the lead rope tied to a bit of baling twine, trusting to luck.

On making for the ring, allow plenty of leeway in front of your stallion, and always keep well back if you are leading any horse behind a stallion; they hate other animals creeping up on them. So long as they are sensibly designed and located, the provision of horse walks to and from the ring is a definite improvement; there is less chance of a distracted mum with a pushchair crossing just in front of you, or a small child running up to hug a hairy leg.

When leading, whether in the ring or outside it, you should use a good long halter shank for a stallion, but in no circumstance should you wrap it around your wrist. This is worth repeating, since severe hand injuries have been caused to people who thought it gave them more purchase. You are nothing like so strong as a stallion (or even a foal, for that matter) and wrapping the lead shank round your wrist will just reinforce, rather than disprove, this point. A leather strap as a lead shank is preferable to a chain, but it must be in good condition. A half-chewed, saliva-drenched strap is asking for trouble.

One advantage of having a long halter shank is that it gives some leeway to both horse and handler if the animal goes up on its hind legs. A tug on too short a shank at a moment of imbalance can result in the horse going over backwards. Stallion harness is designed to prevent rearing, but it cannot be entirely ruled out with any animal, so always be prepared.

When showing stallions, it is especially important that safe distances between horses, and between handlers and horses, are observed at all times. A horse striking out with its hind legs does no harm if proper distances are observed, but could prove fatal if they are not. Striking out with the forelegs is perhaps less predictable, and it may arise from discomfort caused by ill-fitting or unaccustomed tack. This is another reason for plenty of practice and schooling at home.

The Grand Parade is a particularly trying time for stallion handlers. Judging is over, rosettes won, and concentration tends to diminish. Yet it is a time of bustle and hurry, with more animals trying to enter the ring than at any earlier time in the show. The circle of parading animals is so large that there is a natural temptation to tighten up, but the stallion handler must not succumb to it. Crowd applause is likely to be louder than for single classes, adding to the dangers. Concentration is the watchword until the safety of the box is regained.

Showing Foals

If stallions require special consideration so, too, do foals. There is no official stipulation about the youngest age for showing foals, but only in exceptional circumstances should foals be shown at less than one month old.

Foals require competent handling at all times, and this is especially so at a show. The home training described in Chapter 11 will be an enormous help, but a foal enters a completely new world at the showground, with flags flying, the crowds buzzing and lots of unfamiliar horses. When leading a foal in this environment, be either close up to it or at a safe distance. A foal is the sharpest creature alive, and every season someone is kicked by a foal in the ring, either because it is overwhelmed by its surroundings or loses sight of its dam, and instinctively tries to protect itself by lashing out.

If the foal has become accustomed to being parted from its dam at home, albeit for very brief periods at a short distance, this first vestige of independence should assist generally, and in particular when the mare is run out in-hand. There is no hard-and-fast rule here regarding the foal: there is no harm in it 'coasting along' at some little distance from the mare, provided that it does not interfere with the judge's view, but this is rather different from the panicky foal that rushes after its dam, gets in the judge's way and probably spoils the mare's show through causing distraction. That said, it is a simple fact that foals vary

Pat Carmen, groom for E. Bailey & Sons, showing a Percheron filly foal out of Willingham Phoebe at Newark.

A mare and foal class at Soham, Cambridgeshire. Les Christopher shows his Shire mare, Chipstead Gillie and foal, Turnbrook Jodie. The dark colouring around the foal's muzzle suggests that the whole coat will darken to that shade in due course.

M. J. Bradley's mare and foal, Lynside Grace and Lynside Viscount. Lynside Viscount's calm, confident manner is evidence that showing can do youngsters a power of good, provided that they are correctly handled and not 'overdone'.

Pat Carmen leads a foal with a sensible length of halter shank. Gordon Bailey is in the front.

enormously in the time they take to show themselves properly. Some are naturals, standing quietly in line at their first show, behaving impeccably, while others take a lot of time and patience. Whatever patience is required should be considered a sound investment, since all experienced horse people agree that showing a foal teaches it lessons that remain with it throughout its life.

Turnout Classes

If the class you have entered has a pre-judging element, you should make every effort to ensure that all aspects of your turnout are immaculate, since the judge will examine them in minute detail. Indeed, it is often through minor faults coming to light in these inspections that the novice exhibitor improves, so any comments made by the judge should be welcomed and acted upon for the future.

You, the driver, should be smartly attired, comfortable and always wearing a hat. If the groom's outfit matches the driver's, so much the better. However, expense may be a limiting factor here, especially if more than one groom is involved, and no one should refrain from competing simply because he cannot afford matching uniforms. These things take time to acquire.

This painting by Nina Colmore, which has pride of place at Young's Brewery, depicts former head horse keeper, Harry Ranson, driving their four-horse team at Windsor. Harry worked for the brewery for forty-six years and his team was unbeaten in the show ring during the period 1947–54.

The highly professional Bob Stobbart driving Vaux Breweries' Percheron, Scorpion, at the British Percheron Horse Show.

Tom Henfrey with his company's Bob and Amy, winning the Pairs class at the British Percheron Horse Show.

As a driver be sure that you are able to use your whip. It is a functional piece of equipment, and its important role in giving signals has been discussed in Chapter 10 Turnout Driving. It should really be carried all the time and not stuck in its holder. Indeed, some show schedules stipulate that exhibitors in driving classes are expected to carry the whip. In any event, to have put the whip in its holder because both hands are needed for the reins can cost you a place. However, if

Bruce Smith driving Paul Rackham's turnout of three Suffolks in a unicorn hitch.

you feel you must put your whip down to have both hands free to control your horse or team, you should do so.

Shortly before the main part of the class is due to start, the steward or a tannoy announcement will give the word to make for the collecting ring. Once there, you are under the ring steward's control, and must move off as he directs. When you receive his signal, try to keep fifty yards or so behind the turnout in front, so that the judge has every chance to note your entry. If, however, your horse or horses show signs of edginess, or are not so reliable as you would like, get in close to the others!

Give a 'click' to begin with, to set your horse or team up on their toes. Good harness horses should know exactly what is expected of them. With novices, however, remember that all horses act differently in the show ring from how they do at home, no matter how many times you may have practised. Apart from the different venue, there are flags, bunting and tannoys to contend with. The place is crowded with strange horses and even more unfamiliar people. If you are unfortunate in respect of the show's organizers, you might also have to contend with display motorcyclists, forklift tractors, and planes that drop parachutists from the sky. Should you have the misfortune of your horse or team being seriously alarmed by any such apparitions, or if you feel a real 'explosion' is imminent for any other reason, you must endeavour to inform the judge of your intention to leave the ring, while putting safety first. Leaving the ring without informing the judge is a serious misdemeanour, but it is also an exhibitor's responsibility to leave the ring with as much control as possible, for the safety of all concerned.

Assuming that all is in order, the first thing to do is establish as impressive a trot as possible. This does not mean an unduly fast trot, but one that gives the impression of balanced power. It will be much easier for you to concentrate on showing off the turnout if you have an alert and efficient groom. In fact, your groom should be your second pair of eyes from the moment you enter the ring, watching for any other horses that approach dangerously close, and warning you accordingly. However, the groom's priority is to keep an eagle eye on the steward, and be ready to tell you instantly when you are signalled into line. This is important. Some competitors will try to steal a march by cutting in before they are called, or moving up a place beyond the steward's intention. Although the latter should redirect them, you will

Vaux's four grey Percherons worked delivering beer on the streets of Sunderland and, driven by Bob Stobbart, competed against other teams kept simply for showing. Note the grooms or 'trouncers' in attendance.

Bruce Smith driving Anti-Waste Ltd's dray to a team of four Suffolks, accompanied by two alert grooms.

help your cause by being prompt in your own responses, without cutting up others in the process.

In brewery teams, grooms called 'trouncers' assist the driver. They should stand smartly to attention, one hand behind the back. The left

In the line-up, the grooms stand in front of their horses, but not necessarily holding them, while others are put through their paces.

hand should be behind the back if standing on the vehicle's left or near side, and the right hand if on the off side. Their role is the same as for other grooms, to keep an eye out for other vehicles and to convey signals from judge or steward promptly yet discreetly to the driver.

A good Turnout judge will not require exhibitors to trot round the ring ad nauseum, but will call them into line quite promptly. If there has been no pre-judging, it is here that the detailed examination of horses, equipment and vehicles will take place. As with other classes, the basic rules of polite formality and not speaking to the judge unless spoken to hold sway. Following the inspection, turnouts will circle the ring once more, while the judge makes his final decision. At this point, even if there seems no chance of being placed, driver and groom should remain alert to the proximity of other vehicles and to the steward's signals.

After the Class

After the class, always accept the verdict with good grace, whether you think your entry was correctly placed or not. In brief, do your best and then be a good sport. If you have a legitimate query on a point of detail, any judge worth his salt will be happy to answer it, provided it

In Turnout classes, the rear of the dray is important to the judge, who looks for the requisite buckets and nosebags. Like everything else, they must be immaculate.

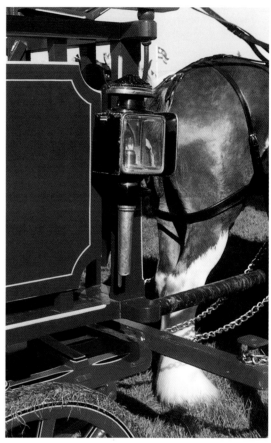

Accessories are all-important. Lamps must be bright and shining, and fitted with candles that have already been lit, making them easier to light next time.

is broached at a time convenient for him to do so, and in a civil manner. An expert opinion may help you to achieve a better placing at your next show, so long as it is sought and acted upon in the right spirit.

The other mark of an equestrian sportsman is that, win or lose, his first concern after the class is the well-being of his charges. Although, as we saw earlier (Grooming and Rugs), heavy horses generally do not have much need for rugs, shows – especially in extreme weather conditions – can be an exception. For example, a horse returning to its quarters after a long class in hot weather will need an anti-sweat or cooler rug until it cools down. Turnout horses will have undergone quite vigorous exertions, and need rugging as soon as they return from the class, possibly even before unharnessing on a cold or windy day. Stock people have long been aware of the 'wind chill factor', so beloved by modern weather forecasters, and act accordingly. They know that a wild, wet day is much more unpleasant and dangerous for any stock than a severe frost in still air.

For providing temporary protection before unharnessing, don't decry the effectiveness of clean hessian sacks. These once-common items may be obtained through builders' yards and the like. A pair may be stitched together to give a double thickness and are then very handy just to sling over the horse's quarters when it first returns from the ring, keeping the loins warm until the horse is unharnessed and a proper rug fitted.

Once they have been made comfortable after the class, if you

Leaving the arena: a poignant moment as this was the last show ring appearance of Tetley's former head horse keeper, the late Albert Hobson. A great character and an urban heavy horse man of the old school.

are staying at the show, the horses should be bedded down in their temporary boxes and you will have some time to relax and enjoy the camaraderie. If you are travelling home, while it is perfectly acceptable to stay long enough for a beer and a much-needed bite to eat, do not loiter for hours, leaving weary horses standing in the horsebox.

CHAPTER 14

Other Classes and Events

Not every owner of heavy horses wishes to get involved in the serious business of competing in major In-hand or Turnout classes; there are many who derive great pleasure and satisfaction from exhibiting their charges in a more relaxed atmosphere. For such people, participation in the traditional Decorated Harness classes, or Agricultural classes may fit the bill, and in some areas nowadays, there is a rekindling of interest in town parades. Another possibility is the Tradesman's Turnout class. Obstacle Driving and Ploughing Matches are other specialized forms of competition and these have been given chapters of their own. For the more agile, Ridden Classes are becoming an increasingly popular part of the heavy horse scene and these now appear at a number of major shows. The fundamental point is that there are many opportunities for all who wish to become part of the colourful show scene.

Decorated Harness Classes

These are rightly becoming more popular. Although many people enter them for personal pleasure, they also enable the one-horse owner to compete against the professional stables, since so much preparation time is involved that few enterprises are likely to pay staff to enter more than one horse at any show.

In these classes, the value of the horse in the judge's eyes should count nil. In theory, this is a 'poor man's class', allowing a moderate or elderly horse to compete with in-hand prize-winners, as it is the decorations and not the animal being judged. Realistically, however, a tall, upstanding horse of bright colour is eye-catching even without its harness, and so has a flying start. A horse such as Royal, Kenneth Keir's tall Shire, is difficult to overlook even before his owner has decorated him.

Yet no one should be deterred from entering Decorated classes, even if their pride and joy is not a potential in-hand winner. Two of the most vital aspects are the time spent and the artistic eye, and this hobby is one for all the family. Remember that, while the heavy horse can carry an almost limitless amount of decorations, in aesthetic terms there is a point at which decorations can be overdone, and bulk is not the aim. Thus the artistic newcomer always has a chance against old hands who might have gone 'over the top' in seeking fresh ways of beautifying their animals. Colour, balance and cleanliness are the important criteria in the Decorated Harness classes.

Decoration is another aspect of the heavy horse world that is enriched by a wide variety of regional styles. The south of England has its own patterns, while in northern England alone the Lancashire pattern is distinct from the West Riding just over the Pennines, which again is different from the East Riding decorations as practised on the large arable farms of the Wolds and Holderness. Further north in

A decorated Suffolk (left) and Shire (right).

Andrew Wager with his Suffolk gelding, Blaxhall Blossom, a breed show winner of the Best Decorated class. This picture shows that a horse need not be plastered all over with brasses and flowers to look effective. Although the basic cart harness is enhanced by a few droppers, the horse could readily be put-to.

'Neatest and Cleanest Harness and Horse' – G. R. Wadsworth & Sons' Shire gelding Monarch, shown by Dick Cooper. The title of this class at the Shire Horse Show goes back to the nineteenth century, when the buzz and excitement of such classes relieved the hard work and tedium of everyday life.

County Durham, the Clydesdale and the Scottish peak collar herald further variations.

Whatever regional traditions are followed, it is of major importance that the decorations should be balanced. There should be no obvious gaps, no high and low places. When viewed from behind, the tail decorations are the starting point, and embellishments along the line of the back should continue upwards in a gentle sweep, until the plume or highest point between the ears is reached.

At the sides, all flowers or wool pieces should be level, not in and out. Colours must complement both each other and the horse. For example, Leeds brewers Tetleys choose red, white and green for their grey Shires, the flowers being red and white, backed by green asparagus fern. A Suffolk horse exhibitor, however, may prefer green and gold against the horse's chestnut coat. Sometimes, experimentation is necessary. Kenneth Keir tried a blue and white colour scheme, but this clashed with Royal's black coat. However, black shows up brasses very well, so Kenneth had fifty-four brass cups made specially, each cup holding flowers to bedeck the 18.3 hand animal. This proved a great

The grey dapples on this Shire, shown by Jessica Field, provide a bold backcloth for some innovative decorations. Note the matching decorated whip. Entrants in the Decorated Harness classes tend to be families rather than companies, and such displays are a labour of love.

Decorated Harness class winner Mr D. Heaps, with his grey Shire. A subtle and elegant blend of colour, with handler's attire co-ordinated with the horse's decorations.

success, but highlights the need for attention to detail. For example, buckles should match the cups and be very, very clean both on top and below. A day and a half is needed for preparation of this sort and all exhibitors agree that there is no easy way.

At one time horse brasses were the main, and sometimes the only, means of beautifying a heavy horse and they changed hands as lots in heavy horse and carriage sales. Nowadays, they have become so collectable that specialized sales dedicated to brasses are held by firms such as Thimbleby and Shoreland of Reading.

Terry Keegan, of The Oxleys, Clows Top, Kidderminster, Worcestershire, is a major supplier of harness decorations. He states that the main show ring requirements are brasses of good quality; their age matters less. While a few exhibitors have collections of superb antique brasses, which they use, in general these do not have much advantage in the show ring over bright, modern ones. Judges, in fact, may not know whether the brasses are old or new. 'Old' ones can be faked, and their detection is beyond the scope of the Turnout judge, who is likely to double as judge in the Decorated class. Brasses, in fact, figure little in Turnout classes in most areas. There will be a face piece, and perhaps a breastplate or martingale sporting four or more brasses, but generally few others.

Aside from decorative brasses, horsemen in the Midlands and south and south-west of England favour brass bells and terrets, the latter being rings, usually on the hames, through which the reins pass. 'It grieves me that the only bells obtainable do not have a nice ring', said Terry Keegan. 'For a good tone a bell must be turned rather than cast, but the cost of that operation simply prices itself out of the market.'

Right: *A brass nameplate adds to the effectiveness of brass decorations.*

Nothing adds to decorations better than winning rosettes.

Earmuffs are another form of decoration in demand in the Midlands and south-east, but seldom elsewhere. Their original function was to guard against flies. They are obtainable in bright colours, to very smart effect.

In Decorated classes, the decoration can sometimes extend to the driver: Kenneth Keir sports a sun hat with a brim that matches Royal's colours, a detail that cannot fail to impress judges. Since the judges in such classes are often ladies, it is by no means uncommon for gentleman exhibitors to attempt to impress them with various exhibitions of gallantry, and the success or otherwise of their endeavours is the stuff of showground legend.

Tradesman's Turnout Classes

These classes were originally introduced in the mid-nineteenth century and had, among their aims, the promotion of better care of working horses. They also brought a little glamour into the lives of the carters, whose normal lot was an unremitting round of long hours and low pay.

Ken Taylor fulfilled a longstanding ambition when he owned and drove a heavy horse turnout. His horse, Majestic, won a large number of Single Trade classes before 'retiring' to the Agricultural scene.

While these classes remain popular today, they normally contain turnouts drawn by both heavy breeds and light, vanner types. This mixture can pose problems for some exhibitors because, while the former usually lead, the pace they set may prove uncomfortably slow for the latter. Therefore, the choice to participate in such classes may depend upon one's individual horse and personal preferences.

Agricultural Classes

These classes are inherently more varied than the Trade classes: as against the near-perfection of every trade dray, the Agricultural, or Farmers' class will have a wide range of carts, waggons and – in many cases – wheeled implements as well. In respect of this last category, it is always imperative to study the schedule closely: while some shows accept certain farm implements in the Agricultural bracket, others confine these classes to carts and waggons. For guidance, the usual definition of an Agricultural Turnout is: 'Mare or gelding any breed,

The usual definition of an Agricultural Turnout is 'mare or gelding any breed, exhibited in gear with two- or four-wheeled vehicle built specifically for an agricultural purpose and still in an original state except for maintenance. No high seats or patent harness are permitted'. The late Mervyn Ramage and his Clydesdale, Blueprint, seen here to a Scotch corn cart.

Bob Claridge driving Jeff Briscoe's farm waggon in the East of England Agricultural class. The red-painted wooden racks, or gaumers, enabled more hay or sheaves of corn to be carried.

exhibited in gear with two- or four-wheeled vehicle built specifically for an agricultural purpose and still in an original state except for maintenance. No high seats or patent harness are permitted.' However, it is always wise to check the specific rules of the class you intend to enter.

At one time, the Agricultural class seemed to be the poor relation, but now it is attracting growing interest. From the exhibitors' viewpoint, it offers an outlet to those with an interest in farm working traditions and restoration skills, and a chance to participate with less outlay than the cost of running a large vehicle and a team. For the spectator – especially if implements are allowed – there is the chance to see a roller competing against a Scotch cart, a sugar beet plough or a hayrake – a more obvious diversity than a succession of drays, no matter how fine the

Mr Evans driving a dark grey Percheron to a waggon in an Agricultural Turnout class at Hertford.

latter. A good commentator, who will ascertain details about the age, history and use of the entries, can make such a class very interesting indeed.

Unlike Trade classes, walk is the only gait allowed. While drivers will not be wearing smart brewery livery, neat, tidy dress is still the order of the day. Similarly, while rope reins ('strings') are sometimes permitted, there should be nothing slapdash about the exhibit.

Participation in these classes may be especially attractive to those with an interest in the traditions of working the land with horses – particularly if restoration is one of their skills.

Town Parades

During the late nineteenth century, these parades had a valuable function, similar in essence to the Tradesman's Turnout classes. They were a positive means of improving the often miserable lot of the town horse, and a day in the limelight for his overworked and underpaid driver. As Keith Chivers wrote in *History with a Future*, 'For the first time,

Not so much a town parade – more a city spectacular: Whitbread Shires pulling the Lord Mayor of London's coach, a scene no motorcade can match.

people became aware of cruelty, carelessness or filth when they saw it'.

The outbreak of war in 1939 was the death knell of most of these parades. However, in 1985, Mike Millington, then chairman of the Southern Counties Heavy Horse Association, instigated the first of the modern parades in conjunction with the City of Portsmouth. Other cities have followed suit. These events do nothing but good. They encourage appearances from some who would not venture into a show ring, and promote the use of serviceable and correctly adjusted harness and the suitability of horse to vehicle. They also encourage enthusiasm for the heavy horse among the general public. In the north of England, the Walkington Hayride has done a magnificent job both in raising money for charities and in providing a ten-mile drive with halts where the horses and vehicles can be approached at close quarters.

Those wishing to participate in such parades will need to obtain details as and when they are promoted by local authorities. Since experienced personnel from the heavy horse world are normally involved on the organizing committee, specialist advice should be readily available.

Ridden heavy horses taking part in a much less formal modern town parade –Sue Everson and friends participating in the Blackpool Carnival.

Another role in pageantry for heavy horses: Shires in medieval costume outside Lichfield Cathedral – part of the medieval market day.

Ridden Classes

Traditionally, the riding of working horses was limited to their being ridden at walk to and from the fields. For this expedient, their drivers invariably rode in a side-saddle posture. One reason for this is that many heavy horses are too wide for most people to ride astride comfortably. The other reason is that, with the side-saddle posture, contact with a sweaty horse is made only through the backs of the rider's trousers, and not with the insides of the thighs as when astride. These factors were even more significant when the handlers were boys in short trousers.

It is a considerable step from this traditional practice to the Ridden classes, which are a new aspect of the heavy horse scene. The 'active' riding of heavy horses, and especially Shires, is a phenomenon that developed in the last decade of the twentieth century and is now increasing by leaps and bounds – sometimes literally, as low jumps are included in certain classes. This is particularly the case in Continental

A more formal style of side-saddle than that formerly adopted by farm boys – Emma Marsden riding one of the Pegg family's Austrey Shires at a Midlands Heavy Horse Association training day.

Europe, where a significant proportion of recently exported Shires are being trained as ride-and-drive animals.

The whole concept of riding heavy horses in this way is anathema to many traditionalists, who point out that the natural gait of the heavy breeds, excepting possibly the Percheron, is the walk. There is a concern that riding a heavy horse at the trot may be stressful upon the joints. Yet the trot is used in Turnout classes, and in the constant speed of Obstacle classes. One practising equine vet and horse owner assures me that there is no reason why a heavy horse should not trot under saddle. Given that assurance, the Ridden classes are another outlet for the heavy horse and all agree that any breed will only survive in the long term if there is a real need and a market for them.

The main potential drawback lies in the fact that the body of the average heavy horse is too wide for the average rider's comfort. It would be of great concern if judges of Ridden classes began to favour a smarter, more active animal rather than the true draught horse. We would then be at risk of animals being bred that lacked the bone and feather, temperament and strength that characterize the heavy breeds.

There are many examples of half-bred horses that have done very well in dressage and showjumping, and it is also the case that some heavy breed shows, including the National Shire Horse Show, now hold Ridden classes for half-breds. However, there is a distinct difference between cross breeding for a specific purpose and 'watering down' within a breed in an attempt to turn it into something it is not. To elaborate on this (while it might be anathema to heavy horse traditionalists), crossing a

Hayfield Poppy, ridden by Sue Everson of Hayfield Coloured Shires, winning the Ridden Heavy Horse (Non-pedigree) class at the Midlands Heavy Horse Association Winter Show.

good Shire with a good Thoroughbred in an attempt to produce a heavy hunter type might be a legitimate endeavour. However, inbreeding poor examples of Shires (i.e. those that lack bone and substance) in an attempt to produce a lighter riding animal would be a folly to be greatly deprecated. In this respect, we would do well to remember Arlin Wareing's dictum: 'Ride Shires by all means, but don't breed for riding'.

As mentioned, the National Shire Show is one show that now includes Ridden classes. The first of these is for pure-bred Shires and the second for half-breds. Both are judged on performance and obedience as a riding horse, rather than as In-hand classes. Plaiting of manes is permitted for safety, but for the same reason there must be no flags or standards. Competitors in either of these classes are eligible to enter the Ridden Dressage Test, details of which are obtainable from the organizers.

Since events of this nature are so much in their infancy, the best advice for exhibitors is to contact show secretaries well beforehand, to

Ann Croft's coloured Shire cross gelding, Samson, in the process of winning an Elementary level dressage competition. This horse was also placed at Medium level on the same day.

If you think that heavy horses can't jump, think again – and check your field boundaries. Riding instructor Tina Reaney with her Shire gelding, Macaulay.

ascertain just what Ridden classes are included, what they entail and what rules are applied. This last point may be especially pertinent: for example, in conventional dressage circles there are always rules relating to permitted tack and equipment. In classes for heavy horses, such rules may have various implications, for example, the horse may be used to working in winkers or blinkers, which may not be allowed, or to going in a driving bit, when the Ridden class requires a snaffle. As with entry to any competitive class, such points have to be considered by both organizers and competitors, if friction and disappointment are to be avoided.

Further to this, another contentious issue which organizers must address is whether ridden horses' legs should be shaven. The lighter type of pure-bred heavy horse with shaven legs may appear to be half-bred, and some have been known to appear in the half-bred class, whereas if the show society had checked the validity of every entry, there would have been no doubt that these horses should have been in the pedigree section.

One positive aspect of Ridden classes for part-breds is that they provide scope for an interesting array of colours that would not be acceptable in pedigree classes, yet which appeal greatly to many owners and the general public. Stallions registered as heavy vanners by the Coloured Horse and Pony Society can throw some marvellous stock. Similarly, dun, liver chestnut and palomino are not recognized Shire colours, nor are chestnut or sorrel recognized in Percherons, yet all such colours can look magnificent under saddle.

For anyone contemplating riding a heavy horse, the first consideration should be their own physique and welfare. Most pure-bred heavy horses are considerably wider than even the large riding breeds, and people with lower back or hip problems are putting themselves at risk if attempting to sit astride such animals. Short-legged riders may also struggle on the heavy breeds, and again risk strain to hips and thighs. On a more superficial note, simply mounting unaided may be problematical. A Clydesdale of 16.2 hands may not appear very tall in a breed class among its peers, but can be daunting when a rider has to mount. At home, a mounting block may provide the answer, but with the show ring in mind, the art of giving and receiving a leg up should also be practised, to avoid the possibility of a clumsy and embarrassing failure in public.

An issue that impacts upon the welfare of both horse and rider is the choice of saddle. As with any form of riding, it is important that the saddle is as comfortable as possible for the rider, but it is even more important that it fits, and is comfortable for, the horse. For most heavy horses, the average riding saddle is completely unsuitable. In the first place, it feels insecure to the rider, since it sits on top of the muscles at the withers, so the natural reaction is to over-tighten the girth, thereby exacerbating problems associated with incorrect fit. Even an extra wide saddle (in normal terms) may produce this effect to some extent. Problems associated with ill-fitting saddles include restricted shoulder movement, back trouble in various forms, stilted movement of the limbs and stumbling, and uncooperative behaviour induced by physical discomfort.

The Dunstable Riding Centre has three Percherons, all of which prove to be highly popular mounts.

With correct training, heavy horses can be ridden in various forms of tack. Here, Maureen and Greg Sikora are riding the Shires Rupert and Moss Edge Duchess in Western style, in a display organized by the Midlands Heavy Horse Association.

Since provision of a suitable saddle is crucial some owners will have saddles made to measure. However, the manufacturers 'Balance' claim to have developed a 'soft option' saddle designed specifically for the heavy horse, based on a model used successfully in long distance riding. In addition to other features, this has a small 'tree' in the front section that allows stirrups to be placed correctly for a balanced seat without putting pressure on the spine. It is also less bulky than a normal saddle and is an option that may be worthy of further investigation. Whatever route you take in procuring a saddle, it is wise to seek the advice of an expert, unless you really are one yourself.

So far as riding is concerned, if a heavy horse is to perform well under saddle, it will need training to the riding aids along similar lines to any other horse, subject to the particular requirements of the classes it is to enter. Since most heavy horses are quite willing and tractable by nature, this should present no particular problems to an experienced

Special training is required for a more traditional ridden role: that of the drum horse. Although this is usually a military role, Gareth Blythe's 18 hand Clydesdale, Jerusalem, is used in displays by a civilian organization, The Welsh Horse Yeomanry. Here, Sue Everson (mounted) is preparing horse and drums for the display.

rider. However, if you have decided to branch into riding from a background of driving, you will find proper instruction invaluable.

Further information and advice on showing heavy horses under saddle can be obtained from the breed societies that have ventured into this area, and enthusiasts may also wish to view the website www.heavy-horse-riding-club.co.uk.

CHAPTER 15

Obstacle Driving

Obstacle Driving is a test of driving skills. A vehicle with either one or two horses is driven between a series of pairs of cones, and the competitor who completes the course without knocking over any cones and within the time limit is the winner. Only if two or more vehicles have a clear round does the time factor apply.

Unlike many equestrian events, which have been pushed up from the grass roots, Obstacle Driving was introduced into the heavy horse world, as it were, from the top. It began when two experimental classes for heavy horses were included in the 1986 National Carriage Driving Championships, under the chairmanship of Joe Moore. The six competitors in both Single and Pair reached so high a standard, and spectator interest was so great, that the Royal Show offered similar classes in 1987. In the same year, the East of England Show also staged an open competition, and the Heavy Horse Obstacle Driving Club (H.H.O.D.) was formed.

Sparked on by its initial successes, and now with an official organizing body, Obstacle Driving was introduced into many more heavy horse shows, giving entrants in classes such as the Open Trade Turnout an additional opportunity to extend their range of activities and exhibit further their driving skills. Indeed the H.H.O.D. recommends that exhibitors in Team or Turnout classes should not have to pay a separate entry fee for the Obstacle Driving class. As well as being popular with exhibitors, these classes continue to attract large numbers of spectators, both lay public and dyed-in-the-wool heavy horse enthusiasts. For the former, it is an inherently exciting class, and one in which the onlooker can readily identify

John Peacock neatly between the cones with his pair of Shires at Portsmouth Heavy Horse Weekend.

with the driver, judging for himself whether an obstacle is likely to be negotiated successfully – perhaps more readily than might be the case with showjumping. For the latter, there is the additional appreciation of the finer points of skill, which echo the rapport between driver and horse established in the days when narrow alleys and doorways had to be negotiated as heavy horses worked for their living.

Rules For Obstacle Driving

Nowadays, virtually all Obstacle classes are run under the rules of the Heavy Horse Obstacle Driving Club, which can be contacted as follows:

Heavy Horse Obstacle Driving Club, Secretary Sally Moreton, c/o Campney Grange Farm, Bucknall, Woodhall Spa, Lincs. LN10 5DX, England. (Tel. 01526 388643)

Since the rules provide a useful insight to what is involved in these classes, they are reproduced here in full.

These rules cannot provide for every eventuality but should be interpreted with intelligence and in the spirit of the sport.
    Heavy Horse Obstacle Driving is designed to show the versatility of the Heavy Horse using traditional harness and vehicles.
1. Fault competition for singles and pairs of Heavy Horses. Horses must be at least 16.0hh and cobs and vanners are not allowed. Drivers must be members of the Heavy Horse Obstacle Driving Club and have valid third party insurance, which must be

declared when the subscription is paid. [At the time of writing, the subscription is £10.]

2. Horses must be 4 years old and over.

3. Vehicle must be a recognized four-wheeled heavy horse traditional-type vehicle – no customized vehicles are allowed.

   The distance between the markers will be 30 cm wider than the track width of a vehicle for singles, and 40 cm wider than the track width of a vehicle for pairs. The vehicle will be measured at ground level on the rear wheels and all vehicles will be check-measured as they leave the arena.

   Competitors are required to provide two clearly named measuring sticks for each class of a length equal to the track width of their vehicle plus the allowance as specified above for each class as appropriate. Any competitor unable to produce the required sticks to the Ring Steward will be unable to compete.

4. Harness must be in good condition, clean and safe, uniform in appearance and of an appropriate style.

5. Competitors and grooms must be properly dressed as for the show ring (i.e. shirt, tie, jacket, hat and apron) – jeans are not allowed – this includes for the inspection of the course and presentation of awards. They must be suitably dressed to drive or groom. Only the driver may inspect the course. Whips may be carried at the discretion of the driver. [The judge or umpire has the responsibility of deciding whether horses, harness, vehicle and the driver's and assistant's dress conform with acceptable show ring standards.]

6. A groom must accompany the driver and must remain on the vehicle at all times during the competition, and must not give directions to the driver. Grooms must be 14 years old or over. Drivers must remain seated – on a bale of straw or plank if necessary – at all times.

7. Any driver deliberately breaking pace out of a trot at any time whilst in the ring or during the competition or prize giving will be eliminated and forfeit his prize money. Excessive use of the whip will be penalized by elimination.

8. Exhibitors may make as many entries as they wish in each class, but each entry must have a different driver, horse(s) and vehicle.

No horse(s) may compete more than once in any one class, but a horse that competes as a single may also compete as a pair. No horse, driver or vehicle may go more than once in any class.

NB. In all cases it is the driver not the horse that qualifies but this does not nullify the above rule and, should more than one driver qualify the same horse, it will be necessary for all but one of the drivers concerned to find another horse to drive in the championship.

9. Horses must be named on declaration and any substitution must be notified to the judges.

10. Drivers may be substituted but the judge must be informed prior to the start of the competition. Only qualified drivers may compete in the Final.

11. Any persons receiving an invitation for a Heavy Horse Obstacle Driving competition must notify the Heavy Horse Obstacle Driving Club stating details of the competition(s) and any financial implications for the competitors.

Any preference by sponsors and/or organizers as far as competitors and/or horses are concerned should be looked upon favourably.

12. The course to consist of a minimum of 8 obstacles and a maximum of 12 obstacles depending on the size of the arena and should include one multiple obstacle in addition to a serpentine.

The distance between the markers in a serpentine, which must not consist of more than four posts in a straight line, must be at least 12 m.

Multiples must have a minimum track-width of 3 m for singles and 3.5 m for pairs and those in the form of a 'U' or 'L' must have a minimum track width of 5 m and may not consist of more than three lettered gates.

No water obstacles or bridges are allowed.

All obstacles must be clearly numbered in a way that ensures that the number of the next obstacle is clearly visible as soon as a competitor has passed through the preceding one. (It is recommended that the numbers be placed with the rounded end in.)

The starting line may not be more than 30 m or less than 15

m from the first obstacle. The finishing line may not be less than 20 m or more than 40 m from the last obstacle.

13. The maximum length allowed for the course is 500 m and the time allowed will be calculated from the speed of 150 m per minute. The time limit is twice the time allowed. Competitors will be timed by electronic timing or stop watch from the moment the nose of the horse(s) crosses the starting and finishing lines. [Shows are urged to use electronic timing and a public display clock if possible.]

14. The order of going will be drawn and competitors must enter the ring within one minute of the bell being rung and must start the competition within one minute of the bell being rung after entering the arena. Failure to comply will result in elimination.

15. Circling before an obstacle or stopping will be a disobedience. If a competitor has a disobedience and knocks over the obstacle without completing it correctly, the bell will be rung and the clock stopped for the obstacle to be rebuilt and 5 penalty points will be added. When the obstacle has been rebuilt the bell will be rung and the clock started and the competitor will retake the obstacle.

   If a competitor takes the wrong course but corrects himself before passing through another obstacle, he will not be penalized unless he crosses his original track. In the event of a competitor taking the wrong course and not rectifying his mistake, the Judge will ring the bell after he passes through another obstacle and the competitor will be eliminated.

   Penalties for disobediences are cumulative, whether they are incurred at the same obstacle or throughout the same course.

16. Faults will be penalized as follows:

   For exceeding the time allowed, every commenced period of one second, 0.5 penalty points.

   For knocking over or displacing an obstacle, or if the ball on top is dislodged (whether it is on one or both), 5 penalty points.

   For knocking over or displacing an element of a multiple obstacle, 5 penalty points.

   For knocking down any part of a multiple obstacle other than a cone, the bell will be rung and the clock stopped. The obstacle will be rebuilt and at the sound of the second bell, the clock will be restarted and the competitor will retake the whole of the obstacle. 5 penalty points will be added.

For knocking over or displacing an obstacle other than the one being driven, 5 penalty points will be added. If it is an obstacle in advance of the one being driven, the bell will be rung, the clock stopped and the obstacle rebuilt; 5 penalty points will be added. If it is an obstacle that has already been driven, the bell will not be rung, but 5 penalty points will be added.

For knocking over a start or finishing flag, 5 penalty points.

For first disobedience, 5 penalty points.

For second disobedience, 5 penalty points.

For third disobedience, Elimination.

For groom dismounting first time, 5 penalty points.

For groom dismounting second time, 10 penalty points.

For groom dismounting third time, Elimination.

For taking wrong course, Elimination.

For exceeding the time limit, Elimination.

For starting before the bell, Elimination.

For failing to pass through the start or finish flags, Elimination.

For knocking over the automatic timing equipment, Elimination.

For receiving outside assistance (including from groom), Elimination.

17. In the event of equality of faults, time will decide.
18. Competitors will drive the course as presented, i.e. if an obstacle has not been rebuilt from a previous round and competitor has started, he will not be penalized.
19. Any contravention of paragraphs 2–10 inclusive will be penalized with elimination or disqualification. Repeated contravention of these rules by a competitor will result in a referral to the Heavy Horse Obstacle Driving committee.

Unaffiliated events

Members of the Heavy Horse Obstacle Driving Club may not take part in unaffiliated shows, except minor shows. Panel Judges and Course Builders may not officiate in competitions at an event/show which is not affiliated except a minor show/event.

Minor events/shows are those at which the aggregate value of any prize and/or the proceeds of any sweepstake, whether in cash or kind given to a competitor or competitors in each and every competition at an event/show does not exceed £50.00. [Although this rule remains in existence, in practice virtually all shows affiliate to the H.H.O.D., since the club provides support, equipment and officials to assist with the running of the classes.]

Preparing and Competing

A glance through the rules above, perhaps coupled with some time as a spectator, will give you some idea of what is involved in Obstacle Driving, and perhaps fire your enthusiasm to compete. In that case, an approach to the Heavy Horse Obstacle Driving Club will doubtless provide further guidance. Hopefully, the following points will also be of value.

The very first aspect of preparation begins at home, and concerns familiarizing your horse, or horses, to cones. You must therefore acquire or have access to some cones – if you cannot source them elsewhere they may be obtained from firms supplying highways contractors. The key point about cones, apart from their value for practice, is that some horses shy at them. If they continue to do so after an initial introduction and a few practice rounds, it is seldom worth persevering, as they might let you down at a crucial time. There must be total trust between horses and driver, and that must be both ways. The most successful horses really enjoy Obstacle Driving: once out of the collecting ring and in the main arena, they become keyed up at the sound of the bell. However, if the driver is continually wondering whether the flying hooves of his Shires or Clydesdales are going to knock over the next cone, or if his charges will spook at it, they probably will. This is a sport that requires enthusiasm from both horse and driver.

So far as vehicles go, any type of vehicle may be used, provided it falls within the rules. Since the external wheel width of each vehicle is measured before the start, and cone widths altered accordingly, there should be no advantage of one type over another. One might think that a lighter vehicle and a lighter type of horse might have an advantage, but experience does not bear this out. Tom Brewster's big Clydesdale, Ambassador, topped 18 hands, yet he was a consistent Single Obstacle winner. Partnered with Baron, another big Clydesdale, he beat smaller and apparently sharper animals hauling lighter vehicles in pairs events. As with so many forms of equestrian competition, ability and rapport between man and horse are often more significant than factors such as size.

Regarding the day of the competition, first ensure that you are fully familiar with the rules in good time – don't try to learn them while you are yoking up. In order to be even remotely competitive, it is essential to walk the course thoroughly beforehand. Take note of the angles, for you can only hope for a clear round by taking each obstacle squarely, that is at right angles to the pair of cones. Try to plan the best way out of the box containing a 90 degree spin turn, which the course designer has cunningly devised for you. Consider how tightly you can weave in and out of the serpentine. Note the length of the final straight when the last obstacle has been cleared.

These considerations are very similar, in their way, to walking the course when showjumping and, as with showjumping against the clock, when your turn arrives the bell will sound, and then you pass through the start gate, at which point the clock is activated. At this point, set your horses off with a click or a word, not with a great whoosh like a B-movie stagecoach driver fleeing from the Indians. The key to a fast time, without penalties, is to make the course as short as possible and to flow round it without checking. If you dash on, then have to check, you really do waste time, and it is also hard on the horses. Also, if your urgings are too frantic, you risk the horses breaking into canter, or missing an obstacle, with the consequent penalties.

Judging

Judges for H.H.O.D. affiliated competitions must be either a List 1 or 2 British Horse Driving Trials Association Judge, or an Official Scurry or H.H.O.D. Judge. The judge should be accompanied by a timekeeper and there should also be another responsible person (other than the course builder) in the ring to indicate 'knock downs' to the judge.

In contrast to the role of a judge in showing classes, the Obstacle Judge is really an umpire, whose main job is to check that the rules are not broken. It is obvious, therefore, that the judge must be intimately familiar with the rules, hence the specific qualification requirements. The most contentious issue is likely to be whether a horse broke from a trot into a canter. Sometimes a horse does so for just a very few strides, and the judge must decide whether an offence has been committed and, if so, its severity.

An eye must also be kept on the groom. The groom is there for safety and must not speak to the driver, nor gesticulate.

Timing, if based on showjumping equipment, is done electronically and clearly, which should save the judge from any harassment. However, a stopwatch gives a double check, just in case there is a problem with the electronic equipment. At a small show, there may be no electronic aids, and a stopwatch may be the sole form of timing. In such cases, close co-operation is required between timekeeper and judge.

CHAPTER 16

Ploughing Matches

With summer's end, the show season draws to a close, and ribbons and polished harness are put away. There is a sense of relief for the busy exhibitor, coupled with a tinge of autumnal sadness for spectator and showman alike. This need not be so. The 'season of mists and ploughing matches' is upon us, heralding highly skilled workmanship and engendering deep passions and inquiries about where the next match is to be staged.

Nowadays, most routine farm ploughing is done by tractors, using multi-furrow ploughs. Even where horses are used, they are in teams of

The Ploughing Match, by Malcolm Coward. These matches are part of the crowded autumn rural calendar.

three, four or more, pulling a gang plough. This implement, which has more than one furrow and a seat (marking it out from other double furrow ploughs), may appear at a ploughing match for demonstration purposes, but it will not be used in a competitive role. So, if farm ploughing is no longer done with a pair, why stage pairs matches?

The reason is that straight and true ploughing is the peak of the horse handler's art. It is also a delight for the spectator. Even those who have never driven a straining pair and guided them onto the headland and into the next furrow can appreciate the pencilled lines of newly turned earth, and the exactness of each new furrow laid upon its fellow. To plough supremely well indicates mastery over every conceivable skill in the handling of a team of horses.

In *Care and Showing of the Heavy Horse* (Batsford 1981), I wrote:
It has been shown that the plough is the most useful invention in the history of man. Of course it has its detractors. Direct drilling, with the seed going straight into the unploughed stubble, is proving practical. Weed sprays have taken over one of the plough's functions. Yet ploughs have been discarded in the past, only for a return to be made to traditional methods of cultivation.

The last sentence has been proved correct, even more quickly than I anticipated. The expense of weed sprays and the continued emergence of certain weeds difficult to kill chemically have meant a return to the plough by several of the most forward-looking and practical farmers in the land. An effectively ploughed field gives a fresh start.

Ploughing matches began in the late eighteenth century. They probably originated when one ploughman challenged another to draw a straighter single furrow. They then developed into matches for preparing the land to grow the best crops with the fewest weeds. Small's horse plough, driven by one man, replaced the old 'twal owen' heavy wooden plough, which had required eight to twelve oxen and a total of four men and boys. At a ploughing match in Alloa in 1791, all forty ploughs were of Small's design. This in turn led to a demand for quicker-stepping, powerful horses, and Clydesdale breeding took off.

Aided by railways and a spreading banking system, major plough

Oxen, used for ploughing in centuries past, are rarely seen in Britain nowadays, but as these pictures show, coloured mules add variety to the ploughing scene.

manufacturers reached out to replace local makers. The firm of Ransomes kept teams of horses and ploughmen especially to compete in matches and thus show off their products in the most practical way.

The modern ploughing match is a popular spectator sport. Organizers of the many excellent autumn country fairs realize that horse ploughing is the number one crowd-puller. In consequence, they offer appearance money, which enables the heavy horse fraternity to travel from match to match, sometimes three or four in a week, to display their skills. Hundreds of colour films and vast yardages of videotape are used to capture the scene, and repeat it on winter evenings.

Organization and Judging Criteria

Match ploughing in Britain is organized nowadays through the Society of Ploughmen, Quarry Farm, Loversall, Doncaster, South Yorkshire, DN11 9DH (Tel. 01302 852469, Website www.ploughmen.co.uk), who will send a list of all British fixtures on request.

The Society's aims are:

To promote and encourage the art, skill and science of ploughing the land.

To promote an annual British Ploughing Contest.

To cooperate with similar organizations in other countries in organizing World Championship Ploughing Competitions.

To provide facilities whereby local winners can compete in National and World Championships, thus fostering and maintaining a high standard of ploughmanship.

To provide facilities for demonstrations, works and trade displays at the British National Ploughing Contest.

The Society of Ploughmen's score sheet indicates what is required in assessing the standard of work. The total of 220 points allocates a maximum of 40 for the Start, which consists of the first eight furrows. These, sometimes termed the 'crown', must be uniform, level and straight. The Finish consists of the last eight furrows, which must be uniform, shallow and straight, and also attracts a maximum of 40 points.

Uniformity overall commands 40 points. Furrows must be even and straight throughout, with no sign of those unsightly 'pig troughs' which indicate that the plough had lost depth. The 'Ins and Outs' are the places where the plough point breaks the headland mark, which is scratched by a non-competitor before the match begins. Few things spoil neat ploughing more than an untidy and irregular headland, with some furrows projecting on to the headland, and others falling short. 'Neat and accurate' is the official description, for which a maximum of 20 points may be awarded.

The remaining 80 points relate to the practical use of the ploughing as a seedbed preparation. The seedbed is judged by the efficiency of weed control and by the use of 'skimmers', or skim coulters, to bury the trash. These miniature plough bodies skim a little furrow only an inch (2.5 cm) or so deep to turn grass or stubble neatly into the path of the advancing mouldboard. If set too shallow they are ineffective: if too deep they add enormously to the draught and the horses' task. For the seedbed itself, 40 points maximum are allowed. Firmness attracts 40 points. Each new furrow must be laid firmly against its neighbour, with no unsightly gaps into which seed might trickle and be lost. It should not bear hoofprints in which water might stand, causing faulty germination.

So far as assessing the fine detail of the work is concerned, Henry Stephens' *Book of the Farm*, revised by James Macdonald in 1891, analyses good ploughing in a way that cannot be bettered more than a century later:

Characteristics of correct ploughing
The furrow-slices should be quite straight: for a ploughman that cannot hold a straight furrow is unworthy of the name.
They should be quite parallel as well as straight, which shows they are of uniform thickness: thick and thin slices lying upon another present irregularly parallel and horizontal lines.
They should be of the same height, which shows they have been cut of the same breadth: slices of different breadths, laid together at whatever angle, present unequal vertical lines.
They should present to the eye a similar form of crest and equal surface: where one furrow slice exhibits a narrower surface than it should have, it has been covered with a broader slice than it should

be. They should have their back and face parallel: to discover this requires minute examination.

They should lie easily upon each other, not pressed hard together.

The newly ploughed ground should be equally firm under the foot at all places. Slices in a more upright position than they should be feel hard and unsteady, and allow seed corn to fall between them.

When too flat, they yield considerably to the pressure of the foot: and they cover each other too much, affording insufficient mould for the seed.

They should lie over at the same angle, presenting crests in the best possible position for the action of the harrows.

Crowns of ridges formed by the meeting of opposite furrow slices should neither be elevated nor depressed with regard to the rest of the furrows in the ridge: although ploughmen often commit the error of raising the crowns too high into a crest, the fault being easily committed by not giving the first furrow slices sufficient room to meet, thereby pressing them against each other.

The last furrow-slice should be uniform with those of the rest of the ridge: ploughmen are very apt to miscalculate the width of the slices near the edges of the ridges. If the space between the last furrows is too wide, the open furrow must be made too deep to fill all the space: if too narrow, there is not sufficient mould to make the open furrow of the proper size.

When the last furrows of adjoining ridges are not ploughed alike, one side of the open furrow will have less mould than the other.

A horseman who has not his horses under strict command cannot be a good hand. A regular pace is the best for men, horses and work.

Henry Stephens continues:

> The judges ought to be present all the time of the competition, when they could leisurely, calmly and minutely ascertain the position and depth of the furrow-slices, and mature their thoughts on points, which might modify first impressions. Inspection of the finished surface cannot furnish information whether the land has in all respects been correctly ploughed, which can only be obtained by comparing the soles of the furrows

while the land is being ploughed. There is also something to be gained in observing the manner in which the ploughman guides his horses in making the best work in the shortest time.

Participation in Ploughing Matches

As with any show or competition, entries to ploughing matches must be made in time to comply with local rules. Although dress standards for ploughing are different from those of the in-hand exhibitor or turnout groom, tidiness helps. No livestock should be let down through their attendant's sloppy dressing, and some ploughing matches have categories for best-dressed or neatest ploughman! Generally, clean, strong boots are recommended footwear, although it is a fact that some top competitors plough in wellingtons. Similarly, although there is nothing to match the traditional breeches and leggings, jeans, flannels and overalls are acceptable.

Naturally, so far as the horse's turnout is concerned, brasses and harness must be properly cleaned and prepared. The Society of Ploughmen can give advice on the acquisition of appropriate match ploughing equipment, and on acquiring the skills to put it to good use.

Assistants

Rules regarding assistants vary between associations. These must be ascertained and adhered to. Some societies allow an assistant for setting the ridge and taking up the last furrows. Others allow help throughout, mainly from the safety angle. Many of today's ploughing teams are underworked compared with their predecessors on the land, who plodded through an eight- or ten-hour day, week after week. Any excitability caused by underwork can be compounded by the crowds surrounding the horses, by the whirr of cine-cameras and, worst of all, by flash bulbs.

However, too many helpers undoubtedly mar a match. They are a source of scorn among former horsemen, and provide ammunition for any who decry the working horse as an economic unit. The situation is by far the worst in Scotland, where half a dozen men may be seen patting and firming each newly turned furrow, and generally making a mockery of proceedings. The horses themselves may be hidden from view by these gangs of helpers, to the detriment of spectators, photographers and reporters alike. The fault lies more often in the lax way the rules are 'enforced' rather than in the rules themselves.

The Start

A good Start is essential in match ploughing. Standards are such that a mistake with the opening 'cop' or ridge can never be retrieved sufficiently to give the competitor a chance. The ploughman's starting point is indicated by a peg at either end of where his ridge is to be. He then sets his own white pegs along the line of the ridge. These pegs are invaluable; it is surprising what help a shiny white peg is on a dull day, compared with any old bit of stick.

The ploughman sets his plough up squarely to his starting mark. He may then couple his horses slightly wider, the better to see his line of pegs between them. But he should only be able to see one peg; the rest should be in a dead straight line. If helpers are allowed for the Start, two are better than one, walking on the outsides of the horses, leaving a clear view between them. A single helper might obstruct the ploughman's view if he walked between the horses.

Champion ploughman Jim Elliott takes up a furrow with his two Clydesdales, one of which was noted for an ability to 'creep' up a furrow like a tractor in low gear. One assistant is usually allowed in the final stages, although rules vary depending on the organizing body.

The first furrow is a 'scratch' or 'rippling' furrow. On its completion another similarly shallow furrow is turned towards it, usually 22 to 24 inches (55–60 cm) from it and running exactly parallel. The object is to leave a tidy mark from which the ridge proper can be set. These first true furrows are termed 'heavy', contrasting with the light scratch furrows. The 'heavy' furrows are not quite as deep as those ploughed later when leaving the ridge, the object being a fairly flat crown. They are made by tilting the plough to the left, with the wing of the point, or share, almost out of the ground. They follow the 'ripple' furrows, and are dropped on to them. In this way they are given a slight angle, rather than being flat.

Plough Attachments

Two items of equipment used by match ploughmen, but seldom used in ordinary work, are the boat and the press wheel. Neither is fitted for the first two furrows. The next time round, the boat may be attached. This is a rectangular steel piece, the function of which is to smooth the furrows. It is not universally employed, for in uneven or stony conditions it does not work, and it may even jump out of the furrow and make things worse than if it were absent.

The press wheel seals loose soil dropping from the furrow top. It may be invaluable on crumbly loam, giving that very desirable clean finish, but on clay where there are no crumbs to smooth, it is seldom used. Both attachments increase the draught (depth), making the horses work harder and therefore more liable to swing out of line. Neither item is used for 'scouring out' or taking up the last furrows. The Society of Ploughmen Rules and Regulations state: 'Boats, presses and other attachments may be used in oat seed furrow ploughing only'.

Leaving the Ridge

The Rules also state 'Horse ploughing – Start to consist of eight furrows'. This involves 'gathering' four times round the ridge, turning right-handed at each end and ploughing up and down on either side of the central ridge. The competitor then starts to 'cast' or 'throw out'. He turns his team left-handed, going down the last furrow ploughed by his neighbour. To avoid penalties for his neighbour's work he is allowed two furrows in which to counter any irregularities.

If these irregularities can be got rid of at such an early stage, the rest of the work becomes simpler. Accurate measurements are essential. If adjustments must be made, the sooner these are done the better.

'The art of ploughing is in setting your plough': that is a well-proven countryman's saying. The frequent adjustments made by the match ploughman look very involved to the unpractised spectator, but are basically simple once the plough's action is understood.

The coulter makes a vertical cut to the required depth. Immediately below it is the share, making a horizontal cut to the required depth. It blends into the mouldboard which is curved to turn the slice cut by coulter and share.

A match plough mouldboard or breast is at least 4 ft 6in (137 cm) long; a shorter length would break up the soil too much. The furrow so formed is always turned to the right – except by some modern individuals jumping on the heavy horse bandwagon without either knowledge or capacity to observe!

The furrow size is determined by the plough wheels. The smaller wheel, which runs on the unploughed ground, is termed the 'land' wheel; the larger one running against the furrow wall is termed the 'furrow' wheel. By adjusting these vertically, the ploughing depth is altered. The furrow width is altered by adjusting the furrow wheel standard horizontally on its slide.

At the front of the plough is the hake, the notches of which give a vertical variation. It is altered if the plough point is digging in too deep or rising out of the ground. It slides along the tee head, its place fixed by a pin, and it is moved if the plough is not following the horses in a straight line. The hake is connected to the baulk or cobbletree by a chain, which in match ploughing is longer than for normal work, to allow more play and more time for corrections to be made.

On suitable soil a properly set plough will keep to its work without a hand on the stilts: in fact, there are stories of men hedging at either side of a field being ploughed, turning the team at the ends and setting them off again until they reached the other hedger of their own accord.

Adjustments

The match ploughman's golden rule is to make only one alteration at a time. If that doesn't work, return the setting to its former place and try

The greys in this Malcolm Coward painting are decked out in their best for the ploughing match. Extra classes for Best Harness or Best Decorated are usually staged after the ploughing.

A pair of Clydesdales decked out for a Best Decorated class at a ploughing match.

another adjustment. When making an adjustment against a previous faulty furrow, the full effect of the correction does not come into play until the second time round. A furrow that is too deep, too shallow, or crooked, affects it neighbour. One leading ploughman said that a match competitor is like a joiner: everything he does depends on accurate measurements.

Adjustments are affected by a number of factors. The height of the horses, the amount of wear on the plough point, the type of soil and the pitch of the plough are but a few factors that come into play.

The Finish

The one strict rule is that the finishing furrow and the scouring-out furrow *must* be turned towards the cop or crown of your plot. Failure to comply can result in disqualification.

As people are becoming increasingly interested in doing things with their horses in addition to showing them in-hand, ploughing matches are attracting more and more teams, and are often rounded off with a Best Decorated class. There is a comradeship under the autumn skies which draws ploughmen together and, although competition is intense, it is less cut-throat than at some summer show classes. The 'season of mists and ploughing matches' deserves its own poet to capture those enjoyable days.

THEIR MASTER'S CUE

White nostrils, warm and graced with quiv'ring hair,
The chink of chains across October's air,
Soft creak of leather, clank of iron shoe;
They pull again, upon their master's cue.

High lifted steps which map a stubbled gauge
As silver ploughshare turns its earthen page,
And carves a bed in which the seed may hide
On one small portion of this planet's side.

What pow'r condensed between the gleaming hames,
Such friends are they inside those gentle frames;
Each blazed and blinkered face with kindness spanned,
No countenance more loved upon this land.

Claudia Steele

CHAPTER 17

Photography and Reporting

This chapter offers hints and observations, based on long experience, for those who wish (in either an amateur or professional capacity) to take good quality photographs of heavy horses, and for those who wish to try their hand at reporting for their local Press.

The first important consideration, for both photographers and reporters, is that they will find themselves far more welcome if they are neither obtrusive not intrusive in their manner. A starting point is appropriate dress. No worthwhile owner or groom would let their horse down by being untidy, and judges and stewards have a duty to look smart. Others on the fringe of the event, including reporters and photographers, should dress in keeping with the atmosphere, with reasonable neatness and acceptable attire. Jeans and trainers are out of place when every hair on a Shire gleams and vehicle paintwork shines. Vivid clothes that might scare or distract the animals are definitely out.

In general, reporters and photographers should be as unobtrusive as possible, and must never be in the way of judges and stewards. It is a cardinal sin for a photographer to poke a glinting camera lens around the end of a fence or other cover just as a team is approaching at a spanking trot. But with common sense, the photographer, whether amateur or professional, has a useful part to play in spreading the heavy horse gospel.

Photography

Heavy horses make marvellous subjects for photographs but, as with all photography, attention to detail makes a vast difference to the end result. If you wish to photograph your own entry, or to take a number of shots to recall a pleasant summer day during long winter evenings, try to make as professional a job as possible.

For our purposes, we will assume that the camera is already set up, with appropriate film, speed, and exposure. For stationary shots, the slower the film speed, the better the quality. Never use a wide-angle lens for close-ups. Distance is then judged for each individual shot.

The first essential is to ensure an appropriate background. To achieve this, your position and that of the subject must be right. Check that there is no telegraph pole or flagstaff apparently growing out of the horse's back. See that there are no unwanted horses in the picture (although if you are taking a line-up, that of course is a different matter altogether.) This may also be a good point at which to remind the photographer not to take a stallion while it is exhibiting a 'fifth leg', in other words, whilst aroused by some nearby female and demonstrating its prowess to the world. A Shetland pony mare in season can bring this about just as readily as one of the stallion's own breed, so do watch out.

Judges Messrs Malson Phillips and N. J. Wright approach Lou Harrison's Acle Mystery, seen under the arched neck of Richard Bedford's Hartcliff Spice Girl.

The sun, if there is any, should preferably be behind you, or slightly to one side, but not straight ahead. 'Photographer's shadow' is a common fault among amateurs, who become so absorbed by seeking a good position and background that they fail to look at the ground in front of them.

When your subject is in position

This impressive photograph from times past depicts Jubilee – a massive and well-marked champion Shire gelding.

A first-class stance. Graham Ward with Essex winner Decoy May Queen, captured on film by Roy Fox.

relative to the background, it may not cooperate. If possible, ask the groom to turn the horse round into the best position, and try to fill the viewfinder with a nice clean shot.

For the set piece, you should stand more or less square to the horse. Basically, all four legs should be evident, but not necessarily with a gap showing between the off and near fore, and the off and near hind. Make sure that one leg is not resting. With the Clydesdale and Shire, the amount of feather is such that positioning may be slightly different from the clean-legged breeds. In all cases, the head should be held up, with the ears pricked.

Robert Bakewell was a pioneer improver of the sluggish, massive 'Fen Blacks' of two centuries ago. In 1770 he wrote: 'A horse [stallion] should have his fore end so formed that his ears when he is shown to advantage be as nearly as maybe over his forefeet.' This description of the ideal stallion stance has never been bettered, and it applies to geldings also. Mares are a different proposition. Their long, graceful necks are in proportion to their longer bodies, designed for foal carrying, so they will almost inevitably have their heads somewhat further forward than stallions. However, they should still stand up well, alert and with ears pricked. In addition to the pictures here of Jubilee and Decoy May Queen, other photographs in Chapters 1 and 13 of horses in-hand provide some exemplary examples of correct stance. Good photographers often capture the correct moment and pose, but it must be said that there are some modern artists jumping on the heavy horse bandwagon who have no idea about stance.

If you are an amateur photographer with a limited knowledge of equine subjects, there is no harm in taking a shot of an animal that someone else has set up, but it is courteous to ask first, and essential not to interfere with the professional's shot. Much can be learnt by studying outstanding photographs in equestrian books or magazines, and it is notable that the best early exponents of the photographer's art have seldom been eclipsed. Although some more recent stud book photographs have been of questionable standard, those in specialist horse magazines are usually good.

Some photographers dislike including the groom, but if he is included, his hand must always be on the side away from the camera. It is far better to have the groom stand holding a short length of halter shank rather than the bridle itself, or it may appear that his hand comes out of the horse's face. Historians of the future may appreciate the groom in the photo; it has often proved possible to date old photographs of the Edwardian period, for example, by studying the groom's attire. Even today, photographs are by no means always captioned, and the groom's presence aids identification. An example of this can be seen in the photograph of the Clydesdale stallion Flashwood, on page 35; even if the foaling date were absent, an estimate of the era could be made by looking at the groom who, incidentally, is doing a fine job of showing off his charge.

For photographs of presentations, try to have the owner and presenter looking towards you, and not obscuring the horse's head. Again, the horse's ears should be pricked, and an accomplice standing out of shot making a strange noise or waving a white handkerchief is invaluable. Be ready for the moment, since any sensible horse tires of having its attention attracted to no obvious purpose.

For photographing moving objects a different technique is needed. Heavy horses may be photographed giving their show to the judge. They will first walk and then trot. The general rule is never to take a trotting horse head on – unless it forms part of a particularly imaginary shot, such as the adjacent picture by Adrian Legge. With automatic focus or zoom lens it may be possible to take two shots of the same showing, one when the horse is three-quarters on, and the other when it has just passed. In either case the groom should be on the far side. Some photographers focus on a spot on the ground that they know the horse will pass in order to gauge distance. Wait for the leg nearest you to lead.

Although the national and provincial Press may often use 'pretty-pretty' examples of showing photographs which are unsatisfactory to the real enthusiast, lots of fun can be had taking odd snaps of stable scenes, harnessing, and so on. In fact, a succession of perfectly set-up animals can become boring after a time; there is much to be said for taking shots of horses as they clatter up ramps, or enjoy a nosebag at a ploughing match. Turnouts offer interesting close-ups of harness, chains and such items as buckets and ropes. In the stables, a row of heads looking over doors makes an appealing shot, especially if all are attracted by the same sight or sound.

The amateur photographer may not have professional Adrian Legge's high quality camera, but is presented with the same scenes. This imaginative shot captures the show scene; you can almost hear the judges conferring.

Photography in the field is yet another aspect. This is better done by two people, one of whom should try to position the horses and make them alert. Never forget that a stallion can be a dangerous animal, and that you may be concentrating so much on your work that you do not appreciate your mutual proximity. Although this applies more to some light horse breeds, be wary at all times. Most equine photographers have horror stories of untoward happenings.

Heavy breed foals make wonderful subjects. An ideal shot is difficult to accomplish, but the rewards are great. Foals are inquisitive creatures, and if you sit down on the ground they may approach to see what this strange being is. A mare suckling a foal is fairly easy to take, but when the pair are running loose the foal always tends to retreat to the far

A picture that captures the accord between working man and horse. In the foreground Thwaites Brewery's Shire, Dray King, refreshes himself after work around Blackburn, aided and abetted by a youthful Patrick Flood.

All the drivers' eyes are on the horse completing its show, but John Owen's bay Shire is more interested in the camera.

Working Shires celebrate being let out on holiday – perhaps a moment for the photographer to remain as alert as his subjects.

side, that is with its dam between it and the photographer. Therefore, don't neglect any chance that occurs.

Again, as when taking set pieces, always check backgrounds, remembering that a row of trees will cause the outline of a black horse to be lost, even if the plantation is a hundred yards away. Have the outline against the sky if possible. Incidentally, when photographing black horses, be advised to take several shots with different aperture readings. A couple of other tips: first, if there is a slope, always photograph any stock with their heads slightly uphill, never down. This usually applies more when out in a field, since most showgrounds are level – although this is not always the case at smaller shows. Second, for group photographs, don't, as a rule, have the horses dead in line abreast, but rather each one half a stride in front of its neighbour. However, in situations where horses are inevitably abreast, it is quite possible, by taking a three-quarter angle, to include three or four big horses in an interesting shot.

Finally, for all photographs of any significance, details of horse, event, date and owner – and perhaps any placing – should be typed or written on an adhesive label and affixed to the back of the print as soon as it is enlarged. If not done there and then, this may well be overlooked. On no account write on the back of the photograph with a ballpoint pen, which will show through. A soft pencil is acceptable, though inferior to a label.

Reporting on the Show

Newspapers and magazines are frequently on the lookout for accurate reports of heavy horse events. For anyone fancying their hand at writing, here is an ideal opening.

The twin essentials are accuracy and timeliness. Mistakes cause friction, and a time- and space-consuming apology in the next issue. There is seldom an excuse for mistakes, although at some smaller shows the veracity and completeness of cataloguing leaves much to be desired.

All publications work to a deadline, and the reporter must know when that is. It is no use preparing a brilliant report for an evening paper, and delivering it two hours late. There is always pressure on space, so the earlier the copy is delivered, whether by post, fax, phone or e-mail, the more chance it has of appearing.

At the show there may be a results board, otherwise it may be necessary to approach the awards secretary direct. At shows where entries are taken on the field there will be no detailed catalogue, and then the reporter really has to work.

Even where accurate catalogues are compiled, they tend to use the horse's name and the owner's name and initial. Today's Press demands Christian names, so these must be sought and memorized. People are rightly very touchy about the correct spelling of their names, so the reporter must be acutely aware of this fact and double-check any name that may have alternative forms. Surnames such as Gardner/Gardener/Gardiner pose a trap for the unwary scribe, as do the variants of forenames such as Derek, Alan, Sydney, Debbie, and so on. For the regular reporter, it pays to compile a notebook of the correct variations for future reference. It is also worth remembering that owners consider their horses' names at least as important as their own!

This talk of names brings to mind the possibility of other forms of confusion. One year, at the East of England showground, I was admiring William Tudor Jones's champion Shire mare, Caerberllan Gold Gift, when the lady Town Crier of Peterborough asked me (as I thought): 'Have you seen the mare?'

'Yes' – indicating Gold Gift – 'that's her, going out of the ring.'

'No', she replied, 'I meant the Mayor of Peterborough!'

If a report as well as the actual results is required, this is likely to consist of interviews with judge or winners, or both. Their observations must be put down accurately. With quoted matter, their exact words must be used. You are recording what the judge or winner said about the winning animal, not what you think ought to have or might have been said.

William Tudor Jones at the East of England showground with his champion Shire mare, Caerberllan Gold Gift, the winner of many awards but never elected to mayoral office! (See text.)

If the words are faithfully and accurately reported, you will gradually acquire a reputation for reliability, and officials and exhibitors will talk to you. If you try to embroider the story, news of your efforts will spread like wildfire around the show circuit, people will refuse you an interview, and the editor will cease to employ you.

It is a matter of courtesy that, during the final stages of preparation, exhibitors should be left alone. A friendly word is in order, but generally owners and grooms have their thoughts full of the coming event, and need to check their preparations. After the judging, the atmosphere is altogether more relaxed.

Many a good feature story has originated from contacts made at the show. That is the next stage for the heavy horse reporter, and a worthwhile aspect of the ever-fascinating heavy horse scene.

In their different ways, good photography and good reporting both serve to convey the atmosphere of the heavy horse scene.

Conclusion

In the new millennium, we naturally consider the heavy horse's future in the show ring. Fifty years ago it looked bleak. There was a bevy of old hands who stuck to their charges through thick and thin, but their numbers diminished year by year, with few replacements. We have to accept that those whose whole working lives were spent with the big horses are now very scarce. Prior to the Second World War no one was 'taught' about heavy horses. Youngsters simply imbibed the knowledge as part of everyday life, and learnt safety and driving techniques through the gradual process of taking more and more responsibility each time they went out with an expert.

Although those days are now gone, recent years have seen a resurgence of interest in the heavy horse, and in the traditional skills associated with it. Today, a number of well-organized training classes and a wide range of literature have helped to keep the ball rolling. Furthermore, no longer is the heavy horse world a male preserve. Female grooms and drivers have earned their place in the summer scene. They have taken over the reins and proved their worth in equal competition.

Men and women from many walks of life now look to horses as a safety valve from the daily pressures of running a business or a profession. Perhaps surprisingly, those in the motor trade can be found among them – and a number of racing motorcyclists have turned to heavy horses when they thought they had risked their necks quite often enough! It seems that close contact with animals is a real antidote to dealing with people and machines.

Others may have slipped into the heavy horse world on a more casual basis: perhaps they simply had some grazing and a basic affinity for the large breeds, or perhaps they were offered one to keep their children's pony company. Whatever the reason, the next step was to take their charge to the local show, even if this was initially just for a day out and to support the event. Of course, once returning with a rosette, children and parents alike became hooked, and the lure of showing had begun to exert its influence on their lives. As George Bernard Shaw remarked: 'Go anywhere in England where there are natural, wholesome, contented and really nice English people; and what do you find? That the stables are the real centre of the household'.

It is a fact that many people prefer to spend their money on a Shire or a Percheron rather than holiday abroad. For them, the constant bustle, the meeting with friends old and new and the change of scenery engendered by the show ring suffice. To stay overnight with one's own stock adds a fresh dimension; the showground takes on a different aspect

Harry Ranson, former head horse keeper of Young's Brewery, pictured on the day of his retirement, with some of his much-loved Shires.

once the crowds have gone home and the stock people congregate and celebrate. As horseman and Suffolk sheep breeder Tom Midgley said, at the age of eighty-nine: 'Showing is about going all out to win with guns blazing, and then having a drink afterwards'.

Harness Makers' Directory

Reproduced by kind permission of *Heavy Horse World* Magazine

EAST ANGLIA

BROWN, N.
14 Chelmer Road, Witham, Essex CM8 2EY
01376 518663

HALFORD SADDLERY
5A Reform Street, Crowland, Peterborough
PE6 OAJ
01733 211018

HUNT, C. P.
Malthouse, Scottow, Norwich NR10 5DB
01692 538687

JACKSON, Rebecca
Work Horse Sundries, Beaumont Farm,
2 Main Street, Wardy Hill, Ely, Cambs.
CB6 2DF
01353 778713

MURRAY, Geo.
Unit 9, Vulcan House, Vulcan Road North,
Norwich NR6 6AQ
01603 487102

WOODBRIDGE, Jane
13 Main Street, Wadenhoe, Peterborough
PE8 5SX
07813 072385

MIDLANDS AND WALES

CLIMPSON, Jerry
The Croft, 12 Water Lane, Middleton-by-
Wirksworth, Derbyshire DE4 4LX
01332 344106

COLEMAN, Robin   Saddlers Cottage, Chase Lane, Kenilworth
CV8 1PR
01926 512368

DAVIS, Terry   5 Leamoor Common, Winstanstow,
Craven Arms, Salop. SY7 8DN
01694 781206

HUSKISSON, J. C. & SON   211–219 Pleck Road, Walsall,
West Midlands
01922 611887

KINGTON, J.   The Larches, Four Oaks, Newent, Glos.
GL18 1LU
01531 890445

PARKER, N.   Unit 3, Chapel Farm, Hanshope Road,
Hartwell, Northampton NN7 2EU
01908 511594

NORTHERN ENGLAND

COATES, Peter   Kelbank, Lee Lane, Cottingley, Bingley,
West Yorkshire BD16 1UF
01274 499040

HOUGHTON & SONS   11–13 Bolton Road, Darwen, Lancs.
01254 702282

JOBSON, R. L.   Bondgate Within, Alnwick,
Northumberland
01665 602135

LAMB, Keith   "L for Leather" 61B Liverpool Road, Irlam,
Manchester
01607 878300

MADDISON & SON   Middle Ludhill Farm, Farnley Tyas,
Huddersfield HD4 6UP
01484 661026

NAYLOR, Derrick   Naylors Saddlery & Sportswear Ltd,
470–472 Edenfield Road, Rochdale, Lancs.
01706 631909

ROBINSON & CO   Norton Road, Malton, Yorks.
YO17 9RU
01653 697442

TAYLOR, Chris   "Saddler's Den", 60 Nunwood Avenue,
                        Southport PR9 7EQ
                        01704 228370

NORTHERN IRELAND

HUNTER, S.   Annahilt Saddlery, 19 Ballykeel Road,
                        Hillsborough, Co. Down
                        02892 638999

WALLS, Robert   81 Gloverstown Road, Duneane, Toome
                        Bridge, Co. Antrim BT41 3RB
                        02879 650319

SCOTLAND

BURDEN, John   IV Horse
                        01888 544261

MICHIE, Eric   18 Badenoch Drive, Huntly AB54 5HW
                        01466 793205

SOUTHERN ENGLAND

BLACKBURN, E.   10 The Crescent, Woldingham, Caterham,
                        Surrey CR3 7DB
                        01883 652255

BUTTONS SADDLERY   44 Guildford, West End, Woking
                        GU24 9PW
                        01276 857771

DEAN, Jeff   Kings Parade, 154 Findon Road, Worthing,
                        West Sussex BN14 0EL
                        01903 264066

DIXON CORY LTD   256A St Margarets Bank, High Street,
                        Rochester, Kent ME1 1HY
                        01634 401983

EVANS, G. R.   Hill Grove, Whipsnade, Luton, Beds.
                        LU6 2LN
                        01582 873925

FARMER, M. J. P.   The Workshop, Battle Farm, Five Oak Lane,
                        Staplehurst, Tonbridge, Kent TN12 0HE
                        01580 892560

HOWITT, R. J.	Red Rae Saddlery, 25 Amwell End, Ware, Herts. 01920 463170
LEARY, Craig	31 Greenwich, Fonthill Gifford, Tisbury, Salisbury, Wilts. SP3 6QL 01747 820674
NIGHTINGALE, Luke	126 Hazlebank Cottages, The Street, Ewhurst, Surrey GU6 7RW 01483 277646
RUMBLE, Lester	1 Freeman Close, Northolt, Middlesex UB5 5TH 020 8841 4232
SLADE, Susan	The Saddlers Workshop, Iron Hill, Hollycombe, Liphook, Hants. GU30 7LP 01428 723085
WETTERN, Juliette	Woodlands View, Old Lane Gardens, Cobham, Surrey KT11 1NN 01483 282310
WHITE, F.	New Scotland Farm, Staple Lane, Shere, Surrey GU5 9TE 01483 222501
ZILCO EUROPE LTD (TEDMAN HARNESS)	PO Box 385, Beckley, Oxford OX3 9DW 01865 351128

SOUTH WEST ENGLAND

BLISDALE HARNESS	Bolventor, Liskeard, Cornwall PL14 6SD 01579 320593
GEACH, Robert	Glebe Farm, Churchtown, Redruth, Cornwall 01209 215726
HIGHET, Jasper	Dolphin Street, Colyton, Devon EX13 6LU 01297 553317
MCDONALD, J.	Clayford, Andrews Hill, Dulverton, Somerset TA22 9RH 01398 324040

RENNY, J.   Roseland Harness, Springfield, Umberleigh,
                             Devon EX37 9AE
                             01769 540371

LOGGING HARNESS DISTRIBUTORS

BRAUNTON, M. J.   Tyn-y-Coed, Eglwysbach, Colwyn Bay,
                             Conwy, LL28 5SG
                             01492 650420

MUSGROVE, Andy   Brockfarm Cottages, Brickworth Down,
                             Whiteparish, Wilts. SP5 2QD
                             01794 884828

Heavy Breed Societies

American Belgian PO Box 335, Wabash IN 46992, USA. Tel: (001) 260 563 3205; Website www.belgiancorp.com.

Ardennes Horse Society of Great Britain Secretary Jo Hewitt, White Ash Farm, Starvenden Lane, Sissinghurst, Kent TN17 2AN. Tel: 01580 715001.

British Percheron Horse Society Secretary Muriel Bond, 3 Bears Cottages, Gissing, Diss, Norfolk IP22 5UF. Tel: 01379 740554; Email muriel@bond7675.freeserve.co.uk.

Clydesdale Horse Society Secretary Marguerite Osborne, Kinclune, Kingoldrum, Killiemuir, Angus DD8 5HX. Tel/Fax 01575 570900

Dales Pony Society Secretary Mrs J. Ashby, Greystones, Glebe Avenue, Great Longstone, Bakewell, Derbyshire DE45 1TY. Tel: 01629 640439; Website www.dalespony.org.

Fell Pony Society Secretary Ian Simper, North Craigs Cottage, Waterbeck, Lockerbie, Dumfrieshire DG11 3HA. Tel: 01461 600606; Website www.rarebreeds.com/fellponysociety.

Irish Draught Horse Society of Great Britain Administrator Caroline Collinssplatt, PO Box 1869, Salisbury, Wiltshire SP3 5XA. Tel: 01722 714970; Website www.irishdraughthorsesociety.com.

Shire Horse Society Secretary Andrew Mercer, East of England Showground, Peterborough PE2 6XE. Tel: 01733 234451; Website www.shire-horse.org.uk.

Suffolk Horse Society Administrative Secretary Amanda Hillier, The Market Hill, Woodbridge, Suffolk IP12 4LU. Tel: 01394 380643; Website www.suffolkhorsesociety.org.uk.

Index